THE APOSTOLIC AGE

by

G. B. CAIRD
M.A., D.D., D.Phil.

Grinfield Lecturer in Theology
University of Oxford

GERALD DUCKWORTH & CO. LTD.
3 Henrietta Street, London, W.C.2

First published 1955

Reprinted 1958, 1962, 1966

© GEORGE B. CAIRD 1955

*Printed in Great Britain by Richard Clay (The Chaucer Press), Ltd.,
Bungay, Suffolk*

THE APOSTOLIC AGE

CONTENTS

TO

My Mother

CHAPTER I

THE ROMAN EMPIRE

1

On January 11th, 27 B.C., Octavian closed the doors of the temple of Janus to mark the return of peace, which for two hundred years had been an exile from Roman soil. Five days later an enthusiastic Senate bestowed upon the vindicator of the Roman people's liberty the venerable title of Augustus. Soon the court poet, less restrained, was to celebrate the emperor's sacred Presence,[1] and the eastern provinces, long accustomed to invest their royal bene-factors with divine honours, were keeping the emperor's birthday as the birthday of " the god and saviour of the whole human race ".[2] Nor was this idle flattery, but the spontaneous gratitude of war-weary people, who could now look forward for themselves and their children to a life in which national wealth would no longer be squandered on the weapons of war, in which family ties would not constantly be relaxed by military service, in which the farmer could expect to reap where he had sown.

In the centuries that followed travel became safe and trade prospered.[3] Flavius Zeuxis need face no greater dangers than the storms of Cape Malea on his seventy-two business trips from Hierapolis to Rome.[4] An African glass-worker is found plying his trade in Lyons,[5] a merchant of the Treveri sets up his business in Dacia,[6] and the Purple Dye Company of Thyatira has its representative in Philippi.[7] With growing prosperity there grew also a huge foreign luxury trade, which sent Roman merchantmen to scour

---

[1] Hor., *Odes*, iii. 5. 2; cf. *Epist.* ii. 1. 15–17.
[2] Priene Inscr. 80 and 105.
[3] Iren., *Adv. Haer.* iv. 30. 3 : " Sed et mundum pacem habet per Romanos, et nos sine timore in viis ambulamus et navigamus quocunque voluerimus ". Cf. C. A. J. Skeel, *Travel in the First Century*.
[4] *Inscriptiones Graecae ad res Romanas pertinentes* (ed. Cagnat and Lafaye), iv. 841. [5] *Corpus Inscriptionum Latinarum*, xiii. 2000.
[6] Ibid. iii. 1219. [7] Acts xvi. 14.

three continents for cargoes of "gold, silver, precious
stones, and pearls; fine linen, purple, silk, and scarlet;
every fragrant wood, every article of ivory, every article
of precious wood, bronze, iron, and marble; cinnamon,
spice, incense, myrrh, frankincense, wine, oil, fine flour, and
wheat; cattle and sheep, horses and chariots, and bodies
(that is, slaves) ".[1]

The Roman peace was guarded by a small fleet and an
army which can hardly have exceeded three hundred
thousand men. Its twenty-seven legions were concentrated at points where trouble could be expected, and as
commander-in-chief of the army the emperor governed
those frontier provinces where the presence of the army was
required. The more peaceful provinces were left to the
Senate. Roman government had always rested on the
concept of *imperium*—the authority to command obedience
—which under the Republic had been vested in the magistrates. Under the Empire this *imperium* was in theory
shared between the emperor and the Senate, who delegated
their authority to magistrates and governors. In fact,
however, the power of the emperor was almost without
restriction, for he possessed the *proconsulare imperium maius*
which gave him a legal right to intervene in senatorial
provinces as well as his own; and his instructions to his
representatives by edict, mandate, or rescript tended more
and more to have the force of law.[2]

Good communications, free trade, and the mingling of
races in cosmopolitan seaports accelerated the spread of a
superficial unity across the heterogeneous peoples that
composed the Empire. In the East the process had been
going on for nearly three hundred years, and in what
remained of Alexander's conquests Greek was the universal
language and Greek culture was universally esteemed. The
name " Greek " was no longer a national but a cultural term.[3]

[1] Rev. xviii. 12–13.
[2] *Edictum*—the proclamation by a magistrate of the rules by which
he is to be guided in administering justice; *mandatum*—an imperial order,
usually secret, given to a representative; *rescriptum* or *epistola*—a written
answer to a petition for a legal decision.
[3] Mk. vii. 26 : " A Greek woman, Syro-Phoenician by race ".

In the newer provinces of the West a similar spread of the Latin language and Roman education had already begun.[1]

Augustus must have been greatly tempted to hasten by legislation the growth of imperial unity. But his adoptive father Julius had been assassinated by the old guard of the Republic because they suspected him of planning under his own monarchical rule an egalitarian regime which would have left no room for the privilege of Roman citizenship. Augustus determined, therefore, to avoid uniformity and to restrict the citizenship of Rome to those who could genuinely represent the Roman way of life.[2]

For the administration of his imperial provinces Augustus instituted a bureaucracy which his successors developed into a civil service of many departments. But it was typical of the Roman genius that this strong central government should be combined with many forms of local independence. There were cities which possessed the full Roman franchise : *coloniae* which had been settled by Roman citizens and *municipia* where citizenship had been given to a previously autonomous community. There were free states, some with their rights guaranteed by a perpetual treaty, others enjoying independence at the discretion of Rome. In the outlying districts there were client kingdoms ruled by native kings like Herod the Great. And where no such privileges existed, every town was entrusted with municipal self-government. In each province, too, a *concilium* was held in which the leading men of every city could meet to discuss provincial affairs.

Beneath this apparent multiformity a common loyalty was being evoked and a common civilization established by the leavening influence of the Roman citizen. Veterans of the army were regularly settled in provincial areas to form new colonies. Any subject who served his term in the army received the franchise by *diploma* at his discharge.[3]

---

[1] See C. Bigg, *The Church's Task under the Roman Empire*, ch. I.

[2] Suet. *Aug.* xl. : "Magni praeterea existimans sincerum atque ab omni colluvione peregrini ac servilis sanguinis incorruptum servare populum, et civitates Romanas parcissime dedit et manumittendi modum terminavit ".

[3] For these *diplomata* see R. H. Barrow, *A Selection of Latin Inscriptions*, 74–77.

In some cities municipal office carried with it Roman citizenship and created a local Roman aristocracy. Apparently the honour could also be bought, though we do not know on what terms. But bought, earned, or inherited, the citizenship of Rome was a source of pride to those who possessed it and a coveted prize to those who did not.

It is the highest tribute to the statesmanship of Augustus that this political settlement survived the reigns of his immediate successors : Tiberius, competent general and embittered introvert; Caligula, the spoilt darling of the Rhine army, mentally unbalanced by the corrupting influences of power; Claudius, antiquarian and amiable pedant, ruled by vicious wives and unscrupulous secretaries; Nero, the artist in vice; each in turn caused the capital city to tremble without perceptibly affecting the ordered life of the provinces.

2

All that legislation could effect Augustus achieved, but the real problem of the Empire lay deeper than politics. The welcome peace could not undo the havoc of the long wars. Farmland had fallen into the hands of a few proprietors, and rural populations were drifting to the cities.[1] The slaves captured in many campaigns were a source of cheap labour with which the free peasant could not compete. Prolonged military service had reared a generation accustomed to receive a living from the state. And everywhere there were displaced persons, uprooted from the old social order and unable to find a place in the new.

The yearning of such people for a community to which they could belong led to the formation of every conceivable type of club.[2] So popular were these clubs that in the interests of public order Augustus had to regulate their proceedings by law. But the camaraderie of the club provided only a superficial escape from the tedium of loneliness

---

[1] Pliny, *Hist. Nat.* xviii. 6 : " Verum confitentibus, latifundia perdidere Italiam, iam vero et provincias ".

[2] See G. Johnston, *The Doctrine of the Church in the New Testament*, pp. 5–6.

and left a feeling of deeper need to which the new fellow-ship of the Christian church would appeal.

In a world which had been swept to the brink of doom by forces which seemed beyond the control of man there was also a widespread sense of the futility of human endeavour. Man's destiny appeared to be dominated by an indifferent or even hostile power, and it mattered little whether you called that power Luck, Fortune, Necessity, or Fate. This pessimism, which so often goes hand in hand with political impotence, was reinforced by a pseudo-science from the East. Horace's famous dictum that " captive Greece took captive her fierce conqueror " [1] is only a half-truth; for Greece herself had already undergone a similar conquest at the hands of the conquered Orient. It was but a hybrid hellenism from which Rome took her culture, and one constituent of it was the astrology of Babylon. " Astrology fell upon the Hellenistic mind as a new disease falls upon some remote island people." [2] To a few astrology was a mystic faith in the kinship between the order in the soul and the orderly courses of the stars, between the flame within and the divine fire which feeds the lights of heaven.[3] For others the belief in a cosmic dominion may even have been the ladder by which they ascended from polytheism to the worship of a Creator. But to the many astrology was a horror of great darkness, a rule of principalities and powers, which robbed life of its purpose and its meaning.

When men live without either the incentive of a hopeful purpose or the natural sanctions of a settled community, it is hardly surprising if their morals are not high. For the degeneracy of Roman society we can call to the witness-box of history almost any of the Latin authors of the period. Under the Republic Sallust had already complained that the filth of the world drained into Rome as bilgewater into the hold of a ship,[4] and more than a century later his complaint still found an echo in Juvenal: " the Syrian Orontes has

---

[1] Hor., *Epist.* ii. 1. 156.
[2] G. Murray, *Five Stages of Greek Religion*, p. 144.
[3] See S. Angus, *The Religious Quests of the Graeco-Roman World*, pp. 254–320; and F. Cumont, *Astrology and Religion among the Greeks and Romans*.   [4] *Catil.* 37. 5.

emptied itself into the Tiber." [1] Half of the vast and
crowded population of Rome were slaves. Of the free
inhabitants some two hundred thousand received a dole,
and were kept out of more serious mischief by the sinister
entertainments of the amphitheatre. Nor could the upper
classes boast of any moral superiority. The emperor was
in theory no more than the leading citizen of a restored
Republic, and it was considered undignified for his equals
to take service under him. Caesar's household, therefore,
to which fell an increasingly large share of the administration
of the Empire, consisted of slaves and freedmen. Survivors
of the old regime might despise the imperial palace as a
" gloomy sweatship ", [2] but they themselves, deprived of a
large measure of their ancestral responsibilities, tended to
drift into an even gloomier self-indulgence. Their aimless
existence led to a fall in the birthrate which not even family
allowances could check ; and the education of such children
as they produced was left almost entirely to slaves, who were
less likely to discipline their charges than to pander to their
vices.

In the provinces there were ordinary people living kind
and decent lives. Egyptian papyri and inscriptions from
all parts of the Empire testify to the strength of family
affections and domestic virtues. Yet even into the most
tranquil home there must have entered something of the
general taint. Slavery was everywhere accepted without
demur. It is true that there was a world of difference
between the educated tutor of a noble family and the
semi-animate tools herded into the mines of Laurium. It
is true that slaves were encouraged to save their small
earnings to buy their manumission by a fictitious sale to a
god. Yet even at the best the slave was to his master not a
person but a possession, and the relationship was degrading
to both. Moreover, slavery put a severe strain on the
passions of an age not remarkable for its chastity. The
picture of pagan sensuality delineated in the Wisdom of
Solomon and in the Epistle to the Romans may owe some-

---

[1] *Sat.* iii. 62. Cf. Tac., *Ann.* xv. 44, where the Christian church is meant.
[2] Sen., *De Ira*, iii. 15. 3.

thing to the outraged conscience of a moralist, but it is a recognisable caricature; [1] and the other letters of Paul make it clear that his converts came from a society in which sexual morality was not high. Life, too, was held cheap, and one of the best-attested vices of antiquity was the limitation of families by abortion or exposure. The majority of the exposed children were girls, who were commonly picked up by baby farmers and reared to fill the brothels of the big cities.

3

Believing that the moral crisis was due to neglect of the national religion, Augustus attempted to initiate a religious revival. His own record, preserved in the monument of Ancyra, tells of the rebuilding of eighty-two temples.[2] But the twilight of the gods was already at hand, and no power of man could halt their plunge into oblivion. To the Romans religion meant the awe which they felt in the presence of a *numen*—the gods of agriculture, the Lares and Penates of the home, the spirits of tree and spring, and those darker beings from beyond the grave, *manes*, *larvae*, *lemures*; and worship was the propitiation of these unseen presences by the strict observance of an elaborate ritual. This animism was a breeding ground for magic and enchantment, necromancy and divination, and was to survive for many centuries in rustic superstition.[3] But as a source of spiritual satisfaction and moral power its value was slight. Long since the men, and still more the women, of Rome had been turning elsewhere for comfort and for hope. The aristocratic priesthood, resenting any encroachment on its preserves, had yet been powerless to prevent the growth of competition.[4] In the provinces the old gods still had a hold on the minds of the uneducated, but in many places they survived only by coming to terms with new foreign

[1] Wisd. xiv. 12–31; Rom. i. 20–32. [2] Cf. Hor., *Odes*, iii. 6.
[3] See T. R. Glover, *The Conflict of Religions in the Early Roman Empire*, ch. 1.
[4] See Livy xxv. 1 for the suppression of new cults during the Punic wars, and Livy xxxix. 8–19 for the Bacchanalian disorders of 186 B.C. in which seven thousand people were involved.

deities, and everywhere the ferment of the times had had an unsettling effect on established religion. The civic authorities, both in Rome and in the provincial cities, could indeed demand observance of the civic cult as a condition of citizenship, and could prosecute on a charge of atheism those citizens who failed to conform.[1] But such conformity was little more than a proof of patriotism, and carried with it no truly religious significance.

Among the educated the vacuum left by the decay of religion was filled in part by philosophy—not the disinterested quest for truth which now only the diminishing school of the Peripatetics attempted to maintain, but the more practical creeds of the Garden and the Porch. Both Epicurus and Zeno, confronted by the social and moral chaos which followed the death of Alexander, had addressed themselves with widely differing results to the problem of suffering, and their teaching remained apposite to the similar conditions of the first century A.D.

According to Epicurus the root of all evil was fear, the unnecessary fear with which men tortured their minds. If there were gods, they took no interest in humankind; death was but an untroubled sleep; evil could be avoided by justice, or, if it came, could be endured; happiness could be attained through the quiet life [2] and the cultivation of friendship.[3] To give intellectual backing to this advice Epicurus adopted the atomic theory of Leucippus and Democritus, and argued that the universe was a machine without caprice and without malevolence. Among the Romans he had a small following well represented by Horace and Lucretius, the one delighting in the life of simple pleasures,[4] the other finding in the gospel of natural law a deliverance from the intolerable burden of superstition.[5] But the problem of evil was not to be solved by running away from it, and the Roman world needed a faith which offered not escape but victory.

---

[1] See J. Juster, *Les Juifs*, . pp. 254–9.
[2] Fr. 86 : " Live inconspicuously ! " Cf. Lucr. v. 1129 f.
[3] Fr. 52A : " Friendship goes dancing round the world inviting all of us to awake into bliss ". E. seems to have founded the first Society of Friends.   [4] Hor., *Epist.* i. 4. 16.   [5] Lucr. iv. 580 f., v. 1194.

Zeno diagnosed desire as the fundamental ailment of which other ills were but symptoms, and prescribed suppression of the emotions as the cure for sick souls. For this purpose, like Epicurus, he enlisted the support of an older philosophy. Heraclitus, searching in his own heart for the truth, had there discovered Reason, and had deduced that at the heart of the universe there must be a similar Reason—the rational formula which held in tension the warring elements of the cosmos. This formula or logos he further identified with the divine Fire underlying all existence. The world had emerged from fire, and to fire it would return. Armed with this metaphysic, Zeno taught that virtue consisted in living according to Nature, that is, in allowing the Reason within to live in harmony with the cosmic Reason of which it was a part. Man could be at home in the universe as long as he was content to abandon himself to an all-embracing destiny. He who had thus accepted the universe was self-sufficient and could defy evil things to touch the defences of his embattled soul.

Here was a faith to put steel into the character of the disillusioned Roman, and one which provided the cosmopolitan society of the Empire with a philosophical basis for world brotherhood. In a popularized form which is usually associated with the name of Posidonius it appealed to a large public, and the itinerant Stoic lecturer became a familiar figure in the market-place.[1] Stoicism dominated Roman thought for three centuries, and finally left its stamp upon Christian ethics. Yet it was from the beginning " a system put together hastily, violently, to meet a desperate emergency ",[2] and it never achieved consistency or coherence. It lost much of its crusading spirit by coming to terms with polytheism, and by assimilating astrology it gave undue emphasis to its own inherent fatalism. Its belief in a universal purpose was cancelled out by the cyclic theory of history in which all things were periodically reduced to the primordial Fire. And its life according to Nature was robbed of its attractiveness by a narrow

---

[1] P. Wendland, *Die hellenistisch-römische Kultur*, p. 85.
[2] E. Bevan, *Stoics and Sceptics*, p. 28.

definition of Nature which made pity a vice and sympathy a weakness. The Roman world needed a faith which could bring the emotions as well as the mind into the service of a divine Purpose not restricted to the realm of change and decay.

The desire to escape from the " bondage of corruption " accounted for much of the popularity of the mystery cults. These cults had sprung up independently in many parts of the Orient, but with minor variations they ran true to a common type. In most of them [1] a mother goddess was worshipped with a male deity who was either her consort or her son—Cybele and Attis, Ishtar and Tammuz, Atargatis and Hadad, Aphrodite and Adonis, Isis and Osiris. The worship included a ritual drama depicting the death and resurrection of the god, which represented either the daily setting and rising of the sun or the annual decay and rebirth of vegetation. By initiation into the mysteries the worshipper was identified with the god, and so made to participate in his immortality.

The mystery cults had spread from the lands of their origin when soldiers and refugees, merchants and travellers settled in foreign cities. Greece had her indigenous mysteries of Demeter and Persephone at Eleusis, but already in Socrates' time the Thracian goddess Bendis had arrived at the Piraeus.[2] Cybele reached Rome during the second Punic war,[3] and Isis in spite of many ejections was well established there by the beginning of the Christian era. Rome tried to expel these Nature cults with a pitchfork, but they kept coming back. The meeting of religions soon led to syncretism, and Isis in particular tended to absorb the persons and functions of her rivals. Ptolemy I and Manetho were even able to construct a synthetic deity, Serapis, from elements of various existing cults.

Polytheism has never been noted for its high morals, and in this respect the gods of the mysteries were no better than

---

[1] There was no mother goddess in the Bacchic or Orphic cults, or in the Persian cult of Mithras which became popular among soldiers in the latter half of the first century A.D.

[2] Plato, *Rep.* i. 327a.   [3] Livy xxix. 11

the gods of Olympus. They were holy, and only the holy might approach them; but theirs was not the sanctity which consists in righteousness. As T. R. Glover has remarked : " Neither Demeter nor Isis was very squeamish ".[1] To the ordinary worshipper the mysteries offered a colourful symbolism and the emotional outlet of ecstasy, but their chief appeal lay in the sympathetic figure of the Great Mother. For the initiate were reserved the higher benefits of freedom from the dominion of the stars [2] and a hope of life beyond the grave. But initiation cost Lucius all his money,[3] and there were few who could afford the price of immortality. The Roman world needed a living hope freely offered to all who were thirsty for the life everlasting.

4

From the Greek kingdoms of the East there came yet another candidate for the religious loyalty of men— emperor worship. In Greece the boundary line between the human and the divine had always been a shadowy one. Zeus could take human form either in myth and poetry or in the chryselephantine splendour of Pheidias' statue at Olympia. Heracles could be elevated from manhood to the ranks of the gods. A god could be identified with a local hero to form a syncretistic deity, such as Zeus Trophonius at Lebadeia. And there were some deities—Asclepius, for example—of whom none could tell whether they had begun their existence as gods or men.

There was in Greek philosophy a strong strain which helped to accentuate this native tendency of the Greek mind. The Pythagoreans, Plato, Aristotle and the Stoics all taught that there is that in man which is akin to the divine, and that the chief end of man is to liberate this divine spark so that it may enter into the life immortal.[4] At a less exalted level there was the theory propounded by Euhemerus in the third century B.C., that the gods were but

---

[1] *Paul of Tarsus*, p. 133.   [2] Apul., *Met.* xi. 6.   [3] Ibid. xi. 28.
[4] E.g. Aristotle, *Nic. Eth.* X. vii. 8 : ἐφ' ὅσον ἐνδέχεται ἀθανατίζειν.

B

men who had been promoted to divine honours in recognition of their benefactions to their fellows.

Philosophers might theorize, but it was Aristotle's most distinguished pupil, Alexander the Great, who took the actual step of laying claim to the worship of his subjects. No doubt he was prompted in this by the practice of the Egyptian kings, by his visit to the oracle of Ammon, where he was hailed son of the god, and by the ceremonial prostration which the kings of Persia expected of their people; but his claim was the logical development of Greek religious thought.   His example was followed by his successors, who adopted such divine surnames as Soter, Euergetes, Epiphanes.   Antiochus IV even had himself designated *theos* on the coinage.   These claims were readily accepted by the populace, because the kings often proved capable of conferring benefits which the older deities failed to supply.   If a king could be the saviour of his people, it was felt that he had earned the right to be regarded as an incarnate deity.

When the eastern dynasties fell before the stronger power of Rome, the common people were quite ready to transfer their loyalty and their worship, and Julius Caesar showed himself equally ready to accept both.   It was this more than anything else that led the Republicans to suspect that he intended to found an oriental monarchy.   Rome was not yet prepared to worship a living Caesar.   But a dead Caesar was a different matter, and within a year of his death he had been deified by the Senate, and the superstitious were declaring that a comet which appeared that year was nothing other than the soul of the dead Julius ascending to heaven.

Warned by the fate of his predecessor, Augustus was in no haste to accept worship during his lifetime.   At Rome he allowed himself to be addressed as son of the divine Julius, but refused any nearer approach to divinity.   In the eastern provinces, where the custom of ruler-worship was well established, he gave permission for the institution of an imperial cult, but with the proviso that the name of the goddess Roma must be conjoined with his own.   At his death, however, he, too, was voted the title *divus*, and in his case deification had constitutional as well as religious import. For the *acta* or authoritative pronouncements of the emperor had during his lifetime the effect of law, but this effect ceased with his death. Deification, therefore, meant that these *acta* had a permanent validity. Henceforward, whenever an emperor died, the Senate had to decide whether to ratify his *acta* by making him a *divus* or to allow him to suffer *damnatio memoriae*, which meant that his *acta* would become a dead letter.

The mad Caligula tried to anticipate the decision of the Senate by identifying himself with the Latian Jupiter, and spent the second half of his reign indulging his bizarre conception of divine splendour. In particular, he commanded the Syrian legate to have his statue set up in the temple at Jerusalem, and so almost provoked a Jewish revolt. But even the deliberate extravagances of Caligula discredited the Principate less than the innocent absurdities of Claudius. For when the Senate voted apotheosis for the dead Claudius, the thought of his maudlin figure among the immortals was too much for the gravity of the philosopher Seneca, who published a devastating satire called the Apocolocyntosis or Pumpkinification. After this even Nero's triumphal entry into Rome as the Lord Apollo could do little more than complete the disillusionment.

In spite of this chequered history the imperial cult maintained its influence in the provinces, where even Nero was regarded with enthusiasm. The next development came in the reign of Domitian. The year of the four emperors had proved how precarious an emperor's tenure of office could be, and Domitian lived in constant dread of being supplanted. In an attempt to enhance his personal reputation he had himself proclaimed *dominus et deus*,[1] and arraigned on a charge of atheism all prominent persons who for any reason failed to acknowledge his divinity.

Throughout the century the cult of the emperor had in the eastern provinces an undiminished popularity. The Empire had given to the people peace and prosperity, and they were happy to express their loyalty and gratitude to

[1] Dio Cass. lxvii. 13; Suet., *Dom.* xiii.; Mart. v. 8.

its supreme citizen. But there were two reasons why emperor-worship could never become the universal religion which the Empire needed to give it spiritual cohesion. The character of many of the emperors was a contradiction of the dignity of the office they occupied, and even the best emperors could provide for their subjects only material benefits which distracted their attention from their deeper and more permanent needs. It is the tragedy of Rome that, in the interests of imperial security, she persecuted the one religion that could have brought unity to her heterogeneous peoples.

CHAPTER II

FIRST CENTURY JUDAISM

1

OF all the peoples subject to Rome the most scattered and
yet the most conscious of national unity were the Jews.
Estimates of their numbers in the Empire range from four
and a half to seven millions, and by any computation the
inhabitants of Palestine were but a small fraction of the
total.[1] The evidence of inscriptions has gone far to support
Strabo's assertion that no city was without its quota of
Jews.[2] The Dispersion of the Jews had been brought
about by many causes. The Ptolemies and the Seleucid
Kings had regarded them as useful settlers. Ptolemy Lagos
had established a large Jewish colony in Cyrenaica, where
they occupied one of the four quarters of the city of Cyrene.[3]
Ptolemy Soter had enlarged the considerable Jewish population of Egypt, so that in Roman times they numbered
about a million, and two of the five districts of Alexandria
were exclusively Jewish.[4] Antiochus III had settled two
thousand families from Mesopotamia in Phrygia and Lydia.[5]
Slavery, too, had contributed to the scattering of the Jews.
The Jewish community in Rome, for example, sprang from
the slaves brought home by Pompey, and in 4 B.C. they were
numerous enough to send out eight thousand men to meet a
deputation from Jerusalem.[6] But the presence of Jews in
many other places was probably due to their desire to find a
more profitable field for enterprise than the impoverished
and over-populated land of Palestine.

Whatever the land of his adoption, the Jew remained a
loyal son of the Law, sent his annual contribution to the
upkeep of the temple-worship, and, when he was able, went

---

[1] These figures take no account of the large Jewish colonies beyond the
eastern frontiers of the Empire, particularly in Babylon.
[2] Jos., *Ant.* xiv. 7. 2; cf. Or. Syb. iii, 27; Philo, *In Flacc.* 7; Acts ii. 9–11.
[3] Jos., *Contr. Ap.* ii. 4. 14; *Ant.* xiv. 7. 2.   [4] Philo, *In Flacc.* 6. 8.
[5] Jos., *Ant.* xii. 8. 4.   [6] Ibid. xvii. 11. 1.

on pilgrimage to one of the great festivals in Jerusalem. Of these three bonds of unity the first was by far the most important. The pilgrimages ensured that the interests of the Dispersion were known in Jerusalem and that the teachings of the Jerusalem Rabbis were carried to Alexandria, Antioch, Ephesus, and Rome. But it was loyalty to the Law that separated the Jew from his pagan neighbours; and the synagogue where the Law was taught was the distinctively Jewish institution.

2

The bond of international Jewry was rather a common practice than a common creed. The Jew believed that God had chosen Israel to be the recipient of a special revelation of his will and purpose, and that this revelation was written in the Torah or Law. For every exigency of daily life the Law could provide the necessary instruction, for every problem of conduct it contained the appropriate rule. Every commandment of the Torah was precious to the pious Israelite, since it gave him the opportunity of rendering obedient service to God. For the purpose of theological debate wide latitude of interpretation was allowed, and the use of allegory was especially popular. But in practice the Law was to be obeyed in its literal sense. Thus Philo wrote voluminous commentaries to show by allegory that the Law of Moses was the source from which every Greek philosopher had plagiarized his ideas. Yet he insisted that in practice the Law was to be literally obeyed, and on the basis of this practical orthodoxy he rose to a position of high esteem and authority in the Jewish community of Alexandria.[1] Similarly the author of the Fourth Book of Maccabees made free use of Stoic vocabulary, but his highest praise is bestowed on the meticulous observance of the ceremonial Law.

The Law of Moses had envisaged the formation of a holy community from which all contaminating influences could be banished. But for the Jewish subject of the Roman

[1] Philo, *Migr. Abr.* 16, 89–94.

Empire these conditions nowhere prevailed. The Jew of the Dispersion lived in the midst of pagan neighbours who were a constant embarrassment to his religious loyalty. Nor was the Palestinian Jew in a substantially better situation.[1] Ever since the conquests of Alexander, Hellenistic culture had been spreading throughout the Orient, and the Jews had only partially resisted its encroachments on their ancestral customs. The cities of the coast and of the Decapolis were almost entirely Gentile, and Galilee had a large Gentile minority. Judaea itself did not escape the general trend. At the beginning of the second century B.C. there had been a strong party in Jerusalem which favoured the substitution of hellenism for native traditions, and it had been their policy which precipitated the Maccabaean revolt. The ill-advised attempt of Antiochus Epiphanes to accelerate the process of hellenization had in fact retarded it. But the revulsion of feeling aroused by persecution never wholly eliminated the Hellenistic leaven. Greek words crept into the language of the Jews and Greek practices into their daily life.

Thus it came about that his religious obligations presented a serious problem to the Jew of the first century A.D. How could he remain faithful to the Law in the face of a hostile prevailing culture? This question had been raised in its acutest form during the persecutions of Antiochus Epiphanes and it is to that time and to that cause that we can ascribe the origin of the major Jewish sects.

3

Among the Sadducees, the aristocratic families who supplied the majority of the temple priesthood, and into whose hands had fallen such political power as Rome allowed to her subject nations, the natural opinion had grown up that only by compromise with their pagan neighbours could they hope to preserve national identity and the cultus on which their own prestige so largely depended.[2]

[1] See E. Schürer, *The Jewish People in the Time of Jesus Christ*, II. i. pp. 11–56.   [2] Jn. xi. 48.

Their surrender to the enticements of Hellenism stopped
short of disloyalty to the Torah, which they professed to
follow to the letter, but they strenuously resisted the attempts of their more zealous compatriots to impose upon
them any interpretation of the Law which would render
intolerable their position in the Gentile world. Their
political conservatism thus led them to adopt a religious
conservatism which repudiated any doctrine not expressly
taught by the written Scriptures.[1] The nucleus of this
caste was a small group of high-priestly families. Between
37 B.C. and A.D. 68, when both Herod and the Roman
governors deposed high priests at will, there were twenty-
eight high priests, but all belonged to the same few families.[2]

An entirely different attitude to the Gentile problem was
assumed by the Hasidim and their lineal descendants, the
Pharisees. They believed that obedience to the Torah
involved strict separation [3] from defilement and especially
from contact with " sinners ", in which category they included both the Gentiles and the *'am ha-aretz* or lax Jews.[4]
Being unable to achieve physical isolation, they established
for themselves an elaborate system of spiritual quarantine
regulations to which they gave the name " tradition ".
According to a pious legend this tradition was an authoritative exposition of the written Law, handed down orally from
Moses through the seventy elders to a succession of prophets
and teachers. In fact it represented the cumulative efforts
of successive generations of lawyers to ensure that the
written Law should not be broken. Two principles governed
their procedure. In the first place, many of the written
laws were so antiquated as to be impracticable and had to
be interpreted with creative imagination if they were to be
applicable to current conditions. In the second place, even
the strictest Pharisee was in constant danger of an unwitting

---

[1] Acts xxiii. 8 : " The Sadducees say that there is no resurrection, nor
angel, nor spirit ".

[2] The traditional derivation of the name Sadducee from Zadok the high
priest is, however, on almost every count untenable. For an alternative
theory see T. W. Manson, *The Servant-Messiah*, pp. 12 ff.

[3] The name *Perushim* has usually been taken to mean Separatists ; but
see again Manson, loc. cit.

[4] G. F. Moore in *The Beginnings of Christianity*, i. pp. 439 ff.

breach of the Torah, and the lawyers therefore "set a hedge about the Law", i.e. allowed a margin of safety by prescribing at every point a little more than the Law required. For mutual encouragement in the pursuit of their ideal of holiness the Pharisees banded together in *ḥaburoth* or brotherhoods, the members of which were known as *ḥaberim*. By these means they contrived to cut themselves off from social contact with those who took their religious obligations less seriously. "The garments of the *'am ha-aretz* are unclean for the Perushim." [1] "He who takes upon himself to be a *ḥaber* . . . does not enter the houses of the *'am ha-aretz* as a guest, nor does he receive them as guests within his walls." [2] Yet even this scrupulosity did not guarantee the uniformity of the sect. For the two schools of Pharisaism, the strict school of Shammai and the liberal school of Hillel, disagreed on more than three hundred questions of legal observance. [3]

While the Pharisees were trying to establish their islands of sanctity in an ocean of worldliness, there grew up on the fringe of Pharisaism the Zealot party, who attributed all their national ills to the pollution of Gentile suzerainty, and saw in revolution the sole hope of national holiness. Considerable doubt surrounds the origin of the Zealot party and its relationship to Pharisaism, but the two groups must have had a good deal in common. It is usually assumed that the Zealot party came into being at the time of the revolt of Judas of Gamala in A.D. 6, when one of the leading revolutionaries was a Pharisee named Sadduk. [4]

At the other extreme were the Essenes, [5] who solved the problem of Gentile intrusion by withdrawing to isolated communities in the vicinity of the Dead Sea. There they formed a monastic order to which initiates were admitted only after prolonged training and an oath of secrecy. They practised communal living, observed a strict daily regimen,

---

[1] Hagiga ii. 7.   [2] Demai ii. 3.
[3] G. F. Moore, *Judaism*, I. p. 81. E.g. Shammai opposed proselytism and supported the nationalist movement (Jos. Ant. xviii. 1. 1).
[4] For the contrary view see *The Beginnings of Christianity*, i. 421 ff.
[5] Phil., *Quod omnis probus liber*, 12–13; Jos. B.J. ii. 8. 2–13; Pliny, *Hist. Nat.* v. 17.

undertook frequent lustrations, and renounced marriage. In other respects they appear to have been orthodox Jews for whose extreme devotion even Pharisaic piety was not enough.

The origin of the Essenes has until recently lain in total obscurity. It now seems to be beyond reasonable doubt that the documents discovered at Ain Feshka in 1947 have to do with the emergence of the Essene movement in the first half of the second century B.C.[1] The Habakkuk Commentary and Manual of Discipline, together with the already known Zadokite Fragment,[2] describe the organization of a sect of the New Covenant by a priest known as the Teacher of Righteousness. After his martyrdom at the hands of a Wicked Priest the sect fled to Damascus under another leader known as the Star, but they seem later to have returned to Judaea. There are marked similarities between their organization and beliefs and those of the Essenes, and any differences can readily be accounted for by two centuries of development.

These four divergent groups had one characteristic in common, that they all offered a practical method of dealing with their Gentile environment. The writers of apocalyptic tracts adopted a more pessimistic view of the human situation, by which they are clearly distinguished from their contemporaries. This difference has been ignored by those who have ascribed the apocalyptic literature either to the Zealots or to the Pharisees.[3] Like the Zealots, the apocalyptists attributed Israel's troubles to the successive pagan empires, but, despairing of any programme of active resistance, they trusted for deliverance to the direct intervention of God. Like the Pharisees they were passionately devoted to the Law, but they lacked the Pharisees' confidence in the meticulous observance of rules as a way of salvation. Apocalyptic is best regarded as the product

[1] See A. Dupont Sommer, *The Dead Sea Scrolls*; H. H. Rowley, *The Zadokite Fragments and the Dead Sea Scrolls*; R. de Vaux, " Exploration de la Région de Qumran ", *Revue Biblique*, iv. (1953), pp. 540–561.
[2] R. H. Charles, *Apocrypha and Pseudepigrapha*, II. pp. 785 ff.
[3] See e.g. E. C. Dewicke, *Primitive Christian Eschatology*, and R. T. Herford, *The Pharisees*.

not of a sect, nor even in any strict sense of a school, but of a literary movement in which the message of the book of Daniel was reinterpreted by a series of imitators for each new crisis in Jewish affairs.[1]

The vast majority of Palestinian Jews belonged to none of these sects or movements, though in varying degrees they came under the influence of all of them. In spite of the weighty authority of G. F. Moore, it can no longer be held that first century Judaism was in all important respects identical with the religion of the Mishna.[2] Up to A.D. 70 Judaism was remarkable for the variety of convictions which could be held together by a common loyalty to the Law, and it had ample room for a simple piety which stopped short of Pharisaic scruple and Zealot fanaticism. Nor should it be forgotten that many, Jews only in name, had abandoned all pretence of adherence to their national religion.

4

The Jew of Palestine spoke Aramaic; the Jew of the Dispersion spoke Greek and had a Greek Bible. But the religion of the Septuagint was not radically different from that of the Palestinian synagogues. A study of the vocabulary of the Septuagint shows that, while many Greek words have been compelled to bear new meanings and associations derived from their Hebrew originals, in comparatively few instances have Greek words modified the thought of the Old Testament by retaining from their pagan background connotations foreign to their biblical context.[3] The translation of the Old Testament into Greek opened up the possibility of a synthesis between Jewish and Greek thought; but this synthesis was not attempted by the translators, who left the fundamental nature of Judaism unchanged.

---

[1] See H. H. Rowley, *The Relevance of Apocalpytic.*
[2] Op. cit. pp. 125–134; Moore failed to make allowance for the changes wrought in Judaism by the fall of Jerusalem and the rise of Christianity.
[3] See C. H. Dodd, *The Bible and the Greeks* ; but see also A. Deissmann, *Die Hellenisierung des semitischen Monotheismus.*

The Greek-speaking Jews of whom we read in Acts were fully as zealous for the Law as their Palestinian cousins. It may well have been from religious ardour that Jews born and brought up in Cyrene, Alexandria, and Asia Minor decided to settle in Jerusalem.[1] But as in Palestine, so in the Dispersion, a basic obedience to the Law left wide scope for variety. The most famous of Hellenistic Jews described himself as a Pharisee.[2] Frequent outbreaks of disturbance in Alexandria and elsewhere show that in many parts of the Empire there were Jewish nationalists who were Zealots in all but name. In Egypt there was a quasi-monastic order, the Therapeutae, who were not unlike the Essenes.[3]

Our most detailed knowledge of Hellenistic Judaism comes from Alexandria. Like the Jews of Palestine the large Jewish community in Alexandria was divided in its attitude to the Gentiles. There was a strong literalist party who clung to the traditional interpretations of Scripture without any thought of accommodating their religion to the enquiring Gentile.[4] At the other extreme were the allegorists, who were prepared to come to terms with Greek philosophy even at the sacrifice of the literal meaning of Scripture.[5] Between the two extremes was the school represented by Philo, who insisted that literal obedience to the Torah and an allegorical elucidation of its meaning were related as body to soul.

The attempt by Alexandrian writers to integrate Jewish theology with Greek philosophy had begun at least as early as the second century B.C., when the author of the Wisdom of Solomon combined the Palestinian wisdom tradition with a Stoic belief in a cosmic Reason and a Platonic doctrine of immortality. Later came Aristobulus, whose work is described by Clement and Eusebius, and there must have been other teachers whose names have not survived. Philo, therefore, stood at the end of a lengthy process, and there is good reason to believe that the process was not confined to Alexandria. Paul's education apparently included

---

[1] Acts vi. 9.
[2] Philo, *Vit. Contemp.*
[3] Phil., iii. 5; Acts xxiii. 6.
[4] Id., *Somn.* I. 16 f., 102; *Confus.* 5, 14.
[5] Id., *Migr. Abr.* 16, 89; *Confus.* 38, 190.

some acquaintance with Greek philosophy and rhetoric, which he must have obtained either at Tarsus or at Jerusalem;[1] and he was certainly familiar with the Wisdom of Solomon. Josephus, a lifelong resident of Palestine, wrote competent Greek and had a knowledge of popular philosophy. Even in Palestine, it seems, a Jewish student could acquire a Greek education, presumably for apologetic or missionary purposes.[2] But the presence of the literalists in Alexandria must be a warning to us not to assume that the whole of Hellenistic Judaism was committed to a single point of view.[3]

Although Judaism involved nationality as well as religion, the door had always been open for a Gentile to enter the commonwealth of Israel as a proselyte on equal terms with the native Israelite. There is no doubt that Jewish theology and ethics held a strong attraction for the serious pagan, weary of polytheism and its attendant moral corruption; but two factors combined to limit the number of proselytes. The Roman government refused to extend to proselytes the privileges and immunities granted to those who were Jews by birth, and most Gentiles hesitated to undergo the rite of circumcision, which would bind them to obey not only the moral but also the ceremonial Law. Accordingly, in most synagogues of the Dispersion there could be found Gentiles who were satisfied to participate in the worship and instruction without becoming more deeply involved.[4] They were considered by the Jews to be sufficiently free from Gentile contamination if they avoided the more obvious moral offences, kept the Sabbath, and observed the Jewish food regulations.

Accessions were to some extent offset by losses. Josephus tells us that many converts to Judaism were not strong enough to persevere in their new religion.[5] An inscription from Asia Minor refers cryptically to " former

---

[1] R. Bultmann, *Der Stil der paulinischen Predigt*, pp. 20–46.
[2] Cf. W. L. Knox, *Some Hellenistic Elements in Primitive Christianity*, pp. 30 ff.
[3] Cf. E. Schürer, op. cit. II. iii. p. 2 : " There was Palestinian Judaism outside of Palestine, just as there was Hellenistic Judaism within it ".
[4] By Luke and Josephus they are referred to as οἱ σεβόμενοι or οἱ φοβούμενοι τὸν Θεόν.   [5] *Contr. Ap.* ii. 10.

Jews " with no explanation of their lapse.[1] One reason for apostasy was ambition, as in the case of Philo's nephew, Tiberius Alexander, who rose to a high position in the imperial service, and actually became procurator of Judaea.[2] Intermarriage with pagans was also common and inevitably resulted in laxity.[3]

There is ample evidence also of syncretism between Judaism and various pagan cults. In the New Testament we hear of Jews who practised magic,[4] and the Magical Papyri are full of references to the Septuagint. Several of the tracts of the Corpus Hermeticum reveal a similar influence. These two collections are admittedly much later than our period, but they are generally thought to include earlier material and ideas. In the Aegean provinces there was a worship of Zeus Hypsistos which almost certainly owed something to the use of Hypsistos as a divine name in the Septuagint.[5] In some places also the God of the Jews, under the title Sabaoth, was identified with the pagan deity Sabazius.[6] The Gnostic heresy at Colossae seems to have been a mixture of Jewish and pagan ideas. In addition to all this, Philo gives plentiful evidence of syncretism in Alexandria.[7] It is highly improbable that any such developments ever happened under the direct auspices of the synagogue. They are rather to be attributed to the literary influence of the Septuagint, to the apostasy of Jews, and the lapse of proselytes, or—by far the most likely cause—to the visits paid to the synagogue by partially converted Gentiles.

5

The Romans had first come into contact with the Jews when Judas Maccabaeus made an alliance with them,[8] and even when Palestine had become part of the Empire, they

---

[1] *Corpus Inscriptionum Graecarum*, 3148.
[2] Jos., *Ant.* xx. 5. 2; Philo, *Mos.* I. 6, 30–31.
[3] Acts xvi. 1; Test. Lev. xiv. 5–8.   [4] Acts xix. 13–19.
[5] Pauly-Wissowa, *Hypsistos*; P. Wendland, op. cit. p. 194; *The Beginnings of Christianity*, V. pp. 90 ff.
[6] Philo, *Quaest. Conviv.* iv. 6; Tac., *Hist.* v. 5; Valer. Max. i. 3. 2.
[7] Spec. Leg. I. viii. 58; *Confus.* 2–3; *Migr. Abr.* 89.
[8] I Macc. viii. 17–32.

continued to treat the Jews as an allied nation, and therefore left them free to live by their own religion and laws. By the normal Roman practice this freedom would not have been extended to Jews who had become citizens either of Rome or of any provincial city, except where they constituted a separate *politeuma*, as at Alexandria and Cyrene; for it was a principle of Roman law that no man could be a citizen of two cities at one time.[1] But Julius Caesar had realized that, if the Jewish religion were to be tolerated at all, it must be granted special privileges. He therefore allowed the Jews to become citizens of other cities without thereby forfeiting their Jewish nationality, and his lenient policy was maintained by his successors.

To the Jews, then, whatever their political status, religious freedom was assured. When Augustus " suppressed all but ancient and lawful associations ",[2] the Jews were exempted as a *collegium licitum*. They were further exempted from military service, which would have involved them in idolatry and a breach of the Sabbath.[3] Their right to send the temple tax to Jerusalem was safeguarded, even against the interference of provincial governors.[4] Prayers for the emperor in the synagogues were accepted in lieu of participation in the imperial cult. In Palestine Roman tolerance went to even greater lengths. The daily sacrifice for the emperor, which took the place of the imperial cult, was provided, according to Philo, out of imperial funds.[5] Copper coinage was minted locally without the image of the emperor.[6] And when the Roman armies had occasion to enter Jewish territory, they left their *signa* behind them out of deference to Jewish scruples.

The Jewish Law in its origin was civil and criminal as well as religious, and Rome left to the Jews considerable independence of jurisdiction. In Judaea the Sanhedrin was in charge of local administration and was the supreme court in all matters of purely Jewish concern. Similarly

---

[1] Cic., *Balb.* 28; *Caec.* 100.
[2] Suet., *Aug.* xxxii; cf. Jos., *Ant.* xiv. 10. 8.
[3] Jos., *Ant.* xiv. 10. 13–19.
[4] Ibid. xvi. 6. 2–7; cf. Cic., *Pro Flacc.* 28. 66.   [5] Leg. 23, 40.
[6] The tribute money brought to Jesus was not "a penny" (A.V.) but a denarius, i.e. a silver coin.

the synagogues of the Dispersion exercised a large measure of legal authority.[1]

The privilege of popularity, however, was not in the power of the government to give. Indeed, the very privileges that Rome bestowed upon the Jews accentuated antisemitism. The Gentiles resented having to share the rights of citizenship with Jews who were exempt from the corresponding responsibilities. They regarded Judaism as an absurd superstition, dismissed the conversion of the proselyte as affectation, and despised these Sabbath-keeping worshippers of an imageless deity, whose prime requirement seemed to be that they should abstain from pork.[2] Whatever the government might say, to the average Gentile the refusal of the Jew to join in the national worship was atheism, and his failure to participate in the common social life was due to enmity towards society.[3] To all this the Jew responded with a sullen contempt. To him the Gentile was a "sinner", and social contact with him was a defilement disqualifying the Jew from participation in worship. In cities like Alexandria, Jew and Gentile lived side by side under an uneasy truce which might at any provocation break down in riot and pogrom.

In Palestine Roman generosity was repaid in hostility. Only the Sadducean aristocracy, whose interest was to maintain political stability, made any pretence of friendship toward the imperial power. The Pharisees, who had no political interest, unjustly regarded the Romans as a threat to their religious purity, which they were fanatically ready to defend. The common people treated Rome as a scapegoat on which to load all their economic and political grievances. The grievances were real enough, for Palestine was over-populated, the Jew lived under a double system of taxation, civil and religious, and although Roman taxes were collected by reliable officials, the collection of customs was still farmed out by auction to the *publicani*, who were hated alike for their exactions and for taking service under

[1] See J. Juster, op. cit. II. pp. 110 ff.
[2] Juv., *Sat.* xiv. 96–98; Epict., *Diss.* ii. 7, 19.
[3] Tac., *Hist.* v. 5; cf. Leopold, *Antisemitismus in der Alten Welt.*

Rome. But in most respects the Roman administration deserved a more appreciative response.

Against the weight of such antagonism the official policy of appeasement could make no headway, and relations between Rome and the Jews steadily deteriorated until the disastrous rebellion of A.D. 66–70. Josephus, the Jewish apologist, tries hard to lay the blame for this catastrophe on a series of unscrupulous Roman officials, and he makes out a sufficiently strong case. But before any such charge against Rome can be entertained, it must be remembered that Rome's intentions were good, and that Jewish nationalism presented the Roman government with an insoluble problem. The first procurator, Coponius, who was sent in A.D. 6 to replace the incompetent Archelaus, had no sooner taken up his office than he was faced with the rebellion of Judas of Gamala. The survivors of the revolt became the Zealot party, whose constant unrest must have been a strain on the nerves of the strongest governor. The next three procurators are no more than names to us, which probably means that Josephus could discover nothing against them. Pontius Pilate is famous for the indiscretions which led eventually to his recall, but he kept the peace for more than ten years.[1] Even in A.D. 40, when Caligula made his insane demand that his statue be set up in the temple, the Jews found an ally in Petronius, the legate of Syria, whose temporising averted the crisis at the risk of his own life. And Claudius made ample amends for his predecessor's blunder by the appointment of Herod Agrippa as king.

All this while, however, Jewish passions had been mounting, and after the death of Agrippa the Romans seem to have abandoned all attempts at conciliation. Certainly in these last twenty-two years before the outbreak of war none of the procurators except Festus showed any aptitude for his post. "When we glance over the history of the Roman procurators, to whom once more the government of Palestine was entrusted, we might readily suppose that all of them, as if by secret arrangement, so conducted them-

---

[1] Philo, *Leg.* 38; Lk. xiii. 1; Mk. xv. 7.

C

selves as most certainly to arouse the people to revolt."[1]
The revolt of Theudas under Cuspius Fadus,[2] the crucifixion
of the sons of Judas of Gamala by Tiberius Alexander,[3]
the massacre of the Zealots by Ventidius Cumanus,[4] only
prepared the way for the repressive government of Felix,
of whom it was said that " he wielded royal authority with
the disposition of a slave ".[5]   In the midst of this period of
rising tension Paul wrote of his fellow Jews : " the wrath
has come upon them to the uttermost ".[6]   Once the cumulative provocation of past years had called into existence
the *sicarii*, a gang of thugs committed to a career of political
assassination,[7] not even Festus could check the march of
events which was leading the nation inexorably to its doom.
And all that could be said in favour of Albinus was that he
did not reach the depths of maladministration attained
by his successor, Gessius Florus.

6

It was a very different Judaism which emerged from the
four years of war.   Even that measure of political independence which the Jews had formerly enjoyed was now
forfeited, and the Sanhedrin was consequently dissolved.
The temple lay in ruins and sacrificial worship had perforce
come to an end.   For both these reasons the Sadducees lost
their importance and disappeared from the scene.

Only the Torah remained, and it became the rallying
point for the resurgent people.   This gave to the Rabbis an
even greater authority than they had previously exercised.
Around Rabbi Johanan ben Sakkai there gathered at
Jamnia (Jabneh) a learned community which appears to
have acted not merely as a religious centre but also as a
supreme court of law.[8]   These Rabbis constituted themselves guardians of Scripture, and with them began the
movement which resulted in the closing of the canon and
the final formation of an authoritative text.   It has usually

---

[1] E. Schürer, op. cit. I. ii. p. 166.
[2] Jos., *Ant.* xx. 5. 1.
[3] Ibid. xx. 5. 2.
[4] Ibid. xx. 6. 1–3.
[5] Tac., *Hist.* v. 9.
[6] I Thess. ii. 16.
[7] Jos., *Ant.* xx. 8. 10.
[8] See E. Schürer, op. cit. II. i, p. 326.

been assumed that the Massoretic text is of a very much later date, but the evidence of the manuscripts from the Judaean wilderness seems to prove that the text reached something like its final form during the period between the two Jewish wars. For while the manuscripts belonging to the A.D. 66 deposit are said to show marked independence of the Massoretic text, those which belong to the A.D. 132 deposit are substantially identical with it.

Although the outward form of Jewish life had changed, Jewish nationalism remained unabated. After the first shock of despair had passed, confidence in the glorious future of the Jewish people returned. One of the principal motives behind the intensive study of the Torah was to prepare for the expected restoration of national independence. Details of the architecture and furniture of the temple were scrupulously preserved against the day of restoration. The sacrificial worship, though discontinued, was diligently rehearsed, and for a time even the priesthood was maintained. The two apocalyptic tracts of Baruch and IV Ezra, which belong to this period, suggest that there was some variety of opinion about the means by which national triumph was to be attained. But the revolt of A.D. 132 shows that the majority of people did not cease to put their trust in a war of liberation, and we know that one at least of the leading scholars, Rabbi Akiba, gave his enthusiastic support to that ill-starred venture.

CHAPTER III

THE FIRST CHRISTIAN COMMUNITY: 1. THE GOSPEL

1

THE first Christians were men with a story to tell, which was so important that they were ready to risk persecution and death in the telling of it. It was the story of Jesus, a man whom many of them had known intimately during the last tumultuous years that led up to his death, a man who after his death had appeared alive to many witnesses. But as they told the story, it was above all a story about God. It was God who had sent forth his servant Jesus to preach and to heal, God who had delivered him up into the hands of wicked men, God who had vindicated him in the triumph of the Resurrection. In accordance with his ancient promises to his people Israel, the God of their fathers had accomplished a new thing, the ends of the ages had come upon them, the curtain had been rung up on the final act of God's drama of redemption.

This story was called the Gospel (*evangelion*). In its origin this word had meant simply good news.[1] But before the first Christian preachers used it, it had had a history which had filled it with a deeper meaning. Deutero-Isaiah had used the term to describe his proclamation to Jerusalem that God was about to visit and redeem his people. Superficially this redemption meant release from Babylonian captivity, but the captivity of Judah had been a punishment for her sin, and the gospel of the prophet therefore involved redemption at this deeper level also; and this gospel, made possible through the vicarious suffering of the Servant of the Lord, was to be not for Israel only but for all peoples.[2] This was the term which Jesus chose to describe his own preaching, and the Synoptic Gospels leave us in no doubt that in using it he had in mind the prophecies of Deutero-Isaiah. The good news of the

---

[1] II Sam. iv. 10; xviii. 27.   [2] Isa. xl. 9; xli. 27; lii. 7; lxi. 1.

prophet to Zion had been " Thy God reigns " ; the good news of Jesus to Galilee was " The reign of God has drawn near ".[1] There is ample evidence that Jesus saw in the Suffering Servant his own vocation. It was from Jesus that his disciples learnt to see in the life, death, and Resurrection of their master the Gospel of God.

C. H. Dodd has shown us how the content of this early preaching or *kerygma* may be recovered from the New Testament.[2] Although our earliest documents, the Epistles of Paul, are not preaching but teaching, not the telling of news but the instruction of converts, nevertheless they contain many references to the Gospel which Paul had preached when he founded the churches to which his letters are addressed. From these references it is possible to reconstruct an outline of Pauline preaching. But there is good reason to believe that this outline represents a common pattern of apostolic preaching. Although Paul speaks more than once of " my Gospel ", he also insists that there was no fundamental divergence between him and those who were apostles before him.[3] On a number of occasions he mentions a tradition which he had received from others,[4] and in writing to the Christians of Rome he assumes that they have received from other missionaries a Gospel substantially the same as his own. Paul presumably received the apostolic tradition at the time of his conversion, which cannot be dated later than A.D. 35, and probably occurred somewhat sooner. By his evidence, therefore, we are carried back to a very early point in Christian history. Moreover, the pattern of preaching which underlies the Pauline Epistles appears also in the speeches attributed to Peter in the early chapters of Acts, where there is every indication that Luke is faithfully reproducing early Aramaic sources. These speeches may accordingly be taken to represent the preaching of the church at Jerusalem.

A comparative study of these speeches yields a standard apostolic sermon with six heads. (*a*) The prophecies of the Old Testament have now been fulfilled. (*b*) This has

[1] Isa. lii. 7 ; Mk. i. 15.　　[2] *The Apostolic Preaching and its Development.*
[3] Gal. ii. 1–10.　　[4] I Cor. xi. 2, 23 ff. ; xv. 3 ff. ; II Thess. ii. 15.

happened in the ministry, death, and Resurrection of Jesus.
(*c*) He has now been exalted to God's right hand as Messiah
and Lord.   (*d*) This belief has been confirmed by the gift
of the Holy Spirit.   (*e*) Jesus will return to bring God's
purposes to their consummation.   (*f*) Meanwhile men have
an opportunity to repent and to receive forgiveness and the
gift of the Holy Spirit.

Such a summary may give the impression that the first
Christian preaching was formal and stereotyped.   But the
age of credal formulae lay still in the far future.   We may
be sure that the message was delivered with a warmth of
enthusiastic conviction by men who had experienced the
blessings they proclaimed.   They preached Jesus because
through Jesus they had themselves received the forgiveness
of their sins and membership in the fellowship of the Spirit.
Jesus had imparted to them a new life, and they were concerned to share it with others.   They testified to what they
had seen and heard, because they had now become a part of
all that they had witnessed.   On the other hand, in doing
justice to the spontaneity of their faith we must not assume
that the members of the Jerusalem community were simple
reporters of facts, who took no time to reflect on the significance of the experience they described.   A full heart
does not necessarily mean an empty mind.   The first
disciples would never have begun to preach at all unless they
had believed that their experience was of universal significance, unless they had seen the events of the Gospel
story against a background of interpretation.   The outline
of apostolic preaching set out above shows clearly where that
background was discovered.   The typical sermon began
with a declaration that the Old Testament prophecies had
been fulfilled, and as each new point was introduced it provided a fresh illustration of this general theme.

The first Christians, then, were interpreters as well as
reporters.   But we may be sure that they, like any other
congregation, varied greatly in their powers of intellectual
and spiritual apprehension.   Luke tells us that the church
" continued steadfastly in the apostles' teaching ",[1] but

[1] Acts ii. 42.

among the apostles Peter showed pre-eminently the
ability and authority necessary for leadership; and among
the listeners there must have been similar differences of
capacity. If, then, we claim that a certain view of the
Atonement or a certain interpretation of the sacraments was
pre-Pauline, that does not mean that it was understood by
every member of the church, nor is it any objection to such
a claim if we find traces of a more naïve doctrine still
persisting at a later period.

2

The divine act described in the apostolic preaching was an
act of forgiveness, and the preaching closed with a summons
to accept what God had freely offered. In the theology of
Paul and later New Testament writers this forgiveness was
especially connected with the Cross. Is there then any
evidence to show that this connexion had been made in the
earliest days of the Christian movement? Many scholars
have asserted that in the speeches ascribed to Peter in Acts
there is no such evidence, and have concluded that the Cross
did not have the central place in the Gospel according to
Jerusalem which it certainly had in the Gospel according to
Paul. There are however several pieces of evidence
which point to an opposite conclusion.

Paul records as a tradition which he had received " that
Christ died for our sins according to the Scriptures ",[1] and
we have already noticed that his Gospel of justification by
faith in Christ crucified was accepted by the Jerusalem
apostles as the equivalent of their own preaching. In
writing to the Romans, Paul assumed not only that all
Christians had been admitted to the church by the ceremony
of baptism but that the ceremony had everywhere a common
interpretation : " Do you not know that all of us who were
baptized into Christ Jesus were baptized into his death ? "[2]
His account of the institution of the Lord's Supper is
similarly drawn from tradition and implies faith in Christ's
atoning death.[3]

All these traditions, then, were part of pre-Pauline

[1] I Cor. xv. 3.   [2] Rom. vi. 3.   [3] I Cor. xi. 23 ff.

Christianity. It is, of course, possible that they originated not with the Jerusalem church but with the Hellenistic party of which Stephen and Philip were the first leaders. It has been suggested that, although the Jerusalem preaching applied to Jesus the title of Servant, it was in the teaching of Philip that Isaiah liii was used for the first time as an interpretation of the Cross. But the balance of probability is against this supposition. There were Hellenists in the church from the beginning, so that their point of view must at least have been represented in the councils of the primitive church. But it is unlikely that those who for two years had kept company with Jesus needed to sit at the feet of their Hellenistic colleagues. For the church has preserved two sayings of Jesus which give a redemptive meaning to his death.[1] Neither of them can be repudiated without gross violence to the canons of historical criticism, and both owe their preservation to the memory of the Twelve. They must, therefore, have formed a part of the original Jerusalem tradition.

Moreover, the Jerusalem preaching is not so reticent about the death of Christ as has sometimes been supposed. If Christ was " delivered up by the settled purpose and foreknowledge of God ",[2] then his death had a major part to play in the divine plan of redemption. Still more important is a phrase used in two speeches in Acts, where the Jews are said to have killed Jesus, " hanging him on a tree ".[3] This is not a description of the Crucifixion which would naturally occur to a bystander. It is a quotation from Deuteronomy xxi. 22 f. : " If a man has committed a capital crime and is put to death, and you hang him on a tree, his body shall not remain all night upon the tree, but you shall bury him the same day ; for he that is hanged is under God's curse ". Surely no Christian preacher would have chosen to describe the death of Jesus in terms which drew attention to the curse of God resting upon the executed criminal, unless he had first faced the scandal of the Cross and had come to believe that Jesus had borne the curse on behalf of others.[4]

To these arguments must be added the consentient

---

[1] Mk. x. 45; xiv. 24.   [2] Acts ii. 23; cf. iv. 28.
[3] Acts v. 30; x. 39.   [4] Cf. Gal. iii. 13; I Pet. ii. 24.

witness of the New Testament writings. For the death of
Christ is presented as an Atonement not only in the Pauline
Epistles, but in Mark's Gospel, Hebrews, I Peter, Revelation, and the Johannine writings.[1] This agreement cannot be
explained solely by the dominant influence of Paul. Mark's
Gospel lacks almost all the characteristic terms and ideas
of the Pauline theology.[2] The Epistle to the Hebrews
comes from the circle of Paul's friends, as may be seen from
the mention of Timothy on xiii. 23; yet its doctrine of
Atonement by sympathy and sacrifice suggests that the
author has built his own superstructure on the foundation
of the apostolic faith. I Peter, whoever its author may have
been, has a theological simplicity which cannot have been
derived from the Pauline corpus, and in points of detail it has
been fully acquitted of dependence.[3] The Revelation was
certainly written in a church founded by Paul, but certainly
not by any docile pupil of the church's founder. John
the Evangelist has been called " the oldest and greatest
interpreter of St. Paul ",[4] but he probably had behind him a
distinctive Gospel tradition,[5] and his treatment of the Cross
is quite un-Pauline. It is noteworthy, also, that these
five writers have in common a sacrificial interpretation of the
Cross, which is conspicuously absent from the typically
Pauline theology. The obvious conclusion is that the few
passages in Paul's Epistles where sacrificial language is used
are survivals of an older point of view, and that " the word
of the Cross " is central to all these New Testament writings
because it was the heart of the original, primitive Gospel.

3

That Jesus was believed from the beginning to have died
a vicarious death is made still more probable when we come

[1] Matthew's Gospel, the Pastoral Epistles, and the Epistle to the
Ephesians (if it is not by Paul) may be added, but their evidence is
secondary. The silence of Luke on this theme in both Gospel and Acts
must be deliberate, since he wrote with Mark in front of him.
[2] A. E. J. Rawlinson, *The Gospel according to St. Mark*, pp. xliii–xlv;
V. Taylor, *The Gospel according to St. Mark*, pp. 65 ff., 125–129.
[3] P. Carrington, *The Primitive Christian Catechism*; E. G. Selwyn, *The
First Epistle of St. Peter*, pp. 248–281, 364–466.
[4] A. Deissmann, *St. Paul*, p. 8.
[5] P. Gardner-Smith, *St. John and the Synoptics*.

to study the early preaching about the Resurrection. The very use of the word resurrection is significant. It was clearly used from the first, and its use implies that the appearances of the risen Jesus were already understood in relation to an earlier eschatology. But in the Jewish eschatological hope the resurrection was to be a corporate event, in which Israel, or at least faithful Israel, would be raised to share in the blessings of the coming kingdom. If men reared in this expectation spoke of the Resurrection of Jesus, it could mean to them only that with Jesus the promised resurrection of Israel had begun. Jesus had been raised as the first-born from the dead.[1] A season of harvest had arrived in which the offering of the first-fruits would be followed by the great ingathering.[2] This was surely the chief ground for the belief, so universally held by the first Christians,[3] that the last days had arrived. The Resurrection of Jesus was proof to his followers that they were living in the midst of the great divine event, which they therefore believed must shortly come to its triumphant consummation.

The argument is carried a stage further by the primitive tradition, recorded by Paul, that Christ " rose again on the third day in accordance with the Scriptures ".[4] The only Scripture which mentions a resurrection on the third day has to do not with the raising of an individual man but with the restoration of Israel.[5] We must conclude, therefore, that Paul received his traditional formula from men who believed that in the representative suffering and triumph of Jesus the whole people of God had passed through humiliation to glory. The future resurrection of Christians was assured because it was implicit in the decisive and inclusive event of Easter morning.

According to Mark Jesus thrice predicted both his death and his resurrection on the third day, and the terms of the first prediction clearly indicate that these prophecies were founded on a divine necessity that the Scriptures should be

---

[1] Col. i. 18; Rev. i. 5; cf. Rom. viii. 29.   [2] I Cor. xv. 20–24.
[3] Acts ii. 17; I Cor. x. 11; II Tim. iii. 1; Heb. i. 2; I Pet. i. 20; I Jn. ii. 18.   [4] I Cor. xv. 4.   [5] Hos. vi. 2.

fulfilled.[1] Even if the radical critics were right in regarding
these passages as a reading back of church doctrine into the
teaching of Jesus, we should still have valuable evidence
from a source independent of Paul that the church interpreted the Resurrection as a corporate event which fulfilled
Hosea's prophecy. Whereas if—as is most probable—the
sayings are genuine, then we can safely infer that Jesus
applied to himself Hosea's prophecy and believed that in his
approaching death and Resurrection the purpose of God
for Israel was reaching its fulfilment. In that case we find
once again that Jesus was not only the theme but the
originator of the church's doctrine.

Without the Resurrection there could have been no
Christianity; yet the Resurrection was no isolated event.
The first preachers did not proclaim to the world that a
resurrection had occurred. They preached the Resurrection of the Crucified. Nowhere in the New Testament is
there any justification for separating these twin pillars of
the Gospel. The Resurrection vindicated the innocence
of Jesus and revealed his death as a mystery of divine love,
while the Crucifixion gave to men the assurance that the
Risen One was also the Saviour.

4

The representative character of the work of Christ is
expressed also in the title Messiah which, according to the
early preaching, was bestowed upon him in virtue of his
death and Resurrection.[2] The Messiah was expected to
come as the king over a restored Israel, and the mere fact
that a man had died and risen again could not have earned
for him the right to the name. It was because Jesus had
died and risen as the representative of Israel that he was
believed to have been exalted to the right hand of God
as head over God's new people.

There can be no question that we are here dealing with the
primitive faith of the Jerusalem church. The name
Messiah had significance only to Jews and would not have

---

[1] Mk. viii. 31; ix. 31; x. 34; cf. xiv. 21; Lk. xxiv. 26.   [2] Acts ii. 36.

been used at all in the Gentile mission unless it had been firmly embedded in the earliest Palestinian tradition. Even so, to Paul and his converts " Christ " had ceased to be a title and had become a proper name.

The disciples of Jesus spoke of him as Messiah after his Resurrection because they had already been accustomed to think of him as Messiah before his death.[1] But neither at Caesarea Philippi nor on the day of Pentecost did Peter identify Jesus with a person clearly defined by religious orthodoxy. " It cannot be too strongly emphasized that there was no generally accepted opinion, no organized and consistent teaching, above all no orderly Messianic doctrine possessing the faintest shadow of authority. The thing itself was of faith, all the rest was free field for the imagination." [2] Peter's " Thou art the Messiah " was more than the discovery of a truth about Jesus; it was an insight into the true nature of messiahship. The vague word Messiah was being defined in terms of the known Jesus. Similarly the post-Resurrection faith meant that God had set the seal of his approval on the life and death of the Crucified and on his interpretation of the messianic calling. Those who held this faith were committed to the Gospel of a crucified Messiah.

The Jerusalem Christians preached Jesus not only as Messiah but as Lord.[3] Little support can now be found for Bousset's theory that this title was first ascribed to Jesus by Gentile Christians who derived it from the Hellenistic mystery religions.[4] " Jesus is Lord " was certainly a pre-Pauline confession, and may well have been the regular baptismal formula.[5] The title was part of a tradition which Paul had received concerning the Last Supper.[6] James of Jerusalem, surely the least Hellenistic of Christians, was habitually known as " the Lord's brother ".[7] The universal belief of the early church that the exalted Christ was

---

[1] Mk. viii. 29.   [2] *The Beginnings of Christianity*, I, p. 356.
[3] Acts ii. 36; x. 36.
[4] W. Bousset, *Kyrios Christos*; and for a refutation A. E. J. Rawlinson *The New Testament Doctrine of the Christ*, Appendix A.
[5] I. Cor. xii. 3; Rom. x. 9; II Cor. iv. 5; Phil. ii. 11; cf. Acts xix. 5.
[6] I Cor. xi. 23.   [7] Gal. i. 19; cf. I Cor. ix. 5.

seated at the right hand of God was based on a psalm in
which the Messiah was given the name of Lord.[1] There is
also strong evidence that even during his ministry Jesus
claimed lordship as in some sense an attribute of his own
vocation,[2] and that he applied to himself Scriptures in which
the title occurred.[3] But the decisive proof is to be found
in the prayer *Maranatha* (Our Lord, come), which must have
originated in the Aramaic-speaking church.[4]

5

The apostolic preaching made no mention of a church,
but men who believed that Jesus was both Messiah and Lord
of necessity believed something distinctive about themselves
also. They were the new Israel. This belief is assumed by
all New Testament writers,[5] and can be traced back to
Jesus himself. His appointment of the Twelve and his
solemn inauguration of the new covenant are adequate
indications of his intention to bring into being a new people
of God, continuous indeed with the old Israel, but cleansed
by the remission of sins for the new life of the Kingdom.
The appointment of Matthias to fill up the symbolic number
after the defection of Judas shows equally clearly that the
disciples had understood Jesus' intention.[6]

The new Israel was a community belonging essentially to
the world to come, which in the ministry of Jesus had
irrupted into the present age. All who accepted the invita-
tion to enter it thereby saved themselves " from this
crooked generation ", and joined the ranks of those who
were already experiencing " the powers of the age to
come ".[7]

Owing to our ignorance of Palestinian Aramaic, there is
still some doubt about the exact name by which this

[1] Ps. cx. 1; cf. Acts ii. 33 ff.; v. 31; vii. 55 f.; Rom. viii. 34; I Cor. xv.
25; Eph. i. 20; Col. iii. 1; Heb. i. 3, 13; x. 12 f.; I Pet. iii. 22.
[2] Mt. vii. 21; Lk. vi. 46; Mk. ii. 28.
[3] Mk. ix. 11–13; xii. 35–37; Mt. xi. 14.
[4] I Cor. xvi. 22; Did. x. 6.
[5] Gal. vi. 16; Rom. ix. 6; Jas. i. 1; I Pet. i. 1; ii. 9; Heb. xii. 22–24;
Rev. vii. 4 ff; Jn. xv. 1–8.
[6] See also R. N. Flew, *Jesus and His Church*.
[7] Acts ii. 40; Heb. vi. 5.

community was known to Aramaic-speaking Christians.[1] But we do know that, when Paul joined the Greek-speaking branch of the church, the term *ecclesia* was already in use.[2] This word is used in the Septuagint, together with *synagoge*, to translate the Hebrew *'edhah* and *qahal*—the assembly or congregation of Israel. *Synagoge* later came to mean particularly the local gathering of Jews for worship, and even the building used for that purpose. The choice of *ecclesia*, therefore, by the Greek-speaking Christians as a designation for the Christian community constituted a claim that that community was no mere sect of Israel but the true, messianic people of God. But this claim was not a Hellenistic innovation. Whatever the word they used, the Jerusalem Christians certainly believed that they were the church of God.

To this community Jesus had a double relationship. Firstly, he was its messianic head who had been exalted to God's right hand and given the name of Lord. This can only mean that from the first he was the object of worship. To share the throne of God is to share the attributes of deity.[3] Paul tells us, whether in his own words or in a quotation from an earlier hymn, that the purpose of Christ's exaltation was " that at the name of Jesus every knee should bow," [4] and this is but a logical corollary to the citation of Psalm cx. Paul's own practice of praying to Christ has an earlier counterpart in the prayer of the dying Stephen,[5] and *Maranatha* is evidence that prayer was offered to Christ by the Aramaic-speaking church. An attitude of worship is implied also in " calling upon the name of the Lord," which Paul assumed to be the universal Christian response to the preaching of the Gospel.[6]

From another point of view Jesus was Israel. We have already seen that the church prior to Paul applied to Jesus a prophecy of Hosea which originally referred to Israel.

---

[1] K. L. Schmidt, *The Church* (tr. from Kittel's *Theologisches Wörterbuch zum N.T.* by J. R. Coates), pp. 47–50; G. Johnston, *The Doctrine of the Church in the N.T.*, pp. 35–45.　　[2] Gal. i. 13; I Cor. xv. 9.
[3] See H. Sasse, " Jesus Christ the Lord ", in *Mysterium Christi* (ed. G. K. A. Bell and A. Deissmann), pp. 93 ff.　　[4] Phil. ii. 10.
[5] II Cor. xii. 8; Acts vii. 59 f.　　[6] Rom. x. 13; I Cor. i. 2.

Similar uses of the Old Testament in the New Testament could be multiplied. To take the most important example, the description of the suffering of the Servant of the Lord in Isaiah liii is quoted by so many different writers that the application of the prophecy to Jesus must go back at least to the primitive church, and almost certainly to Jesus himself.[1] But who is this Servant of the Lord, who by his suffering was to bear the sins of many? This is a notoriously difficult question to answer. Did the prophet mean Israel? Or the Remnant? Or the Messiah? Champions of all three theories have come forward, and it is probable that each contains a measure of truth. For to the Semitic mind a group had a corporate personality which could be embodied in an individual, and the individual was bound up in the bundle of life with the group. Israel, the Remnant, and the Messiah were three different facets of the one idea. Deutero-Isaiah knew that God would bring salvation through his servant Israel, but he could not tell with certainty whether God would save by many, by few, or by one. On any interpretation of Isaiah liii, therefore, Jesus could become the Servant of the prophet's vision only by fulfilling the divinely appointed destiny of Israel.

All that is implicit in this type of old Testament exegesis was fully developed by Paul in his doctrine that Christians have died and risen with Christ and that to be in the church is to be in Christ. But these implications cannot have been entirely hidden from his predecessors through whom the Synoptic traditions were handed down. For in the Synoptic Gospels the corporate nature of the work of Christ is eloquently expressed in the title of his own choice—Son of Man. In view of his confession before Caiaphas,[2] his use of this title must be explained primarily by reference to Daniel vii. 13, where the Son of Man is a symbolic figure representing the kingdom of the saints of the Most High. As Son of Man Jesus united in his own person the whole people of God. When he predicted that as Son of Man he

[1] Mt. viii. 17; Mk. x. 45; Lk. xxii. 37; Acts viii. 32; Jn. xii. 38; Rom. iv. 25; x. 16; Heb. ix. 28; I Pet. ii. 22–25.
[2] Mk. xiv. 62.

must suffer and rise again, he was proclaiming the representative quality of his death and Resurrection. It is true that this title makes only one appearance in the records of the primitive church,[1] but the fact that the early Christians preserved in their Gospel tradition a usage of Jesus which they had not adopted into their own vocabulary suggests that they were better able to distinguish their own ideas from the remembered words of the Master than some modern scholars have been inclined to suppose.[2] Whatever be the explanation of its disuse, the title Son of Man provides us with yet another argument to show that the foundations of Pauline theology are to be sought in the teaching of Jesus accurately preserved by the first disciples.

6

From the early church Paul inherited also the traditions of baptism and the Lord's Supper, both of which he interpreted as sacraments of union with the crucified and risen Christ. In each case there is a high degree of probability that the interpretation as well as the sacrament was pre-Pauline.

The two New Testament sacraments are best explained as symbolic acts like those of the Old Testament prophets. When Jeremiah broke his pitcher in the valley of Hinnom, he believed that his act was not merely a dramatic representation of the coming destruction of Jerusalem but that it helped to bring about that which it symbolized.[3] Prophetic symbolism has sometimes been compared with sympathetic magic, but the two practices arose from totally different motives. The magician tried by potent formula and action to coerce the deity into giving him what he wanted, but the prophet uttered under a sense of constraint a message given to him from above. The prophet believed his symbolism to be effective because it was a visible preaching of the word of God, and the word of God is always effective. He speaks and it is done. His word does not return to him

---

[1] Acts vii. 56.
[2] Cf. I Cor. vii. 25; and see also F. C. Burkitt, *Christian Beginnings*, p. 136; B. S. Easton, *Christ in the Gospels*, pp. 40 f.   [3] Jer. xix.

void, but accomplishes that which he pleases. In the same way the sacraments of baptism and the Lord's Supper were a visible preaching of the word which God had spoken in Jesus Christ. God had promised to those who believed in Christ forgiveness and the gift of the Spirit, new life and membership in the messianic community. Of all this baptism and the Lord's Supper were the symbols, and because God is always true to his promises, the sacraments conveyed that which they symbolized. This Hebraic interpretation of the sacraments is attested by I Peter, where newly baptized converts are described as " begotten again . . . through the living and abiding word of God " ; [1] and by Paul who calls the Lord's Supper a preaching of the Lord's death.[2] If then we can discover what the sacraments meant to those who first administered them, we shall have an additional insight into the meaning of the apostolic Gospel.

Christian baptism was a lineal descendant of the baptism of John. It is probable that the Jews were already practising the baptism (*tebilah*) mentioned in the Mishna as part of the ceremony of cleansing by which proselytes were admitted to Israel, since they would hardly have introduced the practice after the institution of Christian baptism.[3] But John gave to the rite a new eschatological meaning by demanding that the Jews also should undergo a baptism of repentance for the remission of sins as an initiation into the messianic community, into which the Coming One would gather the true sons of Abraham as wheat into the garner. Mark, Q, and Acts all agree in making John's baptism the beginning of the Christian Gospel, and the baptism mentioned in Peter's first sermon is still associated with the remission of sins.[4]

According to Acts, baptism was practised from the day of

---

[1] I Pet. i. 23; cf. Jas. i. 18; Acts ii. 41; xvi. 32 f. Reitzenstein's theory that baptism was introduced into Christianity from the mystery religions no longer needs refutation. The metaphor of a new birth is adequately explained by the connexion of Ps. ii. with the baptism of Jesus and by Rabbinic parallels (see W. D. Davies, *St. Paul and Rabbinic Judaism*, pp. 119 f.   [2] I Cor. xi. 26.

[3] Pesachim viii. 8; see F. Gavin, *The Jewish Antecedents of the Christian Sacraments*, pp. 30–40.   [4] Acts ii. 38; cf. iii. 19; x. 43.

D

Pentecost, and this is confirmed by Paul, whose references to baptism imply not only that he himself had been baptized at the time of his conversion, but that he assumed the same to be true of all other Christians.[1] But it must be admitted that we have a problem here. All our sources agree that John drew a distinction between his own baptism with water and the coming baptism with the Spirit, which he expected to supersede his own.[2] How then did baptism with water come to be the symbol of baptism with the Spirit?

Two explanations may be discarded at once. In the Fourth Gospel we are told that Jesus allowed his disciples to practise baptism during the early period of his ministry while he was working with John in the Jordan valley.[3] But the tendency of the Fourth Gospel to read back later developments into the story of the ministry should warn us not to put too much weight on this statement, and in any case there is nothing to show that the practice was maintained after John's arrest. Again, Matthew has recorded a command of the risen Jesus to baptize all nations in the name of the Trinity,[4] but there are two good reasons for questioning its authenticity. In the first place, early baptism was administered in the name of the Lord Jesus, or of Jesus Christ, and not with the Trinitarian formula.[5] Secondly, it is difficult to explain the reluctance of the Jerusalem church to embark on a mission to the Gentiles, if they had received from Jesus an explicit command to do so. It is, of course, possible that Matthew or one of his sources has elaborated a simple command to the disciples to baptize

---

[1] Gal. iii. 27; I Cor. xii. 13; Rom. vi. 3 f.

[2] Some modern scholars would dismiss this evidence in favour of a theory that John predicted only a baptism of fire (i.e. a judgment), and that a baptism with the Spirit was erroneously introduced into the tradition of John's preaching because in the Pentecostal experience tongues of fire were a symbol of the coming of the Spirit. But John predicted more than a judgment. The Coming One was not only to burn the chaff but also to gather the wheat, i.e. the new Israel, with which the gift of the Spirit was already firmly connected in O.T. prophecy. For our present purpose, however, all that matters is not what John actually said but what the early Christians believed him to have said; and about this there is no doubt.

[3] Jn. iii. 22; iv. 2.

[4] Mt. xxviii. 19.   [5] Acts ii. 38; viii. 16; x. 48; xix. 5.

their converts,[1] but even if we accept this precarious suggestion, it does not solve our problem. Whether the association between water baptism and Spirit baptism was made first in the mind of Jesus or in the minds of his followers, it still requires explanation.

There remains, therefore, the probability that Christian baptism was modelled on the baptism of Jesus. The disciples must have heard from Jesus of the descent of the dove at the moment when he rose from the waters of baptism, and it would be natural for them to feel, even without an explicit command from Jesus himself, that the gift of the Spirit should come to the followers of Jesus through the same rite in which it came to him, and that those who were admitted to the fellowship of Christ's people should be baptized with his baptism. This much at least is certain, that the early converts were baptized " in the name of the Lord Jesus " or " in the name of Jesus Christ ", and that in his name remission of sins and salvation was offered to them.[2] Thus in baptism they were brought into some sort of union with Christ.

The precise nature of this union depends on the interpretation they gave to the baptism of Jesus, and here we have to be guided mainly by the Synoptic tradition. The voice from heaven implies that this was Jesus' anointing as Messiah,[3] but there are indications that at that time the concept of Messiah was fused in his mind with that of the Servant of the Lord—he heard himself addressed as Son, but also as " my Beloved in whom I am well pleased," [4] and he introduced the idea of service into his first answer to the temptations of Satan.[5] The baptism of Jesus, then, was his anointing as Servant,[6] and he was sufficiently at home in the prophecies of Isaiah to realize, even at this early date, that it was also his initiation into his death. Two sayings which belong to the later part of the ministry show that at that time the ideas of baptism and death were closely associated in his mind. As a baptism of water had

---

[1] See W. F. Flemington, *The New Testament Doctrine of Baptism,* pp. 105–109.
[2] Acts ii. 38; iv. 12.
[3] Cf. Acts x. 38.
[4] Mk. i. 11; cf. Isa. xlii. 1.
[5] Mt. iv. 10; Lk. iv. 8.
[6] Lk. iv. 18.

inaugurated his earthly ministry, so the baptism of death
was to be the inauguration of a ministry freed from present
restraints and hindrances. " I have a baptism to be
baptized with, and how I am restricted until it is accomplished ! " [1] What he had anticipated in the prophetic
symbolism of Jordan was to be acted out in the grim
realism of Golgotha. In the other passage Jesus not only
spoke of his own death as a baptism, but declared that it was
possible for others to share that baptism. " With my
baptism you shall be baptized." [2] The way was therefore
open for his followers to interpret baptism as a symbolic
sharing in his death.   It is surely significant that Paul, who
regarded baptism as a putting on of Christ crucified, a
symbolic dying with Christ, assumed that this was the
commonly accepted interpretation. [3]

7

The other Gospel sacrament was known to Paul as the
Lord's Supper. [4] At Corinth, and presumably in every
Pauline church, it consisted of a fellowship meal, in the
course of which bread was broken and a cup shared according
to the example set by Jesus at the Last Supper and in
memory of the Cross, of which the Last Supper had been
the prophetic symbol. The bread and the cup were the
tokens of a new community and a new covenant, which had
been inaugurated by Christ's Passion and would be perfected
by his Second Coming. Paul claims that in instituting this
rite he was following a pattern which he had " received from
the Lord." These words have sometimes been taken to
mean that Paul's knowledge of the Last Supper was derived
from a direct revelation, or that Christ had conveyed to him
in a vision the true meaning of a rite which the church had
formerly practised with uncomprehending fidelity.   But the
commonly accepted interpretation is that Paul was ack-
knowledging one of his many debts to the traditions of the
primitive church.

---

[1] Lk. xii. 50.   [2] Mk. x. 38 f.
[3] Gal. iii. 27 ; Rom. vi. 3 f.   [4] I Cor. xi. 20–34.

This view is strongly supported by Mark's account of the Last Supper.[1] The form of the narrative suggests that it was preserved for its importance in worship, and we may safely take it to represent the eucharistic tradition of the Roman church. The absence of any command to repeat the rite, the words " poured out for many " and the eschatological saying in verse 25, the difficult Greek of the phrase " my blood of the covenant," and the identification of the meal with the Passover all combine to prove Mark's independence of Paul.[2] Yet, for all these minor differences, the two accounts are in substantial agreement, and the tradition which has their united testimony has every right to be regarded as primitive.

If we had only the evidence of Paul and Mark to consider, we should certainly conclude that the Lord's Supper as they understood it had been observed by the Christian church from the beginning. But before we can accept this conclusion, we must meet three objections based on other New Testament writings. Firstly, there is no eucharistic teaching to be found in Acts, I Peter, the Pastoral Epistles, Hebrews or Revelation, and this has been taken to mean that there was no general agreement about the relation of the Last Supper to the death of Christ.[3] But the argument from silence is notoriously weak, and in this case its weakness can be demonstrated. If there had been no disorders in the conduct of public worship at Corinth, Paul would have left no hint that he had ever heard of the Last Supper or that he had handed on to his converts a command to repeat the rite; and from his silence we might have concluded that no such sacrament was celebrated in the churches he established, or indeed in any other churches.

The argument from Luke's account of the Last Supper [4] is almost as precarious, since this narrative has produced a plethora of theories and a minimum of agreement. The

---

[1] Mk. xiv. 16–25.

[2] " The vocabulary, style, and ideas are Jewish, and there are strong reasons for thinking that the narrative is of Palestinian origin." V. Taylor, *The Gospel according to St. Mark*, p. 542; cf. J. Jeremias, *Die Abendmahlsworte Jesu*, pp. 80–99.

[3] V. Taylor, *The Atonement in N.T. Teaching*, pp. 234 ff.

[4] Lk. xxii. 14–20.

theories fall into three main types. (1) There are still a few champions of the longer text, which has the great majority of manuscripts in its favour.[1] For them there is no problem, since Luke is then in complete agreement with Paul and Mark, whose accounts he has conflated. But most scholars prefer, with Hort,[2] to follow the text of D and to treat vv. 19b–20 as a second-century harmonization. (2) The shorter text may be regarded as a free adaptation of Mark. According to this theory vv. 15–18 are a literary expansion of Mk. xiv. 25, and the Marcan saying over the cup has been omitted because of a doctrinal prejudice which also caused Luke to omit Mk. x. 45. In the opinion of J. M. Creed Luke could not have treated Mark's account in this way unless Christian rites and institutions had been still in a fluid state,[3] but it is doubtful whether the theory will bear the weight of this deduction, since *ex hypothesi* Luke was not reflecting any eucharistic tradition which would constitute an independent source. (3) Luke may have drawn all or part of his material from his special source. According to one view, vv. 15–17 and 19a were drawn from L and v. 18 from Mark,[4] according to another vv. 15–18 were from L and v. 19a from Mark.[5] In either case Luke must have had a non-Marcan account of the Last Supper which gave special emphasis to the eschatological hope and barely mentioned the Cross. It does not, however, necessarily follow from this that the Lucan source is more accurate or more primitive than the tradition attested by the joint evidence of Mark and Paul.

The third difficulty arises out of Luke's references to " the breaking of the bread ".[6] In view of the normal Jewish practice of giving a religious significance to every meal by breaking bread and pronouncing a blessing, it is conceivable that these passages refer to ordinary meals, but the contexts

[1] A. J. B. Higgins, *The Lord's Supper in the N.T.*, pp. 43 f.
[2] F. J. A. Hort, *Introduction*, pp. 63 f.
[3] *The Gospel according to St. Luke*, pp. 260 ff; cf. H. Lietzmann, *Messe und Herrenmahl*, pp. 216 f.
[4] B. H. Streeter, *The Four Gospels*, pp. 216, 222.
[5] V. Taylor, *Behind the Third Gospel*, pp. 35–40.
[6] Lk. xxiv. 30, 35; Acts ii. 42, 46; xx. 7, 11.

in which the phrase occurs suggest rather that the meals in question had a specifically Christian character, though the nature of the ceremony is not explained. It is clear, however, that the practice of holding these meals did not originate at the Last Supper, since we are told that Jesus was recognised in the breaking of the bread by two disciples who were not present in the upper room.

In *Messe und Herrenmahl* H. Lietzmann put forward the hypothesis that there were two distinct types of early eucharistic practice, the Jerusalem and the Pauline. The Jerusalem disciples, who had been accustomed to sharing meals with Jesus during his ministry, continued to hold fellowship meals in the presence of the risen Christ. These meals, which were known as " the breaking of the bread ", included no cup and had no connexion with the Last Supper or the Cross, but were a joyful anticipation of the messianic banquet to be held at the return of Christ. The other type of celebration was derived from the Last Supper and from a special revelation in which Paul " received from the Lord " the true meaning of the sacrament as a memorial of the Lord's death.

This theory of dual origins is open to serious objection. Paul's description of the Last Supper reads much more naturally as a formal church tradition than as the record of a visionary experience.[1] Luke, on whose evidence the theory was erected, knew of no such difference, for he used the same language to describe the rite over which Paul presided at Troas—at which he himself was present—as he used to describe the fellowship meals held in Jerusalem under the auspices of Peter. Nor can a rigid distinction be sustained between Paul's memorial sacrament and the eschatological feast of the primitive church. Paul combines both ideas in a single sentence (" You preach the Lord's death until he comes "), and the same combination of ideas is found in Mark, and to some extent even in the shorter text of Luke. It is also extremely difficult to believe that those disciples for whom the meals with Jesus had culminated in the Last Supper could have prolonged the

---

[1] R. Otto, *The Kingdom of God and the Son of Man*, p. 276.

series without any thought of the one meal to which Jesus had given a special and solemn meaning.

Not all of Lietzmann's theory needs to be discarded. We may well believe that Jesus broke bread at many a meal with a wider circle of disciples than the Twelve, and that from his characteristic action these meals came to be known as " the breaking of the bread ". The name would persist even when, under the influence of the Last Supper, a new interpretation was given to the broken bread and a cup was added to the symbolism of the meal. It is possible that even during his ministry Jesus taught his disciples to regard their common meals as anticipations of the messianic banquet. But even if we grant all this, there is in the Lucan writings no evidence sufficient to outweigh the impressive agreement of Paul and Mark that the Lord's Supper was from the earliest times a memory of the Lord's death as well as an expectation of his return.

Where there is so much room for doubt and dispute, dogmatism is out of order. But the only reliable evidence points to the conclusion that the members of the primitive church shared the bread and the cup as a sacrament of the Lord's death, so that, having been united with him in his Passion, they might be united with him also in the glory of his eternal kingdom.

CHAPTER IV

THE FIRST CHRISTIAN COMMUNITY: 2. THE SPIRIT

1

THE faith of the first Christians that in Jesus God had visited and redeemed his people was founded on the Resurrection, attested by living witnesses; but it was confirmed both to them and to later converts by the gift of the Spirit. When the author of Hebrews reminds his readers that the Gospel preached to them by eye-witnesses had been accompanied by an impressive display of divine energy, including " distributions of the Holy Spirit ", he is true to the earliest tradition, preserved for us in Peter's Pentecostal sermon, where the gift of the Spirit has the same evidential character.[1] A modern Christian might be embarrassed at being asked, " Did you receive the Holy Spirit when you believed ? "[2] But to such a question the Christian of the first generation expected a precise answer. For the Spirit made his presence known unmistakably by the gift of revitalizing power, and the sense of newly acquired power was one of the marks of apostolic Christianity. At first it was natural that attention should be directed to the obvious and dramatic signs of the Spirit's activity, and we find accordingly that tongues, prophecy, and miracle bulk large in the early records. But we shall see the early period of church history sadly out of perspective if we imagine that the Holy Spirit was regarded merely or mainly as the source of wonders and portents. The Holy Spirit in the Bible is always the immanent power of the Living God, who through human agency is shaping history to his own ends; and in the New Testament the Spirit is always the gift of Christ, whereby men are enabled to participate in his ministry and purpose. The works of the Spirit, therefore, were never mere marvels. Even those which to modern sophistication appear to be " unspiritual " had a

[1] Heb. ii. 4; Acts ii. 33; iv. 32.   [2] Acts xix. 2.

positive religious value to which we must be ready to open our minds; and they were accompanied from the first by other works which were of more permanent worth for the building up of Christian character and Christian society. But whatever the form it took, the experience of power was so universal among believers that Paul could appeal to it with confidence as a proof that the old order had given place to new, and that God was fulfilling his promise of creating for himself a new people.[1]

From the time of Ezekiel the promise of the Spirit had been part of Israel's eschatological hope,[2] a promise renewed in three prophecies which can be shown to have received particular attention from Christian teachers.[3] This association of the Spirit with the last days was a familiar idea in first-century Judaism.[4] In the light of this tradition it is not surprising that Jesus should have pointed to the obvious activity of the Spirit in his own ministry as a proof that the kingdom of God had arrived,[5] nor that his followers should have found the same argument convincing.

The Holy Spirit in the New Testament is always an eschatological gift, a proof and an anticipation of the coming End. To Paul the Spirit is the earnest or first-fruits of our inheritance,[6] in Hebrews the partaker of the Holy Spirit is said to have " tasted . . . the powers of the age to come ", in I Peter the Spirit of God rests on those who are following Christ through suffering to glory, in the Revelation the Spirit is the spirit of prophecy which enables the martyrs to bear their last triumphant testimony, and in the Fourth Gospel the coming of the Paraclete has almost taken the place of the Parousia.[7] Any belief that has such universal support is likely to have been a part of the primitive faith, and this conclusion is borne out by the speeches attributed to Peter in Acts, where the gift of the

[1] Gal. iii. 5.
[2] Ezek. xxxvi. 27; xxxvii. 14; xxxix. 29.
[3] Isa. xliv. 3; Joel ii. 28–32; Zech. xii. 10. See C. H. Dodd, *The Old Testament in the New.*
[4] Test. Jud. xxiv. 2 f.   [5] Lk. xi. 20; Mt. xii. 28.
[6] II Cor. i. 22; v. 5; Rom. viii. 23; Eph. i. 14.
[7] Heb. vi. 4 f; I Pet. iv. 14; Rev. xi. 3; xix. 10; Jn. xiv. 16 ff.

Spirit is intimately connected with the eschatological crisis that has been brought into existence by the death and Resurrection of Jesus.

2

The earliest and most spectacular manifestation of the Spirit's presence was glossolalia or speaking with tongues. Of all the activities of the early church this is the furthest removed from the range of normal modern experience, and it is therefore the more imperative that we should try to enter into a sympathetic and imaginative understanding of it, if we are to have an accurate picture of primitive Christianity. From Paul's full treatment of this subject in I Corinthians xii–xiv, and from the records of similar phenomena in more recent times,[1] it is possible to obtain a fairly clear conception of this form of speech. Men and women undergoing a profound religious experience found themselves compelled by an upsurge of emotion to give utterance to thoughts and feelings far beyond the range of their normal powers of expression; and this they did with an outpouring of vocables which was usually unintelligible both to the speaker and to the audience,[2] though there were some people who claimed the ability to interpret the ecstasies of their fellow Christians.[3] As the name "tongues" indicates, those who were endowed with this gift were popularly supposed to be speaking foreign languages. To this belief Paul himself subscribed, as may be seen from his mention of different types of tongues and his quotation from Isaiah,[4] but he left it open whether in any given case the language was human or angelic.[5] There can be no doubt, therefore, that glossolalia gave the normal impression of articulate utterance and not of hysterical raving.

In Acts there is good evidence that glossolalia was a

---

[1] P. G. S. Hopwood, *The Religious Experience of the Primitive Church,* pp. 145–162.
[2] I Cor. xiv. 2, 14, 16, 19.
[3] I Cor. xii. 10.
[4] Ibid. xii. 10; xiv. 21.
[5] Ibid. xiii. 1.

common experience in the early church,[1] and there is no reason to doubt that it made its first appearance on the day of Pentecost, since the bystanders' charge of drunkenness shows that we have here to do with ecstatic speech. Luke's account of Pentecost has been subjected to much ill-considered criticism, on the grounds that he has wilfully transformed an occurrence of glossolalia into a linguistic miracle. But Luke did not invent the theory that glossolalia was foreign speech. Like Paul he accepted the current explanation. If he is in any way responsible for heightening the effect of the story which had come down to him, it is because he assumed that each of the inspired disciples was speaking a different language, so that in a crowd drawn from every nation under the sun many would be bound to recognize their native tongue. Nor can we rule out the possibility that his assumption had a basis of historic truth. We have already seen that on occasion glossolalia could be interpreted. It may well be that at its first appearance, while some of the pilgrim crowd recoiled in disgust, communication was established in the minds of the more sympathetic listeners, so that they felt themselves carried by the speakers' enthusiasm into new realms of religious experience.

According to Luke, Peter at once concluded that the tumultuous experience which he and his companions had undergone was the outpouring of the Spirit foretold by the prophet Joel. They had been taught by Jesus to regard his ministry as the beginning of the new age, and to await the gift of the Spirit. But it is worthy of note that they should have regarded their glossolalia as the fulfilment of this promise. It is to this fact that we must look if we would understand what Pentecost meant to those who heard the rushing, mighty wind and saw the tongues of flame descend. They must have felt themselves exalted by an access of energy which demanded immediate expression. Later it would be directed into more useful channels, but for the moment it found what outlet it could. Paul, to be sure, insisted that it was both necessary and possible to

[1] Acts x. 46; xix. 6.

confine glossolalia within the limits of decency and good order,[1] and he spoke from personal experience, for he possessed the gift in a high degree.[2] But it should also be noted that in the midst of an impassioned attack on disorder in worship Paul never suggests that glossolalia is anything but a profound religious experience. " He who speaks in a tongue speaks . . . to God." [3] His speech may be unedifying to the listener, but it is a genuine communion. Provided that order be maintained, the Spirit is not to be quenched when with inexpressible groanings he assists in the intercessions of the saints.[4]

3

Superficially similar, but of immeasurably greater religious significance was the gift of prophecy. The two gifts are mentioned together,[5] presumably because both were forms of ecstatic speech, whose only outward difference was that prophecy was intelligible to the hearer. But though glossolalia died out within a generation, the prophet came to share with the apostle the place of pre-eminence in the church.[6] A study of Old Testament prophecy helps us to understand why this should have been so. Even the greatest of the prophets were subject to ecstasy and trance, but these abnormalities never constituted the essence of their vocation. A. Guillaume has compared the ecstasy of the prophet with the facial contortions and gestures of the high jumper. " Ecstasy and trance are, as it were, the postures of prophecy. There are accidents, but not inseparable accidents. They are common to monotheism and heathenism; they do not affect the inner reality of inspiration, which is to be sought in the divine use of the human instrument." [7] Whatever may have been the psychological mechanism of his calling, it was the nature of the Old Testament prophet that he spoke the word of the Lord; and it was the nature of the New Testament prophet that through him the Spirit spoke to the churches.

[1] I Cor. xiv. 40. [2] Ibid. xiv. 18. [3] I Cor. xiv. 2.
[4] I Thess. v. 19; Rom. viii. 26 f. [5] Acts xix. 6; I Cor. xii–xiv.
[6] Eph. ii. 20; iii. 5; iv. 11. [7] *Prophecy and Divination*, p. 364.

In first-century Judaism prophecy was confined to apocalyptic predictions of the End with all its preliminary woes. Some modern scholars have held that Christian prophecy conformed to the same pattern, and that the famine prediction of Agabus,[1] for example, was only a part of a larger forecast of disaster provoked by Caligula's threat to have his image installed in the temple.[2] Apocalyptic is, indeed, magnificently represented in the New Testament by the Revelation of John of Patmos. and Rawlinson may be right in treating Mark's " Little Apocalypse " as the work of a Christian prophet.[3] But there is no need for us to suppose that the primitive church was in any way circumscribed by Jewish precedent, and all the evidence is to the contrary. First John the Baptist and then Jesus had revived prophecy in its classical form, and in the New Testament prophecy covers many types of inspired utterance. Moreover, the Christian prophet lived in an inspired society, and many of his spiritual gifts were shared by other Christians, so that we might easily get the impression that in the early church all the Lord's people were prophets.

Prophecy certainly included inspired preaching. At Thessalonica and again at Corinth Paul had the experience of preaching the Gospel and knowing as he did so that the Spirit was helping his infirmities and winning conviction in the hearts of those who heard.[4] Along with such preaching went *paraclesis*—" the moral strengthening which comes from the presence and guidance of those who are strong in faith ".[5] This word and the corresponding verb occur frequently in Acts and in the Epistles. In one passage *paraclesis* is expressly said to be the work of the Spirit.[6] In another a pastoral letter from Jerusalem to the churches of Syria and Cilicia is called a *paraclesis*, and in the following verse we are told that Judas and Silas, the bearers of the letter, because they were prophets, added a verbal *paraclesis* from which the church of Antioch derived

---

[1] Acts xi. 28.
[2] P. Carrington, *The Meaning of Revelation*, pp. 57–61; W. L. Knox, *St. Paul and the Church of Jerusalem*, pp. 34–38.
[3] *The Gospel according to St. Mark*, p. 181.
[4] I Thess. i. 5; I Cor. ii. 4.
[5] E. G. Selwyn, op. cit., p. 262.   [6] Acts ix. 31.

strength.[1]   Paul too makes *paraclesis* one of the characteristics of prophecy when he declares that the prophet
" speaks to men edification and strengthening and
comfort ". [2]

John of Patmos includes under the head of prophecy the
martyr's testimony to Jesus,[3] and there is good evidence
that the early church considered bold confession to be one
of the outstanding gifts of the Spirit, though not one that
was confined to the ranks of those properly called prophets.
Jesus had promised that in time of persecution the Holy
Spirit would tell his disciples what to say,[4] and Acts records
the keeping of that promise.[5]   According to Luke's second
tradition of the descent of the Spirit, the presence of the
Spirit was revealed when the disciples " began to speak the
word of God with boldness (*parrhesia*) ".[6]   Along with
the gift of fearless confession went the gift of joy; for the
apostles who spoke out boldly before the Sanhedrin also
rejoiced that they had been counted worthy to be dis-
honoured for the name of Christ.[7]   In the Synoptic
tradition we read of one occasion when Jesus experienced
an exultant joy which led him to make an inspired utterance,[8] and in the records of the early church joy and bold
confession go together as the gifts of the one Spirit.

It was part of the prophetic gift also to lead the prayers
and praises of the church.   Luke has drawn for us an
illuminating little picture of the church of Antioch meeting
for worship under the leadership of five prophets, whose
spiritual gift was exercised to such effect that under the
guidance of the Spirit the church decided to commission
Paul and Barnabas for a new missionary enterprise.[9]   In
the Didache, too, a rubric provides that the prophet is not
to be bound by any set form of worship but is to be free to
employ his gift of prayer.[10]   Luke also describes the Bene-
dictus as a prophecy.[11]   We know that most of the Old
Testament prophets delivered their messages in poetic form,
and the poetic structure of the teaching of Jesus is one of the

[1] Acts xv. 31 f.   [2] I Cor. xiv. 3.   [3] Rev. xix. 10.
[4] Mk. xiii. 11; Lk. xii. 12.   [5] Acts iv. 8.
[6] Acts iv. 31.   [7] Acts iv. 41.   [8] Lk. x. 21.
[9] Acts xiii. 1–3   [10] Did. x. 7.   [11] Lk. i. 67.

many indications that he belonged to the goodly fellowship. The hymns of the Revelation are the work of a prophet, and so are the many elevated and rhythmical passages in the writings of Paul, who was also among the prophets. It is possible, therefore, that we owe to the inspired words of Christian prophets the beginnings of our hymnody.

But the greatest source of the prophet's authority and influence and the gift which distinguished him from his brethren was his power to pronounce specific instructions for the conduct of church affairs. When the Holy Spirit ordered the church of Antioch to send Barnabas and Paul on a missionary journey, the command came, without doubt, from the lips of Simeon, Lucius, or Manaen.[1] When on a later journey the Spirit forbade the missionaries to carry out their plan of preaching first in Asia and then in Bithynia, the spokesman was almost certainly the prophet Silas.[2] Timothy, too, is said to have been designated to his office by prophecy.[3] I Peter attributes to Christian prophets the revelation which initiated the Gentile mission of the church, and the same thought is expressed in the Epistle to the Ephesians.[4] It was in fact through the prophet that men might " hear what the Spirit says to the churches ".

4

Besides these two forms of inspired speech the most obvious indication of the Spirit's activity was miracle. Luke has often been accused of credulity because he has packed his narrative with signs and wonders,[5] but it would be more in keeping with the evidence to commend him for his faithful reproduction of one of the major constituents of early Christianity. For the Epistles bear their concurrent witness that the preaching of the Gospel was everywhere accompanied by exorcisms and healings and by other forms of miracle which are expressly distinguished from miraculous

[1] Acts xiii. 1–3.   [2] Acts xvi. 6 f.
[3] I Tim. i. 18; 4. 14.   [4] I Pet. i. 10–12; Eph. iii. 4–6.
[5] Acts ii. 43; iii. 1–10; iv. 32; v. 12–16; ix. 32–34; 36–42; xiii. 11; xiv. 8–10; xvi. 16–18; xix. 11–12; xx. 9–12; xxviii. 7.

cures.[1] Paul not only ascribes these powers to the energy
of the Holy Spirit, but in one place actually questions the
right of any man to call himself an apostle unless his claim
is attested by " the signs of an apostle " [2]—a phrase which
certainly covers miracle, though it may include much else.
In this argument Paul was on sound ground, for during the
earthly ministry of Jesus the missionaries he sent out were
given " authority over unclean spirits ", and were able to
report success in the use of it.[3] On the one recorded
occasion when this power failed them they were surprised
and disappointed.[4] At that time their mission had been
an extension of Jesus' own ministry of preaching and
healing. The healing work of the early church was a con-
tinuation of the same ministry, carried on in the name of
Jesus and in the power of his presence. Particularly significant are the words of Peter to Aeneas : " Jesus Christ
heals you ".[5]

We may take this stand with regard to the New Testament
miracles in general without being compelled to defend the
authenticity of every single miracle story. It is possible
that tradition has made some episodes in the life of Jesus
more miraculous than they really were, but only because he
was the sort of person round whom stories of marvel would
readily gather. It is possible that in the annals of the early
church the miraculous element has been at some points
exaggerated, but only because in that period men were
daily experiencing the afflatus of divine power, and tended
to ascribe to that power all that was extraordinary.

5

Not only in the ministry of healing but in all the opera-
tions of the Spirit Jesus was believed to be continuing his
work. The Spirit was indeed the Spirit of Jesus. The
risen and regnant Lord had poured out the Spirit upon his
disciples, and through the Spirit he exercised his sovereign

[1] I Cor. xii. 9–10, 28–30; Gal. iii. 5; Rom. xv. 19; Heb. ii. 4.
[2] II Cor. xii. 12.   [3] Mk. vi. 7; Lk. x. 17.
[4] Mk. ix. 28.   [5] Acts ix. 34.

E

authority over them.[1] In Acts every new development in the story is brought about by the guidance of the Spirit. Stephen was appointed to office because he was seen to be filled with the Holy Spirit, and by the Spirit he was given what he was to say in the hour of his opportunity.[2] The Spirit directed the missionary work of Philip and Peter,[3] and overcame the hesitation which the conservative Christians of Jerusalem felt about admitting to church membership the Samaritans and the Gentile Cornelius.[4] When an evangelistic mission to the Gentiles was started at Antioch, Barnabas was sent to investigate, and because he was full of the Holy Spirit he gladly recognized this new development as an act of God's grace.[5] It was the Spirit who inaugurated the mission of Paul and Barnabas,[6] the Spirit who brought unanimity to the council meeting at Jerusalem,[7] the Spirit who compelled Paul and Silas to forsake Asia for Europe.[8]

In all this Luke is undoubtedly preserving the authentic quality of primitive Christianity. If he had been disposed to read back into the age he was describing the characteristics of the age in which he wrote, we should presumably have had from him a story of a mission planned and directed from Jerusalem by the Twelve. But of such ecclesiastical theory there is not a trace in his narrative. Instead he shows to us a church in which all authority belongs to Jesus, exalted at the right hand of God, and making his royal commands known to his disciples through the Spirit.

6

In the New Testament the Holy Spirit is Christ's gift to his church. Those who became " partakers of the Holy Spirit " entered the *koinonia*, the fellowship established by common participation in Christ and in his heavenly gift.[9]

---

[1] Acts ii. 33; Eph. iv. 8.
[2] Acts vi. 3, 10.
[3] Acts viii. 29, 39; x. 19 f.
[4] Acts viii. 17; x. 44.
[5] Acts xii. 23 f.
[6] Acts xiii. 3.
[7] Acts xv. 28.
[8] Acts xvi. 6 f.
[9] Heb. vi. 4; II Cor. xiii. 13; Phil. ii. 1 f.; cf. I Cor. i. 9.

To belong to Christ, to receive the Spirit, to be a member
of the church—all these were but different and inseparable
aspects of the same experience, and the Spirit was recognized from the first as the source of unity and harmony.
" They were all filled with the Holy Spirit . . . and the
company of believers was of one heart and soul; and none
of them said that any of the things he possessed was his own,
but they had everything in common." [1]   Community of
possessions was the outward symbol of an inner community
of thought and purpose, and both were the product of the
Holy Spirit.   This passage is the best commentary on the
one use of *koinonia* in Acts : " They continued steadfastly
in the apostles' teaching, in the *koinonia*, in the breaking of
the bread, and in the prayers ".[2]   Some scholars have conjectured that in this list of typical activities *koinonia* must
have been a technical term for the sharing of goods which is
mentioned two verses later,[3] but it is much more likely that
it refers to the unity of spirit of which that sharing was the
visible expression.   *Koinonia* frequently means fellowship
in the New Testament, and there is no need to search for
another meaning in this case.

Paul, too, believed fellowship to be the creation of the
Holy Spirit.   *Koinonia pneumatos* could, to be sure, mean
simply " participation in the Spirit ", but in the two contexts where Paul employs the phrase it almost certainly
means more—the fellowship which participation in the
Spirit entails.   In Philippians ii. 1 f. Paul is enumerating
all the bonds of sympathy which unite the minds of Christian
brethren—encouragement, comfort, fellowship, and a heart
of compassion; and in the threefold benediction with which
II Corinthians ends he is bespeaking for his friends the grace
which Christ supplies, the love which God bestows, and the
fellowship which the Spirit creates.[4]

It was one of Paul's most constant and earnest desires
that the churches should conduct their affairs not by
argument and division but by reaching a common mind

---

[1] Acts iv. 31 f.   [2] Acts ii. 42.
[3] E.g. F. Hauck in Kittel's *Theologisches Wörterbuch zum N.T.*, III,
pp. 789–810.   [4] II Cor. xiii. 13.

under the guidance of the Spirit.[1] And we find the same
ideal expressed in the words of the pastoral letter from
Jerusalem : " It seemed good to the Holy Spirit and to us." [2]

A remarkable feature of the primitive *koinonia* was that it
embraced two language groups. In his account of Pentecost Luke clearly means us to understand that the first
Christian converts were a cross section of the cosmopolitan
crowd of pilgrims, and that the converts remained in
Jerusalem as members of the primitive church. There was
also resident in Jerusalem a considerable colony of Hellenists
—Greek-speaking Jews of the Dispersion [3] who for one
reason or another had decided to settle in the holy city—
and it is very probable that further converts were won from
their ranks. Thus from the beginning the Christian community included some members who spoke only Aramaic,
some who spoke only Greek, and probably only a few who
were equally at home in either language; for it must be
remembered that the disciples of Jesus were for the most
part " uneducated and ignorant men ". Humanly speaking, it was inevitable that the difference of language should
create two distinct social units within the church, and the
evidence that this actually happened is to be found in
Luke's reference to a dispute between the Hebrews (i.e. the
Aramaic-speaking Christians) and the Hellenists over the
administration of the common fund.[4] This quarrel proves,
what we should in any case have suspected, that the life of
the Christian community was only imperfectly subjected
to the Spirit's control; but it proves also the Hebrew and
Hellenist, in spite of the language barrier, had been sharing
in the one fellowship of which the common fund was the
symbol. Moreover, Luke assures us that any possible
breach of the fellowship was averted by the prompt and

[1] Rom. xv. 5 f.; I Cor. i. 10; II Cor. xiii. 11; Phil. i. 27; ii. 1 f.; cf.
I Pet. iii. 8.   [2] Acts xv. 28.
[3] See *The Beginnings of Christianity*, pp. 59–74, for the view that
Ἑλληνιστής means Gentile. It is, however, impossible to make sense of the
story of Cornelius and the later controversy between Paul and Jerusalem
if the Gentiles were admitted to the church from the beginning, and Acts
ix. 29 seems to be decisive evidence in favour of the view adopted above.
It follows that in Acts xi. 20, which describes the first preaching to Gentiles,
the reading Ἕλληνας is to be preferred.
[4] Acts vi. 1.

generous decision of the apostles to hand over the charge of the fund to a board of seven men, all of whom appear from their names to have been Hellenists.

7

Members were admitted to the church by baptism, and it was therefore at baptism that the gift of the Spirit was to be expected. At his baptism Jesus had seen the Spirit descend out of the cloven heavens, and so for his followers baptism with water had become the symbol both of baptism with the Spirit and of union with Christ. " By one Spirit we were all baptized into one body." [1] " Be baptized every one of you in the name of Jesus Christ, for the remission of sins, and you shall receive the gift of the Holy Spirit." [2]

In the story of Cornelius the Spirit is given first and baptism follows.[3] But this episode does not involve a modification of the general rule. Luke clearly meant us to understand that this was an exceptional case, an instance of the guidance of the Spirit. By the obvious descent of the Spirit on a Gentile household Peter was led to a new conception of the scope of the Gospel. Baptism followed the gift of the Spirit, not as the empty symbol of a gift already bestowed, but as the formal admission to the church of those who were manifestly qualified for membership by the gift they had received.

The story of Philip in Samaria,[4] however, might seem on a superficial reading to represent quite a different practice. Philip preached and baptized in Samaria, but the Spirit was not given to the Samaritans until Peter and John came and laid their hands on them. This has sometimes been taken to mean that baptism by men of less than apostolic rank required to be completed by the subsequent laying on of apostolic hands. But there is not a shadow of support for this theory to be derived from any other passage in the New Testament. Baptisms and the

[1] I Cor. xii. 13.   [2] Acts ii. 38; cf. ix. 17 f.; xix. 1–6.
[3] Acts x. 47 f.   [4] Acts viii. 5–17.

laying on of hands are mentioned together in Hebrews, but without anything to show how they were related.[1] Twelve men at Ephesus received the Spirit by the laying on of Paul's hands, but the conversation which preceded shows that Paul believed baptism to be the occasion on which the Spirit was given, so that the laying on of hands must be regarded here as a part of the baptismal rite.[2] Paul himself received the Spirit at his baptism by the laying on of hands, but they were the hands of " a certain disciple of Damascus named Ananias ", who laid hands on him for the double purpose of restoring his sight and imparting to him the Spirit.[3] The fact is that the laying on of hands, whatever it may have signified, was not an apostolic monopoly.[4] In the church of Antioch hands were laid on Paul and Barnabas—themselves apostles—to commission them for a new undertaking, and by the laying on of hands of the presbytery Timothy was ordained to his office.[5]

The evidence of the Pauline Epistles is likewise fatal to this theory of apostolic ratification. Paul had been baptized,[6] but in view of his solemn oath to the Galatians it is incredible that any apostle had ever " added anything " to him.[7] He regarded baptism as the decisive moment when a man put on Christ, was united with Christ, received the Spirit.[8] Yet he considered it a matter of complete indifference by whom baptism was administered, and he could hardly have written to the Corinthians, " I thank God that I baptized none of you except Crispus and Gaius", if baptism by one of his assistants had required his own

[1] Heb. vi. 2.   [2] Acts xix. 1-6.   [3] Acts ix. 17 f.
[4] Simon the sorcerer undoubtedly thought it was, but he was not a very reputable ecclesiastical authority. In the O.T. the laying on of hands indicates identification : a worshipper lays his hand on the sacrifice in order to identify himself with his offering (Lev. iii. 2 etc.), the congregation lay their hands on the Levites to identify themselves with this offering of the first fruits of Israel (Num. viii. 10), and Moses lays his hands on Joshua to make a public identification of himself with his successor, so that Israel may obey Joshua as they have obeyed Moses (Num. xxvii. 18). In the N.T. the laying on of hands accompanies healing, baptism, the commissioning of missionaries, and ordination. If we insist on finding a rationale for this practice, the only one which covers all cases is that of Augustine : " What else is the laying on of hands but prayer over a man ? " (*De Bapt.* iii. 16).
[5] Acts xiii. 3 ; I Tim. iv. 14.
[6] Rom. vi. 3 ; I Cor. xii. 13.   [7] Gal. i. 20 ; ii. 6.
[8] Gal. iii. 27 ; Rom. vi. 3 ; I Cor. xii. 13.

apostolic seal.[1] And in all his controversies with Jerusalem and the Judaizers there was never any suggestion that his practice was deficient at this point.

In the face of this evidence it cannot be maintained that the procedure followed in Samaria was the regular practice in the early apostolic age. Nor is it probable that Luke has read back into the early period a practice current in his own day, since there would be no point in doing this unless he did it systematically. We must try, therefore, to find a simpler explanation of the episode in Samaria, unencumbered by later controversies about church order. Fortunately Luke's own view of the matter is sufficiently clear. He tells us that the apostles had no part in the first missionary movement which carried the Gospel far and wide throughout the country. The evangelists were persecuted men, unauthorized by any save the Holy Spirit that was in them, and they brought the Gospel as far as Antioch.[2] Inspired by their success, the apostles began to follow their example,[3] but only on two occasions did they think fit to intervene in the work of the missionary pioneers. On both occasions a change of policy was involved, once when Philip preached for the first time to the half-pagan Samaritans, once when men of Cyprus and Cyrene began to preach to Gentiles.[4] It appears, then, that the visit of Peter and John to Samaria was necessitated, not by routine ecclesiastical administration, but by an event which promised to be a crisis in the affairs of the church. Word had come to Jerusalem that Samaritans were being baptized, but without any of the accompanying signs of the descent of the Spirit. This naturally made the apostles anxious, for it might have been taken to mean that the Samaritan mission lacked divine sanction. But when Peter and John were sent to look into the matter, their prayers were answered and the Spirit was bestowed on the new converts by the laying on of their hands. This was the sign of divine approval for which they were looking, and, convinced by it, they joined in preaching to the Samaritans.

[1] I Cor. i. 13–17.   [2] Acts viii. 1–4; xi. 19–21.
[3] Acts viii. 25.   [4] Acts viii. 14; xi. 22 ff.

Thus in this case, as in the case of Cornelius, the gift of the Spirit guided the apostles to approve a new departure in policy. But these two exceptions leave unaltered the general rule that the Spirit was the gift of Christ to those who accepted him as Messiah and Lord, and who by the ceremony of baptism were admitted to membership of his messianic people.

CHAPTER V

THE FIRST CHRISTIAN COMMUNITY: 3. THE WAY

1

FOR those who had accepted the Gospel and had been baptized into the messianic community, in which the crucified and risen Lord exercised his sovereignty through the guidance of the Holy Spirit, there remained a further message. Upon them the new age had dawned, and if they enjoyed its benefits they must also direct their lives by its principles. If they called Jesus Lord, they must do what he had said. If they lived by the Spirit, by the Spirit they must walk.[1]

The name which the New Testament gives to this change of direction is repentance, and there is ample evidence that a call to repentance was part of the earliest apostolic preaching.[2] When the apostles called on men to repent, they were asking not for penitential tears but for a decision to turn back from the path of self-will and to walk henceforward in the way of the Lord; and the reality of this decision was in no way impaired by their profound awareness that repentance came to them not as the result of their own moral striving but as a gift from God.[3] Repentance and faith went together as parts of a single response to the Gospel.[4] For the Gospel offered to men a clean break with the past and a new opportunity for the future; and repentance was the step by which men of faith passed over from the old life to the new.

New converts, then, must be instructed in the practical consequences of their faith, in order that they might perform " works worthy of repentance ". Preaching (*kerygma*) must be followed by teaching (*didache*); and so we are told

---

[1] Lk. vi. 46; Gal. v. 25.
[2] Acts ii. 38; iii. 19; viii. 22; xvii. 30; xxvi. 20.
[3] Acts v. 31; xi. 18; cf. Rom. ii. 4; II Tim. ii. 25.
[4] Acts xxvi. 20.

that from the earliest days the church " continued steadfastly in the apostles' teaching ".[1]   The content of this
teaching is not hard to reconstruct.   In a later chapter we
shall see that the instruction designed for Gentile congregations had to include a considerable amount of elementary
ethics, which a Jew would have taken for granted; but in
the early years, while the converts were all Jews, accustomed
to the moral standards of the Old Testament, the apostles'
teaching must have consisted in a repetition of the teaching
of Jesus, much of which had been entrusted to them alone.

The four Gospels make it plain that during his ministry
Jesus was addressed by friend and adversary alike as Rabbi
(the title is sometimes transliterated, sometimes translated
by the Greek *didaskalos* or *epistates*).   As a Rabbi Jesus
gathered round him a group of disciples to whom he gave
systematic instruction, and engaged in learned debate with
other Rabbis on the interpretation of the Law.   It is true
that Jesus habitually spoke and acted with a more than
Rabbinic authority, but this does not alter the fact that
scholars of his own day, however much they disagreed with
his teaching, were compelled to regard him as one of themselves.

After Pentecost the followers of Jesus found more
exalted terms with which to address their Master, but they
continued to describe themselves as disciples.   The old
relationship was transcended but not forgotten; for it was
still their task to bring the life of the community under the
authority of the remembered teaching of Jesus.   Two of
the earliest names for the Christian religion were " the
Way " [2] and " the Life ".[3]   Long before Christianity came
to be known as " the faith once for all delivered to the
saints ",[4] it was conceived as a life to be lived, a way to walk
in.   This emphasis on practical religion is thoroughly
Jewish, and reminds us of the *halakhah* of the Pharisees.[5]
But the superficial similarity between Christianity and

[1] Acts ii. 42.
[2] Acts ix. 2; xix. 9, 23; xxi. 4; cf. xvi. 17; xviii. 25 f.
[3] Acts v. 30.   [4] Jud. 3.
[5] From the verb *halak*—to walk. Cf. also the use of the verbs περιπατέω,
στοιχέω, and πορεύομαι in Acts and Epistles.

Pharisaism must not blind us to the essential differences between them. The ethical teaching of Jesus was no mere comment on the Law of Moses, but a new commandment directed to those who had already entered the Kingdom of God by the narrow door of repentance. The Christian was called to give his loyalty not to a set of regulations but to a person, who had embodied the Way which he had taught, and who had died that the Way might be opened to others. To set foot upon that Way was to journey in the presence of the ascended Lord and in the strength and guidance of his Spirit. Christian ethics, in short, were seen to be a consequence of redemption; but for a sound understanding of early Christianity the converse is equally important—that redemption was seen to have ethical consequences. Especially when the Gospel was carried to Gentile peoples it was this strong ethical strain that prevented communion with Christ from degenerating into a pagan mysticism, salvation from becoming a ritual transaction, the reception of the Spirit from turning into emotional display and profitless enthusiasm.

2

Our principal source for the reconstruction of the apostolic teaching is the Synoptic tradition. When all due allowance has been made for later interpolation, editorial arrangement, and possible legendary accretion, the authenticity of this tradition stands beyond reasonable dispute; and the bulk of the material must have been handed down by the apostles and other members of the Jerusalem community. We cannot suppose that the entire apostolic teaching has survived, but the Synoptic Gospels undoubtedly preserve that part of the apostolic teaching which, in the course of a generation or more of natural selection, made the most abiding impression on the church. It is for this very reason that we are justified in using the Gospels as a source not only for the life and teaching of Jesus but for the life and teaching of the early church as well. Indeed, it might almost be said that when the Gospels are least satisfactory as sources for the life of Jesus they have their greatest value as sources for early church history. For example, the different versions of the Beatitudes, the Lord's Prayer, and the Lord's Supper make it difficult for us to know with certainty what Jesus actually said; but they prove that these parts of the tradition had worked themselves deeply into the life and worship of the church.[1]

From the Synoptic Gospels we may deduce not only the content of the apostolic teaching but also the manner of its transmission. For the teaching of Jesus was given in two distinct forms, and it is altogether likely that the apostolic teaching followed the same double pattern.

Many of the recorded sayings of Jesus were spoken impromptu, called forth by some episode, question, or debate. The narratives which provide contexts for such sayings—called paradigms by Dibelius, apophthegms by Bultmann, and pronouncement stories by Vincent Taylor— suggest by their lack of descriptive detail that they have been told and retold in ever barer outline to meet the recurrent needs of the churches; and it has been conjectured that many isolated sayings once formed the conclusion of narratives lost in the course of transmission. The questions to which these stories supplied the answers were bound to be raised again and again in the life of the early church and to stimulate the memory of those who had heard the authoritative word from the lips of the Master. In I Corinthians vii we see Paul facing a problem concerning marriage and divorce by asking first whether the tradition he had received contained any apposite saying of the Lord; and we may be sure that the primitive community turned

---

[1] This fact was appreciated long before the advent of Form-criticism. "It is clear that selection among the facts, whether of word or deed, has been at work; and this selection throws back welcome light upon the instinctive wants and ideals of the Apostolic Age." J. V. Bartlet, *The Apostolic Age*, pp. xi–xii. "When we consider how many words of Jesus were never recorded, and concerning how many events in his life we have no information whatsoever, it becomes obvious that those which were remembered and recorded were preserved for the sole reason that they had made a strong impression upon the primitive community. Every narrative that has been preserved, every saying that has survived is evidence of some particular interest on the part of this primitive church." J. Weiss, *The History of Primitive Christianity*, p. 12.

constantly to the apostles for the same light upon their perplexities. What was to be the Christians' attitude to Judaism? Should they keep the Sabbath,[1] observe the fasts[2] and rules of cleanliness,[3] attend the temple and pay its tax?[4] What was to be their attitude to Rome and its tribute money?[5] What stand were they to take on moral questions, such as marriage and divorce?[6] On what terms were converts to be admitted to the church?[7] What place was to be accorded in the Christian scheme of things to John the Baptist,[8] to an unauthorized evangelist,[9] to children,[10] to the relatives of Jesus,[11] to the apostles?[12] To these and many other questions, as they came up one by one in the early meetings of the church, the apostles could reply with a story.

Not all of the teaching of Jesus, however, can have been transmitted in this way. Much of it is concerned not with problems or details of conduct, but with attitudes of mind and principles of general validity. It is precisely this type of teaching which most clearly possesses a poetical structure.[13] This structure cannot with any degree of probability be ascribed to compilers and editors, for they can be shown to have used more artificial methods of arrangement.[14] But if Jesus cast much of his teaching in poetic form, he must have done so, like the prophets before him, with the intention that it should be committed to memory by his disciples; and the poetic form could hardly have survived the process of transmission unless the disciples had in turn adopted the same method of instruction. We know that Paul received from those who were Christians before him an oral tradition of the words of Jesus, that he passed this tradition on to his converts, and that he expected them to have an accurate memory of the things they

---

[1] Mk. ii. 23 ff.; iii. 1 ff.; Lk. xiii. 15 ff.; xiv. 1 ff.
[2] Mk. ii. 18 ff.
[3] Mk. vii. 5 ff.
[4] Mk. xiii. 1 f.; Mt. xvii. 24 ff.
[5] Mk. xii. 13 ff.
[6] Mk. x. 2 ff.
[7] Mk. x. 17 ff.; Lk. ix. 57–62.
[8] Lk. vii. 18 ff.; Mk. xi. 27 ff.
[9] Mk. ix. 38 f.
[10] Mk. x. 13–16.
[11] Mk. iii. 31–35; Lk. xi. 27 f.
[12] Mk. x. 35 ff.
[13] E.g. Lk. vi. 27–38; Mt. vi. 1–6, 16–18. Cf. C. F. Burney, *The Poetry of Our Lord*; V. Taylor, *The Formation of the Gospel Tradition*, pp. 89–100.
[14] E.g. the catchword—Mk. ix. 41–50; Lk. xvi. 16–18.

had been taught.[1] It is a reasonable inference, therefore, that from the first the instruction of converts was carried on in the same systematic way. If T. W. Manson is right in believing that the two collections of sayings which we know as Q and M had a common pattern,[2] this would be a further indication that the teaching of Jesus had already been reduced to systematic form during the period of oral tradition.

3

Luke's interest in the manner of life of the Jerusalem community is concentrated upon one particular, to which he makes frequent references in the early chapters of Acts. This is the so-called communism of the early church. Unfortunately Luke's evidence is extremely difficult to fit into a coherent picture. Twice he tells us that the Christians " had everything in common," which seems to imply communal ownership of all possessions.[3] On the other hand the example of Barnabas is cited as though the sale of his farm was an act of outstanding generosity; and Ananias is reminded by Peter that he had been under no constraint to sell his property or to surrender the money which it brought in.[4] The dispute which arose between the Hebrews and the Hellenists suggests that there was a common fund out of which daily meals were supplied to a limited number of needy persons.[5] In the face of this conflicting evidence it is best to treat " everything in common " as an exaggeration, and to look for the truth in Acts ii. 45 and iv. 34[b]–35 : " they began to sell their property and goods and to distribute them to all according to each one's need "; " all who were owners of lands or houses began to sell them and to bring the price of what they had sold and to lay it at the apostles' feet; and distribution was made to each according to his need ". All the verbs in these two passages are in the imperfect tense, which shows that the sale of property was not a single concerted action but a

[1] I Cor. vii. 10, 25; xi. 23; I Thess. v. 2.
[2] *The Sayings of Jesus*, pp. 22–23.   [3] Acts ii. 44; iv. 32.
[4] Acts iv. 36 f.; v. 4.   [5] Acts vi. 1 f

continuing process. Perhaps it was Barnabas' distinction that, inspired by the story of Jesus and the rich young man, he set the example which others followed from time to time. In this way the church created and sustained a common fund which the apostles administered for the benefit of the poorer members.

This practice reflects the social and economic status of the early church. Jesus had set out to win the social outcast, and from the beginning a high proportion of the church's membership must have been drawn from the lower levels of society. This was certainly true of the churches to which the Epistle of James was addressed, and equally true of the churches founded by Paul.[1] But in spite of the general poverty of his own converts, Paul habitually thought of the Jerusalem Christians as " the Poor ". The point of view of the Jerusalem Christians themselves may very well be preserved for us in Luke's Gospel, which contains a large number of sayings about the disposition of wealth, makes Jesus' command to the rich young man into a general rule for all Christians,[2] and gives the Beatitudes and Woes in a form which assumes that all Christians are poor.

But the common fund of the early church did not owe its origin to economic necessity. Nor is there any suggestion in Acts that Barnabas and the other wealthy Christians were induced to dispose of their property by the hope of an immanent Parousia, which would make all provision for the future unnecessary. The real explanation of their conduct is twofold. According to Luke it was the gift of the Spirit that created a fellowship of heart and soul which found practical expression in the sharing of goods; and Ananias' offence was that he lied to the Spirit.[3] But in following the direction of the Spirit the church was also putting into effect the teaching of Jesus. The Holy Spirit was the Spirit of Jesus, the gift which he had poured out, and there could never be any conflict between the guidance of the Spirit and the authority of the word of Jesus. " He will

---

[1] Jas. ii. 1–8; I Cor. i. 26; II Cor. viii. 2.
[2] Lk. xii. 33; cf. Mk. x. 21.　　　[3] Acts iv. 31 f.; v. 3.

take what is mine and declare it to you." [1]   We are justified,
therefore, in taking this one aspect of early Christianity as
an illustration of the concern of the church to bring its
whole life under the sovereignty of Christ their King.

4

So far we have assumed that the apostles' teaching was
concerned with Christian behaviour; but other questions
also must have been raised in the first assemblies of the
church to which the apostles would be expected to give an
authoritative answer.   The apostolic preaching made the
claim that the events of the ministry, death, and Resurrection of Jesus had happened in accordance with a pre-
ordained plan of God set forth in the Scriptures of the Old
Testament.   This claim involved such a revolution in Old
Testament exegesis that many a convert must have been
beset with doubts and difficulties, and those who undertook
the work of evangelism would be particularly conscious of
the need for further illumination, so that they might be
better equipped to give a reason for the faith that was in
them.   It was therefore incumbent on the leaders of the
church to search the Scriptures for a deeper understanding
of the divine purpose which had been fulfilled in Jesus
Christ.

Ever since Rendel Harris published his Testimonies, it
has been assumed by the majority of scholars that the early
Christians supported their claims by the use of proof-texts,
drawn at random from the Old Testament and isolated
from their contexts; and that at an early date an editor,
possibly Matthew the apostle, produced a collection of these
proof-texts, which remained in current use at least until the
time of Cyprian.   In a series of recent writings [2] C. H. Dodd
has shown that this theory fails to account for the facts;
for a complete list of the Old Testament texts quoted in the
books of the New Testament—Revelation being for obvious

[1] Jn. xvi. 14.
[2] "The Foundations of Christian Theology" in *Theology Today*, VII
(1950–1), pp. 308–20; *The Old Testament in the New Testament; According
to the Scriptures*.

reasons excepted—indicates that the New Testament writers drew heavily on certain passages from the prophets and psalter to the neglect of other portions of Scripture. Dodd shows further that the passages most commonly quoted share a single " plot ", which has three main variations. The first group (Joel ii–iii; Zechariah ix–xiv; Daniel) describes the Day of the Lord : God's intervention in history to destroy the powers of evil, to redeem and sanctify his people, and to establish his everlasting reign. The second group (Hosea; parts of Isaiah; Habakkuk i–ii) tells of the judgment of God upon Israel's sins and the emergence of a new, purified people of God. The third group (parts of Isaiah; Psalms xxii, xxxiv, xlii–xliii, lxix, lxxx, cxviii) depicts the suffering and ultimate triumph of God's righteous Servant, who is in some way identified with Israel. In each group of passages Israel is brought by the grace of God through humiliation to glory ; and the early church saw in Jesus the fulfilment of all these prophecies because he had chosen to be identified with Israel in her ignominy, whether deserved or undeserved, in order that Israel might be identified with him in his Resurrection.

Neither the choice of passages nor the application of the common " plot " to the events of the Gospel story can be attributed to Paul or to any other New Testament author, since all assume without argument the validity of their Scriptural references. Dodd therefore justly concludes that behind the use of the Old Testament by the various New Testament writers there lies a common principle of selection and interpretation, which must be regarded as part of the primitive teaching.

At this point in the argument we have to choose between two alternatives. The method of exegesis employed by the early church was clearly the product of a creative mind. The mind either belonged to an unknown genius, who laid the foundations of Christian theology and disappeared from history without leaving any memory fo his achievement; or else it was the mind of Jesus. Between these two possibilities we need not hesitate for long. There can be no doubt that Jesus possessed the quality of mind necessary

F

for sustained and original thought. He would not have been given the title of Rabbi unless he had proved himself expert in the handling of Scripture; yet his teaching was recognized to be new and totally different from that of the scribes. And in the Gospels we repeatedly find him directing the attention of his disciples to the Scriptures which concerned himself.

All the evidence at our disposal, then, points to the conclusion that in meeting their intellectual difficulties as well as their practical ones the members of the Jerusalem church continued to be disciples of Jesus the Rabbi. His teaching, faithfully preserved by the apostles, determines the whole future development of Christian behaviour and Christian thought.

CHAPTER VI

THE GENTILE MISSION: 1. FROM JERUSALEM TO ROME

1

THE first Christians were Jews, and they did not cease to be Jews on the day of Pentecost. On the contrary, their new enthusiasm led to a regular attendance at the temple, and the Greek-speaking Christians seem to have kept up their association with the Hellenistic synagogues.[1] To what lengths they carried their observance of the Torah in private we have no means of knowing. Luke tells us that, up to the time of his meeting with Cornelius, Peter had scrupulously adhered to the food laws.[2] On the other hand, some at least of the disciples of Jesus belonged to the 'am ha-aretz, and on two occasions Jesus had defended them against criticism from the Pharisees.[3] From the opening chapters of Acts, however, it appears that the members of the primitive church were sufficiently orthodox to allay any fears or suspicions that the Pharisees may have entertained about them. Jewish orthodoxy, as we saw in Chapter II, was a matter of practice rather than belief. The Christians might hold any beliefs they pleased about the Messiah, the Resurrection, or the Age to Come, without incurring any charge of religious disloyalty, provided that their beliefs did not affect their obedience to the Law. The Sadducees, indeed, made some half-hearted attempts to suppress the new movement, but they acted from political, not religious, motives, being afraid that the disturbances produced by the apostles' preaching would give the Romans a pretext for intervention; and their attempts failed because the Pharisees, led by Gamaliel, withdrew their support.[4]

[1] Acts ii. 47; iii. 1; vi. 9; xii. 20; xxv. 42.
[2] Acts x. 14.   [3] Mk. ii. 14, 18–20, 23–28.
[4] Acts v. 33–40; the speech ascribed to Gamaliel cannot be historical, since it contains an anachronistic reference to Theudas; but there is no reason to doubt the historicity of the incident.

83

It has sometimes been thought that the Christians could not have adopted this attitude of continued loyalty to their old religion, if they had been convinced that they were the new Israel and that the new age had dawned; but in fact there was nothing inconsistent in their behaviour. It may seem obvious to us, with our knowledge of the course which events actually took, that the Gospel had implications which made a break with Judaism inevitable; but there were excellent reasons why this should not have been so obvious to the primitive church. Firstly, Judaism was more than a religion: it was a nationality. The Torah was religious precept, social custom, and civil law all rolled into one, without any of the distinctions between law and religion which we have learnt from the Greeks and Romans.[1] A Jewish Christian, therefore, even though the religious centre of his life had shifted from Torah to Christ, could not abandon the Torah as a national way of life without becoming denationalized; and that was a step he could be expected to take only under compulsion. Secondly, there was the teaching and example of Jesus; he had been a Jew, had confined his ministry to the lost sheep of the house of Israel, had claimed that he came not to destroy but to fulfil, had sent his disciples out on preaching tours with instructions not to go beyond the boundaries of Israel. Thirdly, the new Israel had never been envisaged as a totally new beginning, but as the old Israel purified and reconstituted. The church was committed to the task of winning men from the old Israel into the new, and to this end they must keep open their lines of communication.

We need not suppose that arguments such as these were consciously formulated by the Christians. Their behaviour was spontaneous and unreflective, because the relation of the Torah to the Gospel had not yet become a problem to them. The strength of the ties which bound them to Judaism may be estimated by the hold which they retained on Paul even after he had come to the conclusion that Christ was the end of the Law for everyone who believed. For

---

[1] See H. W. Robinson, " Law and Religion in Israel," in *Judaism and Christianity, III—Law and Religion* (ed. E. I. J. Rosenthal), pp. 47–65.

in spite of all that he suffered at the hands of his kinsmen according to the flesh, Paul had still a passionate affection for them; with all his zeal for Gentile equality, he still took it for granted that the Gospel was " to the Jew first and also to the Gentile "; and with all his insistence on Christian freedom, he was still prepared to be a Jew to the Jews, that he might win the Jews.[1]

2

The first breach in the religious truce is associated with the name of Stephen. There is much that is obscure about the story of his sudden emergence and equally sudden death; but this much is apparent, that he was accused of preaching that Jesus would put an end to both Torah and temple, and that, after being arraigned on a charge of blasphemy, he became a victim of mob violence. Luke assures us that the witnesses who testified against him were false witnesses, but at once contradicts himself by putting into the mouth of Stephen a speech that goes far to substantiate the charge on which he was indicted. For the speech undertakes to prove by Scriptural quotation that God had always made his presence known to his faithful servants in whatever part of the world they happened to be, so that the building of the temple by Solomon was a denial of the true nature of God; and that the Law had failed to achieve its purpose because of the constant disobedience of Israel, which had now reached its climax in the repudiation of Jesus. The style of the speech is quite unlike that of the other speeches in Acts and also quite unlike Luke's own style, so that it cannot be treated as a typical apostolic sermon or as a free composition by the author. It is possible, therefore, that Luke had access to a reliable tradition which preserved for him, not indeed a verbatim report of Stephen's defence, but a sample of the arguments which Stephen and other Hellenistic preachers were accustomed to use in controversy with the Jews. We know that Luke had ample opportunity to consult one such

[1] Rom. ix. 1; i. 16; I Cor. ix. 20.

evangelist, who had been a colleague of Stephen from the beginning.[1]

Stephen, then, seems to have been the first Christian to realize that Christianity meant the end of Jewish privilege, and the first to open the way for a mission to the Gentiles. In the Hellenistic synagogues he may well have had contacts with pious Gentiles, to whose religious quest Jewish nationalism and Jewish ritual formed an insuperable barrier. But we must beware of treating Stephen as though he were the product of his environment. There is all too little evidence that a sympathy with Gentile aspirations was a normal product of Hellenistic Judaism. Paul found little enough support for his Gentile mission in the synagogues of the Dispersion, and the Hellenistic synagogues of Jerusalem, which produced Stephen, nurtured also Stephen's persecutors. The real source of Stephen's doctrine was the teaching of Jesus. Up to this point the Jerusalem Christians had emphasized those elements in the teaching of Jesus which united them with Judaism. Stephen drew attention to those elements which had brought Jesus into controversy with the religious authorities, and it was no accident that the charge brought against the first Christian martyr was the charge already brought against his Lord.

Luke tells us that the death of Stephen involved the whole Christian community in persecution, so that all except the apostles fled from the city to Judaea and Samaria.[2] Since J. Weiss wrote *Das Urchristentum*, it has been commonly assumed that Luke's statement was an exaggeration, that only the Hellenists were affected by the persecution, and that the Aramaic-speaking Christians remained in the city, strengthened their ties with Judaism, and finally became the Judaistic church of which James the Lord's brother was leader. But this is an unwarranted simplification of early church history. The later Judaistic Christianity was not produced from primitive Christianity by a simple subtraction of the Hellenists. Moreover, Luke's account is remarkably confirmed by the evidence of Paul. In Galatians i

[1] Acts xxi. 8.   [2] Acts viii. 1.

Paul first confesses to having " persecuted the church of God ", i.e. the one existing church in Jerusalem. Then, in describing his visit to Jerusalem three years later and his meeting with Peter and James, he points out that the other apostles were not in Jerusalem as might have been expected. Finally, he mentions no church in Jerusalem, but only the churches of Judaea, who had heard tell " that he who once persecuted us is now preaching the faith which once he tried to destroy ". Clearly these churches of Judaea were established by Aramaic-speaking refugees from the city of Jerusalem; the Hellenists, as we shall see later, sought safety further afield; and the apostles, in spite of the danger, continued to use Jerusalem as headquarters.

3

At this point Luke, like Paul, stops speaking of the church in Jerusalem (though he does mention some " brethren " in connexion with Paul's visit), and begins to speak of " the church throughout all Judaea and Galilee and Samaria ".[1] The Samaritan churches, like those in Judaea, were founded by refugees from Jerusalem, and particularly by the preaching of Philip the evangelist and the subsequent preaching of Peter and John.[2] But what was the origin of the churches in Galilee? Were they also established by the refugees, or was Galilee an independent centre of Christianity from the beginning?

The theory of an independent Galilean Christianity has been used to provide solutions for many New Testament problems. It has been conjectured that Apollos, who knew the teaching of Jesus but had not received Christian baptism, and the twelve disciples of Ephesus, who had not heard of the Holy Spirit, must have learnt their Christianity from a source that knew nothing of Pentecost;[3] that the Christians of Damascus were evangelized from Galilee rather than Jerusalem; that Q was a Galilean document, independent of the Twelve; that the conflicting accounts of the Resurrection were the divergent local traditions of

---

[1] Acts ix. 31.　　[2] Acts viii. 1, 5 ff., 25.　　[3] Acts xviii. 25; xix. 1 f.

Galilee and Jerusalem.[1] These speculations, however, are
mutually contradictory, and so tend to cancel one another
out; and much of the evidence on which they are based is
capable of another explanation.

The most elaborate argument is that propounded by
Lohmeyer, who started from the obviously Galilean character of Mark's Gospel. Apart from the story of Passion
week, this Gospel is concerned almost entirely with Galilean
material; it represents the Galilean crowd as consistently
on the side of Jesus, unlike the Jerusalem mob which demanded his crucifixion; and it ends with a promise that
the risen Jesus will appear in Galilee. From this Lohmeyer
concluded that, whereas Luke represents the point of view
of the Jerusalem church under the leadership of the Twelve,
Mark represents the Galilean Christians under the leadership of the brothers of the Lord. For Luke Jesus was the
Messiah, who had already appeared to various witnesses;
for Mark he was the Son of Man, whose appearance was still
eagerly expected.

Some of the weaknesses of this theory are obvious and
require only a brief mention. The Galilean character of
Mark's Gospel is sufficiently explained by the fact that the
Twelve were Galileans and shared in Jesus' Galilean ministry. It is highly improbable that the Gospel originally
ended, as it does now, without a Resurrection appearance.
The brothers of Jesus belonged from the first to the Jerusalem church, and James, to whom a special Resurrection
appearance had been granted, was soon sharing with the
Twelve the responsibilities of leadership.[2] The distinction
between the two types of Christology is arbitrary in the
extreme. But behind all these points of detail there is a
more serious criticism, which applies equally to other forms
of the Galilean hypothesis. Although it must be admitted
that Jesus attracted in Galilee a large and enthusiastic
group of followers, who heard his teaching and observed his
works, yet it is clear from Mark's Gospel that to most of

---

[1] E. Lohmeyer, *Galiläa und Jerusalem*; R. H. Lightfoot, *Locality and
Doctrine in the Gospels*; F. C. Grant, *The Gospel of the Kingdom*.
[2] Acts i. 14; I Cor. xv. 7; Gal. i. 19.

them Jesus' conception of the Kingdom and of Messiahship remained a total mystery, and that he was more gravely embarrassed by their uncomprehending enthusiasm than by the enmity of the Pharisees. These supporters gave him their loyalty on the erroneous supposition that he was to be the traditional Son of David, and one of the great dangers of his ministry was that they should attempt to force him into the mould of their own messianic hopes. To them the Cross must have been as great a stumbling block as it was to any other Jew. Even for the more intimate group of disciples, who were to be the nucleus of the Jerusalem church, the Cross became meaningful only in the light of Easter and Pentecost. For those who did not belong to that circle Jesus may well have been a cherished and a poignant memory, but without the apostolic Gospel of the Resurrection and the Pentecostal gift of the Spirit he can hardly have been to them the dynamic presence around whom they could form a new society.[1] To all this we must add the weighty testimony of Paul, who, in spite of his determination to be independent of the Jerusalem apostles, agrees with Luke in regarding Jerusalem as the sole centre of primitive Christianity.

In view of all this it is best to conclude that the Galilean churches, like those of Judaea and Samaria, were founded by the missionary movement which followed the death of Stephen. At a later date Galilee may have developed its own local tradition, but only as a variant on the one apostolic Gospel.

4

Once persecution had provided the first impetus for the missionary enterprise of the church, the progress of the Gospel was so swift that we can no longer follow its course. Unnamed men and women, who have left no record of their

---

[1] This argument would be weakened if it could be shown that the appearance of the risen Jesus to over five hundred brethren at once, recorded in I Cor. xv. 6, happened in Galilee; but the other appearances listed in this tradition were all to apostles, which strongly suggests that Paul's tradition was a Jerusalem tradition.

work, were led by the Spirit to undertake a task of evangelism, which was carried out without organization or plan. It is doubtful whether even at the time any one person ever knew the whole story, and today only a few fragments of it are preserved for us.

Before Saul had completed his self-appointed duties as persecutor in Jerusalem, there was a Christian community in Damascus.[1] Philip had left his first mission field in Samaria, and was evangelizing the coastal cities from Azotus northwards to Caesarea.[2] Soon other refugees— almost certainly Hellenists—" travelled as far as Phoenicia, Cyprus, and Antioch ".[3] Some of the results of this activity could be seen over twenty years later when Paul and his companions on their way up to Jerusalem found churches in Tyre, Ptolemais, and Caesarea.[4]

At Antioch Jew and Gentile seem to have lived together with more mutual toleration than was to be found in other great cities of the Empire. There many of the Jerusalem Hellenists, including some who had come originally from Cyprus and Cyrene, found a new home and a promising new field for their preaching; and there the Gospel was addressed for the first time to Gentiles. This new departure need not have been the outcome of any considered policy. The evangelists found that their preaching was attracting Gentiles and saw no good reason to turn them away. Before long an entirely new kind of church had come into existence, in which Jewish and Gentile converts joined freely in a single fellowship. Barnabas was sent down from Jerusalem to investigate this new development, and was so thoroughly convinced that this was the work of the Holy Spirit that he set off at once for Tarsus to enlist the aid of the man who was best fitted to promote the new Gentile mission.[5] We cannot give any precise dates to this dramatic sequence of events, but we shall not be far wrong if we place Paul's arrival in Antioch some four or five years after the outbreak of persecution.

From this point the brilliant achievement of Paul tends

[1] Acts ix. 19.   [2] Acts viii. 40.
[3] Acts xi. 19.   [4] Acts xxi. 4–8.   [5] Acts xi. 22–26.

to throw into obscurity the lesser lights of the Christian
mission, and our sources afford us only three glimpses of
them. Barnabas, after his first journey with Paul, continued the work in Cyprus with Mark as his partner,[1] and
later tradition attributes to one of them the foundation of a
church in Alexandria.[2] Apart from this not too reliable
hint and the fact that Apollos of Alexandria had some sort
of acquaintance with Christian teaching before coming to
Ephesus,[3] the origins of the Alexandrian church are lost in
impenetrable darkness, but it is difficult to believe that
Paul would have passed over the claims of so great a city
in favour of Spain, except on the principle that he refused
to build on other men's foundations.[4] While Paul was busy
in Greece and Asia Minor, the brothers of the Lord, the
other apostles, and Peter in particular were engaged in
missionary tours, and the fact that they were regularly
accompanied by their wives suggests that these tours lasted
a considerable length of time; [5] but we have no evidence
to show in what areas this work was carried on.[6] Some
time before A.D. 49, when Aquila and Priscilla were expelled
from Rome along with other Jews under the edict of
Claudius, Christianity had reached the capital city.[7] When
Paul wrote his Epistle to the Romans, the Christians had
returned to the city in strength. But about the beginnings
of the church in Rome we have no information. If we
could be sure that Romans xvi was an integral part of the
Epistle, it would afford us an interesting picture of the way
in which the Roman church was built up by the arrival in
Rome of Christians from other parts of the Empire; for
many of the people mentioned in that chapter must have
known Paul intimately at some point in his missionary
career. But a strong case can be made for regarding this
chapter as a separate letter addressed to the church of
Ephesus. If the Epistle to the Hebrews was written to the

---

[1] Acts xv. 39.   [2] Clem., *Hom.* i. 9; Eus., *H.E.* ii. 16.
[3] Acts xviii. 25.   [4] Rom. xv. 20–24; II Cor. x. 16.
[5] I Cor. ix. 5.
[6] Even if we accept the Petrine authorship of I Peter, the address of the
Epistle cannot be taken as proof that the countries mentioned had been
evangelized by Peter.
[7] Acts xviii. 2; Suet., *Claud.* xxv.

church in Rome, then in the light of Heb. ii. 3, we could say that the church was founded by disciples who were with Jesus during his earthly ministry.   But the letter may have been written from Rome to a church elsewhere.[1]

5

By the time that the Gentile mission began in Antioch other Christians had returned to Jerusalem to take up the threads of their former life.   No more is said of the common fund, which must have been discontinued while the congregation was scattered; but otherwise the character of the church was not markedly changed.   Many of the Hellenists had gone, but it is a mistake to think that the Jerusalem church never again numbered Hellenists among its members. We know that Barnabas of Cyprus still held a position of esteem there, and at a later date we hear of another Cypriot, Mnason, residing in Jerusalem, who is described as an early disciple.[2]   But important changes lay not far ahead. Barnabas was sent to Antioch to investigate the new situation there, and was so impressed by what he saw that he chose to remain.   In A.D. 41 Herod Agrippa became king, and tried to curry favour with the Jews by an attack on the Christians, in the course of which James, the son of Zebedee, lost his life and Peter was forced to flee the country.[3]   As the more liberal leaders were thus removed, the direction of the Jerusalem church fell more and more into the hands of James, the Lord's brother.

This James had remained aloof and suspicious during the Galilean ministry, but an appearance of the risen Jesus had convinced him of the truth of the Gospel.   He promptly joined the Jerusalem community and was accepted by them as an apostle.[4]   His great piety and profound reverence for the Torah won him the respect of the Pharisees, and fitted him admirably for the difficult task of leading the church at a time when it had fallen into disfavour with the

---

[1] Heb. ii. 3; xiii. 24.   For a picture of the church in Rome based on Romans and Hebrews see W. Manson, *The Epistle to the Hebrews.*
[2] Acts xi. 22; xxi. 16.   [3] Acts xii. 2, 17.
[4] Mk. iii. 21, 31–35; I Cor. xv. 7; Acts i. 14; Gal. i. 19.

Jewish authorities. His fundamental Christian convictions cannot be doubted; for, when Paul laid before him the Gospel which he was preaching among the Gentiles, he was able to give it his cordial assent.[1] But he believed that for the Jews the Law of Moses had a permanent validity, even when their Judaism had been taken up into the fulness of Christian faith. Without wishing to impose any unnecessary restrictions upon Gentile Christianity, he was firmly resolved that no Gentile Christian should be allowed to frustrate the Jerusalem church in its task of presenting the Gospel to their fellow Jews. For he realized that, if it became known that Jewish Christians were in the habit of fraternizing with Gentiles, Jewish society would be closed to them and their opportunity for evangelism lost.

Under James's leadership the church gained ground among the Jews. Pharisees were received into church membership.[2] But with every new accession the character of the church changed, until James found himself presiding over a large congregation more firmly bound to Judaism than to the churches of the Hellenistic mission.[3] Between such a church and the church of Antioch, energetically pursuing its mission to the Gentiles, friction was bound to arise. Throughout the controversy between the two parties the leaders, Paul and James, acted in complete good faith, and we get the impression that they understood and respected one another's point of view. But Paul had occasion to complain of underhand conduct on the part of some of James's following.[4]

The course of the dispute presents the most perplexing of all the problems in New Testament chronology, and theories have multiplied with little prospect of agreement.[5] But it is clear that James made two attempts at resolving the differences between the two types of Christianity. First, he sent envoys to Antioch with the suggestion that Jewish and Gentile Christians should meet separately for the fellowship meal which included the Lord's Supper. Peter, who

---

[1] Gal. ii. 9.   [2] Acts xv. 4.   [3] Acts xxi. 20 f.
[4] Gal. ii. 4; cf. Acts xv. 24.
[5] For a full discussion of this problem see Appendix A.

happened to be in Antioch, and Barnabas both fell in with the proposal, but the one dissentient voice of Paul ensured its final rejection.[1]   The second solution was first submitted to a church counsel in Jerusalem and then embodied in a pastoral letter to the churches of Syria and Cilicia, which recommended to the Gentile Christians that they should observe a few rules of the Jewish Law, in order to make it possible for their Jewish brethren to eat with them without violation of the Torah.[2]

This was a good working compromise, but it was not a permanent solution.   The two points of view were ultimately irreconcilable, and sooner or later the church would have had to decide whether it was going to live by the Law or the Gospel.   But history took the decision out of the church's hands.   During one of their frequent periods of anarchy the Jews turned against James and put him to death.[3] The Jerusalem Christians, finding their position intolerable in the rising tide of Jewish nationalism, withdrew across the Jordan to Pella, there to disappear from the pages of history.   And within a few years Jerusalem was reduced to ruins by the army of Titus.

---

[1] Gal. ii. 11 ff.   [2] Acts xv. 24–29.   [3] Eus., *H.E.* ii. 23.

CHAPTER VII

THE GENTILE MISSION: 2. THE MISSIONARY'S PROBLEMS

I

WHILE the Gospel was being addressed only to Jews and to the God-fearers, whose attendance at the synagogue had made them familiar with the language and thought of the Old Testament, the pattern of the apostolic tradition, whether in Aramaic or Greek, was sufficient for missionary needs. But when the Gentile mission began, the traditional presentation of the Gospel had to be modified to suit new conditions. In the first place, there were difficulties of vocabulary. The Aramaic Gospel could be translated literally into a form of Greek which was intelligible to the Jew of the Dispersion, even if he were unwilling to accept it; but to the Gentile many of the terms of this translation Greek were either unintelligible or liable to serious misconstruction. The Gospel of the Kingdom, which had been central to Jesus' preaching, could give the impression that the missionaries were putting forward a pretender to the imperial throne.[1] At Athens the crowd laughed at Paul when he mentioned the Resurrection, supposing that he was attempting to introduce a foreign mystery cult with a male and female deity, Jesus and Anastasis. The title Son of Man, full of meaning on the lips of Jesus, sounded in its Greek guise like a barbarism. Similarly the title Messiah conveyed nothing to Greek ears, and some who heard the word Christos automatically substituted in their own minds the homonym Chrestos.[2]

There could be no one way of dealing with linguistic problems such as these. Some words—resurrection, for

[1] Acts xvii. 7. *Basileus* was the official Greek title of the emperor.
[2] Suet., *Claud.* xxv : " Iudaeos impulsore Chresto assidue tumultuantes Roma expulit ". Cf. the variant readings at Acts xi. 26; xxvi. 28; I Pet. ii. 3; iv. 6. By the first century A.D. itacism had removed all phonetic distinction between eta and iota.

example—could not be discarded without irreparable loss.
Nor was the idea of the Kingdom entirely superseded,
though it occupies a much less prominent place in the
Epistles than in the Gospels. But the title Son of Man fell
early into disuse, and Christos almost as quickly ceased to
be a title and became a proper name. To take the place of
these two titles Hellenistic Christianity found in the
apostolic tradition a third title which was full of meaning
to the Gentile. The primitive church from the earliest days
had worshipped Jesus as Lord, and here was a title which
could make an immediate appeal to the religious aspirations
of the Graeco-oriental world. To the devotees of many a
pagan cult the ascription of the title *Kyrios* [1] to Jesus meant
that he was one who claimed their worship and their loyalty,
one to whom they might surrender themselves as "slaves",
and in his service find their true life. Thus in making the
baptismal confession "Jesus is Lord" the Gentile convert
might not understand all that was implied in the formula,
but he was making that complete self-committal which was
the necessary prelude to fuller comprehension.

2

The use of the title *Kyrios* was one of the earliest ways in
which the church tried to solve the problem of making
contact with the Gentile mind, but it led to a more serious
difficulty. In the pagan world there were "gods many
and lords many", and there was a danger that in the prevailing religious hospitality Christ should be accepted into
the pantheon or even identified with other "lords" in a new
syncretism. The attempts of Reitzenstein and others to
show that the Christian sacraments were derived from the
hellenistic mystery religions, wrongheaded as they were in
many respects, prove nevertheless how easily the sacraments
could have been assimilated to pagan practice. The
Christian missionaries, therefore, had to find some way of
preaching Christ as Lord which would preserve the mono-

[1] For the use of this title in the Hellenistic cults see Bousset, *Kyrios Christos*.

theistic heritage that had come to them from the Old Testament. The use of the Septuagint in public worship and the presence of converted Jews or Godfearers gave them some assistance, but more than this was needed. They must in some way define the relationship of Christ the Lord to all those other deities that made claims to lordship; and this they tried to do in three ways.

The simplest method was to dismiss pagan religion as idolatry. Paul recalls how the Thessalonians responded to his preaching by turning from idols to serve the living and true God, and Luke records two sermons in which a similar appeal is made.[1] There were some Christians at Corinth who were so thoroughly convinced by this argument that they felt free to participate in a sacramental meal at a pagan temple, on the grounds that the pagan deity had no real existence and therefore could not be the recipient of worship.

Along with this attack on idolatry went an assertion of the unity of God.[2] In this connexion Cullmann has made the interesting suggestion that the earliest baptismal formula, " Jesus Christ is Lord ", was expanded when Christianity came into direct opposition with heathenism into a bipartite formula, of which a trace has survived in I Corinthians viii. 6 : " One God the Father . . . and one Lord Jesus Christ ".[3] One passage would be a meagre foundation for such a theory if Paul were here expressing his own doctrine, for he was quite capable of couching his own thoughts in quasi-credal form. But he seems rather to be quoting as a basis for further discussion extracts from a letter he had received from Corinth, so that the formula has some claim to be regarded as an accepted confession of faith.

But pagan religion was not so easily disposed of. The Christian might deny to the pagan gods any real divinity, but it was useless to deny the hold which they exercised over the minds of men. Of the gods many might be gods in name only but their dominion was a real dominion. The

[1] I Thess. i. 9; Acts xiv. 15; xvii. 29.
[2] I Cor. viii. 6; I Tim. ii. 5; Jas. ii. 19.
[3] O. Cullmann, *The Earliest Christian Confessions*, p. 32.

G

astral deities in particular influenced by their authority
vast areas of human life. Confronted with this dilemma
the Christian was able to profit by the experience of the
Jew. For the Jew had learnt from the prophets to scorn
idolatry, only to discover that in terms of temporal success
the religions of the great empires seemed to yield better
results than his own worship of Yahweh. So the belief had
grown up that idolatry was the result of a corruption of the
natural order as established by Yahweh. For Yahweh had
created the heavenly bodies to mark out the times and
seasons, and men had given to the creature the worship due
to the Creator.[1] Israel had been accustomed to regard the
heavenly bodies as angelic beings, the heavenly host sur-
rounding the throne of God.[2] Pagan worship, therefore,
appeared to them as the worship of angels to whom God
had delegated some part of his authority. From there it
was a small step to the belief that each nation had been
allotted by God its own angelic governor, and that men had
mistaken God's representative for God himself.[3] But the
angelic rulers must in some sense be held responsible for
what happened under their rule. Indeed, just as an earthly
king could be regarded as the personal embodiment of his
own realm, so the angelic ruler was identified with the kingdom which lay under his authority. The fall of Babylon was
the fall of Lucifer, the morning star.[4] When the armies of
Alexander and Darius met on the field of Granicus or Gau-
gamela, there was a corresponding battle on the heavenly
plane between the angelic princes of Greece and Persia.[5]
It inevitably followed that the angelic rulers of tyrannical
and idolatrous empires were themselves believed to be evil;
they could be identified with the sons of God who had fallen
from grace through lusting after the daughters of men,[6]
and, since even Israel was held in subjection to a series of
pagan nations, the whole world must be considered to lie

---

[1] Deut. iv. 19; Wisd. xiii. 1 f.
[2] Job xxxviii. 7; Judg. v. 30; I Kings xxii. 19; Neh. ix. 6.
[3] Deut. xxxii. 8 f. (LXX); Sir. xvii. 17.   [4] Isa. xiv. 12.
[5] Dan. x. 20; cf. Rev. xii. 7, where the war between Michael and the
dragon is the heavenly counterpart of the Atonement.
[6] Gen. vi. 1 f.; En. vi. ff.

under the control of " principalities and powers " who were in revolt against God. But Israel looked forward to the day when heavenly ruler and earthly monarch would alike come under the judgment of God. " It shall come to pass in that day that Yahweh will punish the host of the height in the height and the kings of the earth on the earth." [1] The present age was subject to the world rulers by a decree which God himself could not revoke, but the age to come would be under the reign of God.[2]

This Jewish doctrine was primarily a theodicy for the encouragement of the Jews themselves in time of persecution and national disaster, but it was capable of being developed for apologetic and missionary purposes also. For there were many Gentiles who were looking for an escape from polytheism, and almost all Gentiles had in some measure felt the impact of astrology with its theory that all human life was controlled by the *kosmokratores*, which directed the orderly motions of the stars and planets.

Thus the Christian missionary had ready to his hand an explanation of pagan religion which did full justice to its power without in any way compromising his fundamental monotheism. Moreover, he could carry the doctrine further than the Jew had done, for he believed that the age to come had already broken in upon the present age, and that Christ had already, in principle at least, vanquished the principalities and powers.

This belief in the subjection of the principalities and powers was worked out most fully by Paul, but there are indications that the Hellenistic church was already thinking in these terms before Paul began to write his Epistles. For Paul's teaching was based on two psalms, one of which had certainly been applied to Jesus from the earliest times.[3] Psalm cx, which was the foundation of the church's belief in the lordship of Christ and in his heavenly reign, declared that this reign meant the subjection of all hostile powers; and Psalm viii showed that the universal supremacy of Christ was the fulfilment of God's design for man. But references to these two psalms are found in conjunction not

[1] Isa. xxiv. 21; En. xci. 15. [2] Heb. ii. 5. [3] I Cor. xv. 25 f.

only in the writings of Paul but also in Hebrews i–ii and in I Peter iii. 22.[1] In neither of the passages concerned is there any clear dependence on Paul either in language or in thought, and the best explanation of the evidence is that each of the three writers was developing in his own way a piece of Old Testament exegesis which was in current use in Hellenistic Christianity. This hypothesis may possibly gain a little support from the credal hymn found in I Tim. iii. 16, where it is said that Christ " appeared to angels ". It is possible too that one reason why the stories of exorcism bulk so large in the Gospel tradition is that they demonstrated to the pagan world the authority of Jesus over the principalities and powers. Nor must it be forgotten that Jesus spoke of his own ministry as a warfare with Satan. He claimed that his exorcisms were the despoiling of the strong man, who till that moment had kept his fortress secure; when his disciples reported success in their mission, he said that he had seen " Satan fall as lightning from heaven "; and behind the human agents who brought him to the Cross he perceived " the power of darkness." [2]

3

To those who had been educated in Greek philosophy a belief in one God presented no difficulties, for the whole course of philosophy had been an attempt to discover the unity behind the plurality of nature. But to the philosophic mind *theos* had come to mean something very different from what it meant to the Jew or the Christian. *Theos* was the rational principle or pattern underlying the manifold phenomena of the sensible world, the universal within the particular. The divine Logos of the Stoic, for example, was but the universal counterpart of the logos or rational faculty which is found in human nature.[3] Greek thought could accommodate itself to belief in a creation, in which the Creator had left the stamp of his own character on all his works, or to a providential ordering of history according

---

[1] ὑποταγέντων is a slight but unmistakable reminiscence of Ps. viii. 6.
[2] Lk. xi. 20; x. 18; xxii. 53.   [3] Plac. I 7. 33; Sen. Ep. lxv. 24.

to a changeless decree. But the biblical faith in a Living God, who had done in the history of one people that which he had done in no other place and at no other time, and whose mighty acts had reached their climax in a particular, unique event—that was the denial of all that the Greeks held dear.

W. L. Knox has shown in great detail how hard it was for the educated Greek to accept eschatology; [1] but this was only part of a larger difficulty. Eschatology is but one aspect of the biblical conception of history, which in its totality was foreign to the Greek mind. Aristotle had preferred poetry to history as a more philosophic and a more serious study, inasmuch as poetry was concerned with universals and history merely with particulars—what Alcibiades did and had done to him.[2] Aristotle's philosophy had lost its popularity, but in this respect he represented a mentality which did not change with the centuries. The Greek of the first century A.D. still found it incredible that what Jesus did or had done to him could have any universal significance.

Along with this depreciation of history went a static conception of God.[3] To be perfect God must be changeless, and to be changeless he must never be acted upon by any other agent. He must be active, not passive; he could not suffer.[4] To those who were accustomed to think in this manner the Gospel of the Cross, which proclaimed that God had been revealed in human suffering, was merely ludicrous.[5] This was particularly true of the Stoics, whose ideal man, emulating the divine attribute of *apatheia*, remained unaffected by the actions of others.[6] Some

---

[1] *St. Paul and the Church of the Gentiles*, Ch. I.
[2] Poetics 1451b5–11; cf. Met. V 11, 1018b32.
[3] Cf. F. M. Cornford, *The Laws of Motion in Ancient Thought*.
[4] Diog. Laert. VII 134. The verb πάσχω meant (1) to be the object of any action; (2) to suffer; and the two meanings were never clearly distinguished. From the same root was derived ἀπάθεια which could mean (1) incapacity to be acted on; (2) inability to suffer; (3) absence of passion.
[5] Lucian, *Peregr.* xiii.: "that gibbeted sophist".
[6] Arist., *De Anima* III 4, 429a10, Philo, *Leg. All.* III 129, Sen., *Ep.* ix. 1 ff.; Epict., *Diss.* III 2. 4; see esp. Plot., *Enn.* I 2. 3: "Of such a disposition of the soul whereby it thinks and remains unaffected (ἀπαθής), if someone should say that it was an assimilation to the divine, he would not be wrong."

concession to this point of view is to be found in the Fourth Gospel, where Jesus suffers by his own volition, so that the Cross becomes an Action rather than a Passion.

Quite a different problem confronted the Christian in his preaching of the Resurrection. From the Orphics and Pythagoreans popular Greek philosophy had inherited a dualism, in which man was regarded as an immortal soul incarcerated in an earthbound body, but destined to escape from the trammels of corporeal existence and to be assimilated to the divine.[1] To such aspirations the Gospel must have sounded pure bathos with its promise that the believer would bear to all eternity the body from which he had so passionately yearned to be free.

The effect of these and other intellectual difficulties on the progress of the Christian mission must be judged mainly from our knowledge of Paul's work. When problems of this sort were raised within the fellowship of the faith, he dealt with them; and his treatment of the resurrection body was a most successful attempt to bridge the gulf between Jewish and Greek thought.[2] He was always ready to discuss theology with the mature, but he did not employ such arguments in his evangelistic preaching.[3] Luke tells us that Paul made one attempt at Athens to speak to the Greek intelligentsia in their own language, and this may have been the scene of his disillusionment.[4] For he himself recounts how he came to Corinth already aware that the preaching of the Cross was foolishness to the wisdom-loving Greeks, and already determined to preach nothing but Christ and him crucified.[5] It is not surprising, then, that in the Pauline churches there were " not many wise, not many mighty, not many noble ".[6] Paul's missionary methods were opportunist; to use his own expression, when he came to an open door, he went in; but he must have felt that the door to the upper classes of Greek society was very firmly closed.[7]

In all probability other missionaries had very much the

[1] Plato, *Crat.* 400C; *Gorg.* 493A; Philo, *Ebriet.* 98; *Leg. All.* I 106, III, 40 ff.; Sen., *Ep.* lxv. 16; cii. 23.
[2] I Cor. xv. 35 ff.   [3] I Cor. ii. 1–6.   [4] Acts xvii. 16–34.
[5] I Cor. i. 23; ii. 2.   [6] I Cor. i. 26.   [7] I Cor. xvi. 9; II Cor. ii. 12.

same experience as Paul. As we shall see in the next chapter, there is growing agreement among scholars that the Hellenistic missionaries used a common form of ethical instruction of which traces have been preserved in several of the Epistles. The long exhortation to slaves and the brief word to masters suggest very strongly that most of the early converts in all the Hellenistic churches were drawn from the lower strata of society.[1]

4

The chief response to the missionary preaching came from the common man, who in the cosmopolitan society of the Roman Empire was not noteworthy for his high moral standards. To judge by the Epistles, denunciations of pagan vice formed a regular feature of Christian ethical instruction,[2] and on two occasions Paul reminds his readers that it was from just such a life of moral degradation that they had been rescued by Christ.[3] In other words the church contained a large number of members whose previous acquaintance with the fundamental rules of morality had been slight, and they presented the missionary with his most urgent and perplexing problem. A form of ethical education had to be devised which was adequate to their needs, but which at the same time was compatible with the essential nature of the Christian Gospel.

The teaching of Jesus had been advanced ethics. He had been able to take for granted what had already been said in the Old Testament, and to go on from the point where the old Testament left off: " You have heard that it was said to the men of old . . . but I say to you . . ." The Jewish Christian had come to the Gospel via the Torah; as Paul put it, the Law had been his schoolmaster to lead him to Christ. The admission to the church of Gentiles who had had no comparable preparatory training compelled the church leaders to define the relationship between Gospel and Law.

---

[1] Col. iii. 22–iv. 1; Eph. vi. 5–9; I Pet. ii. 18–25.
[2] Rom. i. 24 ff.; xiii. 12 f.; I Cor. v. 9; vi. 9 ff.; Gal. v. 19; Eph. iv. 17 ff.; v. 3 ff.; Col. iii. 5 ff.; I Thess. iv. 3 ff.; I Pet. ii. 1; iv. 3 f.
[3] I Cor. vi. 11; Col. iii. 7.

There were some Jewish Christians to whom it appeared self-evident that the Gentile converts must undertake to observe the Law and in token of that undertaking accept circumcision.[1] Doubtless the motives that led them to adopt this attitude were many and complex. But we must do them the justice of believing that foremost among those motives was a genuine concern for ethical standards. The men who caused trouble for Paul at Corinth claimed to be " ministers of righteousness ";[2] and although no defence is possible for their personal attacks on the apostle, it must be said of them that they honestly believed that, in demanding obedience to the Law, they were serving the cause of morality. The hypothetical objections which Paul introduces into the argument of two other Epistles may well have been drawn from actual controversy with Jewish Christians who thought that Paul's repudiation of the Law was an encouragement to Gentile laxity.[3]

It is not likely that the advocates of this policy ever formed a party within the church as a whole, nor that Paul's opponents in Galatia and Corinth were the same men who pursued him from city to city.[4] It is clear, too, that James dissociated himself entirely from this point of view, although he believed that Jewish Christians were still bound by the Law.[5] Peter, apart from one lapse at Antioch, abandoned all attempt to keep the Law and lived like any Gentile Christian.[6] Paul went further and held that to live by the Law was to frustrate the grace of God,[7] though in practice he was prepared to make large concessions to Jewish scruple.[8]

The agreement of these three leaders that the Law could not be made the basis of a Christian ethic opened the way for the development of a new system of instruction, and

---

[1] Acts xv. 1, 5.   [2] II Cor. xi. 15.
[3] Gal. ii. 17; Rom. iii. 7 f.; vi. 1.
[4] τοὺς ἐκ περιτομῆς (Gal. ii. 12) may mean " the Jewish Christians " or simply " the Jews " (see Dom Gregory Dix, *Jew and Greek*, pp. 42–43); it cannot mean " the circumcision party "—the question of circumcision had not been raised in the particular dispute that Paul is describing in this passage.
[5] Acts. xv. 24; Gal. ii. 9 f.   [6] Gal. ii. 14.   [7] Gal., ii. 21.
[8] I Cor. ix. 20; Acts xvi. 3; xxi. 23 ff.

we shall see below that such a system was developed at a very early date within the Hellenistic church. This teaching, however, could not be expected to transform in a moment the character of all the Gentile converts, and we can see from the Epistles that it did not in fact do so.[1] This put a strong weapon into the hands of the Jewish Christian legalists. The missionary, therefore, was forced to fight a battle on two fronts, on the one hand against Gentile converts who resented correction, and on the other hand against Jewish Christians who felt that the correction was not rigorously enough applied.[2]

---

[1] E.g. I Cor. v. 1, 11.   [2] II Cor. x. 10

CHAPTER VIII

THE GENTILE MISSION: 3. THE MISSIONARY'S EQUIPMENT

I.

THE Christian missionary carried with him on his travels a certain basic equipment, which was to assist him both in his preaching and in his teaching. Some of this may have been in written form; for, in a passage which is almost certainly a genuinely Pauline fragment embedded in the Pastoral Epistles, Paul mentions some books and parchments which he had left in safe keeping at Troas.[1] Other Christian writings are mentioned elsewhere in the Epistles as though they were in common use.[2] But in the early period at least it is probable that the missionary's equipment was carried in his memory. That is the implication of the word *paradosis*, which along with the verbs " deliver " and " receive " is used frequently by Paul to denote an oral tradition, both *kerygma* and *didache*.[3]

Little more need be said here about the preaching tradition, since we have already seen that the Gospel of the Hellenistic church differed from that of the primitive church only in the disuse of a few terms and the addition of arguments against idolatry. But there was one point where, for a Gentile audience, the primitive Gospel pattern required considerable amplification. While the Gospel was being addressed to Palestinian Jews who had known something of Jesus during his lifetime, the preacher could pass lightly over the ministry and come directly to the heart of the Gospel—the Cross and the Resurrection. " Jesus of Nazareth, a man commended to you by God with miracles and wonders and signs, which God did through him in your

---

[1] II Tim. iv. 13; see P. N. Harrison, *The Problem of the Pastoral Epistles*, pp. 118 ff.

[2] Rom. xvi. 26; I Pet. ii. 6.

[3] Rom. vi. 17; I Cor. xi. 2, 23; xv. 1, 3; Gal. i. 9; Phil. iv. 9; Col. ii. 6; I Thess. ii. 15; iv. 1; II Thess. iii. 6.

midst, as you yourselves know. . . ." [1] Among the
Gentiles no such appeal to public knowledge could be made;
rather, it became increasingly necessary for the preacher
to have at his disposal a fund of stories which illustrated the
character and methods of this Jesus through whom salvation was proclaimed, and particularly those stories which
explained the clash of beliefs that led him to Calvary. The
end of this process of amplification may be seen in Mark's
Gospel where, though the pattern of the apostolic preaching
is retained and the Crucifixion and Resurrection are still
the heart of the Gospel, these events are shown to be the
climax of a ministry in which the Gospel of the Kingdom,
proclaimed by Jesus in word and deed, was rejected by the
authorities and misunderstood by the disciples.

From the primitive church the missionaries also inherited
a tradition of the sayings of Jesus. As the work of evangelism proceeded, the various missionary centres developed
their own local forms of this apostolic tradition, in which
emphasis was laid on local needs. Synoptic criticism has
made us familiar with three such local traditions. The
teaching material which is peculiar to Matthew's Gospel
(M), because it combines an interest in the Jewish mission
and a markedly Rabbinic quality with violently anti-
Jewish feeling, is usually believed to represent the tradition
current in the Jerusalem church between the conference of
A.D. 49 and the flight of the Christians from Jerusalem
shortly before the outbreak of the Jewish war. The
material common to the Gospels of Matthew and Luke (Q),
on account of its sympathetic attitude to the Gentiles, is
generally assumed to be the Antioch tradition. The
material which is found only in the Third Gospel was
collected by Luke, probably during a prolonged stay in
Caesarea. [2] Yet another collection can be traced behind the
Epistle of James; a table of parallels between this epistle
and the Synoptic Gospels shows that the author's acquaintance with the sayings of Jesus was not confined to any one

---

[1] Acts ii. 22; cf. x. 37.
[2] B. H. Streeter, *The Four Gospels*, pp. 230 ff.; T. W. Manson, *The Sayings of Jesus*, pp. 15–28.

of our Gospel sources, since there are affinities both with M
and with Q.[1] Paul, too, had at his disposal a very compre-
hensive sayings tradition.   Twice he cites a commandment
of the Lord as the authority for his own teaching or practice.[2]
Elsewhere echoes of the teaching of Jesus, and especially
of the teaching which is found in Mark and Q, are worked
into the fabric of Paul's own instruction; [3] but he makes it
clear that in his own mind he drew a sharp distinction
between such dominical sayings and teaching derived from
other sources or from his own judgment.[4]

In one place Paul refers to his sayings tradition as " the
law of Christ ", and in another place he describes himself as
" under Christ's law ".[5] For Paul the law of Christ
exercised its authority not as a written code but by an inner
constraint; it was " the law of the Spirit of life in Christ
Jesus ", a new covenant " written not with ink but with the
Spirit of the Living God, not on tablets of stone but on the
tablets of the human heart ". [6] But the inward and
spiritual nature of their authority did not in any way
detract from the obligation which these sayings of the Lord
imposed upon his disciples. Paul's doctrine of the Spirit
was his own contribution to Christian thought, but in
treating the sayings of Jesus as a new Torah he was not
alone. In the Epistle of James the dominical tradition is
designated " the law of liberty ",[7] and in Matthew's Gospel
Jesus is portrayed as the new Moses who from another Sinai
promulgates the new Law.[8] Any idea which Paul shares
with two other writers who are in other respects so different
from him is likely to have been derived by all of them from
their common background in Hellenistic Christianity.

One part of the teaching of Jesus which was of particular
importance to the missionary was the mission charge,
originally delivered to those disciples who went out on

---

[1] J. B. Mayor, *The Epistle of St. James*, pp. lxxxiv–lxxxvi.
[2] I Cor. vii. 10; ix. 14.
[3] A. M. Hunter, *Paul and His Predecessors*, pp. 55–58; W. D. Davies,
St. Paul and Rabbinic Judaism, pp. 136–141.
[4] I Cor. vii. 25.   [5] Gal. vi. 2; I Cor. ix. 20.
[6] Rom. viii. 2; II Cor. iii. 3.   [7] Jas. i. 25; ii. 12.
[8] See C. Chavasse, " Jesus : Christ and Moses." *Theology LIV* (1951)
pp. 244–250, 289–296.

preaching tours during the Galilean ministry. How highly this teaching was valued and how deeply it penetrated into the life of the church may be seen from the fact that the charge has come down to us in four forms, each one differing in details from the other three.[1] The mission charge would hardly have been preserved in each of the four Synoptic traditions unless it was used by the early church as a manual of instructions. We know that Paul regarded it in this light and quoted one of its provisions as authority for missionary practice in his own day.[2]

2

Not all of the missionary's equipment could be taken over directly from the primitive church. We have seen that the moral condition of the Gentile converts made it imperative that a form of ethical instruction should be devised to meet their needs. The existence of such a form may be inferred from Romans vi. 17, where Paul, writing to a church which he had not founded, assumes that they have received a pattern of instruction in common use throughout the Hellenistic church; and also from I Corinthians xi. 16, where he speaks of a practice uniformly observed by all the churches of God. The content of the teaching must be deduced from a comparative study of the Epistles.

The Pauline Epistles, the Pastoral Epistles, Hebrews, James, and I Peter all contain passages of paraenetic or catechetical material. Some of these passages are written in a bald style which is in striking contrast to the normal style of the epistles in which they occur, there is a large measure of agreement in the subjects that are dealt with, and there is even a small but distinctive vocabulary which is peculiar to this type of writing. These similarities used to be explained as the result of literary dependence of one writer on another, but a much more convincing explanation is that each of the writers was developing in his own way the common themes of missionary teaching. The evidence

---

[1] T. W. Manson, op. cit., pp. 73–78, 179–184, 256–259.   [2] I Cor. ix. 14.

which points to this conclusion has been set out in tabular form by two scholars, Carrington and Selwyn, and for the details their works should be consulted; [1] but the main points can be summarized as follows :

(1) In I Thess. iv. 1–9 Christian converts are exhorted to abstain from Gentile lusts because they have been called to holiness and to brotherly love. The key words—abstain, lust, holy, brotherly love, and the phrase " to love one another "—are all found in I Pet. i. 13–22 ; ii. 11. The verb abstain ($\dot{a}\pi\dot{\epsilon}\chi\epsilon\sigma\theta a\iota$) is a rare one which is found elsewhere in the New Testament only in the apostolic letter (Acts xv. 20, 29) and in I Tim. iv. 3. In this sequence of ideas, reproduced with such close resemblance in two epistles, and with partial parallels in Rom. xiii. 8–14, Carrington sees a " Christian Holiness Code "—a recasting for Christian use of the Levitical code (Lev. xvii–xx), in which a warning to refrain from heathen practices is followed by the two commandments, " You shall be holy, for I the Lord your God am holy", and "Thou shalt love thy neighbour as thyself ".

(2) In I Thess. v. 4–7 there is a sustained metaphor to which there is no complete parallel in other New Testament writings, though the whole passage seems to have been compiled from traditional ideas. Christians are said to have passed from darkness into light,[2] so that they have become children of light,[3] and they are reminded that the darkness is the time for sleep and revelry,[4] but the day is the time to watch and be sober.[5]

(3) There are some close linguistic resemblances between II Thess. ii. 13–17 and I Peter.

(4) A discussion of the place of trials in the Christian life is to be found in Rom. v. 3, I Pet. i. 6, and Jas. i. 2. The idea of testing is common to all three. Two phrases—" various trials " and " the testing of your faith "—occur in

---

[1] P. Carrington, *The Primitive Christian Catechism*; E. G. Selwyn, *The First Epistle of St. Peter*, Essay II ; cf. also A. M. Hunter, *Paul and His Predecessors*; C. H. Dodd, *Gospel and Law.*
[2] Cf. I. Pet. ii. 9; Rom. xiii. 12; Phil. ii. 15; Col. i. 13; Jn. viii. 12.
[3] Cf. Eph. v. 8; Lk. xvi. 8; Jn. xii. 36.
[4] Cf. Rom. xiii. 13; I Pet. iv. 3. [5] Cf. I Pet. v. 8.

I Peter and James but not in Romans. The word " hope " occurs in Romans and I Peter but not in James. The word " patience ", and in particular the phrase " produces patience ", occurs in Romans and James but not in I Peter. It is not easy to see how literary dependence could explain this triangular relationship.

(5) The same three epistles all refer to the Christian's inner warfare, though in terms sufficiently different to preclude literary dependence : " lusts that make war against the soul " (I Pet. ii. 11); " delights that make war in your members " (Jas. iv. 1); " a law in my members making war against the law of my mind " (Rom. vii. 23).

(6) In several of the epistles there is a fourfold form of instruction. Each of the four divisions has its key word, and Carrington has used the Latin translation of these words to designate the divisions they introduce—*deponentes* (put off), *subiecti* (submit), *vigilate* (watch), and *resistite* (resist) : the Christian must put off pagan vices and put on the new life, must be subject to all proper authority (all men to the state, wives to husbands, children to parents, slaves to masters), must watch and pray, must resist the devil. The pattern appears in full in Colossians, Ephesians, and I Peter, and with one omission in James; and various excerpts from it are found in Rom. xiii and elsewhere.

(7) In three cases the *deponentes* section is introduced with a " wherefore " or " therefore ", which suggests that the whole fourfold pattern was dependent on a prior statement.[1] In each case the preceding paragraph contains a description of Christian baptism as a new creation or a new birth.

(8) In Romans xii and I Peter there are several examples of the use of a participle as an imperative, which probably implies a Hebraic background.[2] The occurrences in I Peter cannot be explained on the theory that the epistle was dependent on Romans.

To this material collected by Carrington and Selwyn one

---

[1] Eph. iv. 25; I Pet. ii. 1; Jas. i. 21.
[2] See Selwyn, op. cit., pp. 467–488, an appended note by Dr. David Daube.

important addition must be made. The trinity of Christian virtues, faith, love, and hope, mentioned so often in the Pauline Epistles, is found also in Hebrews and I Peter.[1] At the end of his hymn of love Paul refers to them as " the three ", and there would be no reason in that context for mentioning faith and hope at all unless the virtues had already come to be regarded as an inseparable trio. For the same reason, when Paul exhorts the Thessalonians to " put on the breastplate of faith and love and for a helmet the hope of salvation ", he makes a double metaphor do service for a triple grace; he did not feel disposed either to add to the armour provided by Scripture [2] or to subtract from the threefold virtue of Christian tradition.

All this evidence seems to take us behind the Epistles to the teaching tradition of the early church; but as an argument for the existence of a formal catechism it is not all of equal cogency. Some of the parallels listed above seem to point only to a common vocabulary and a common fund of ideas, drawn partly from the Old Testament, partly from the teaching of Jesus, and partly from the apostolic *kerygma*. In any attempt to reconstruct a hypothetical source behind the Epistles there is clearly ample room for difference of opinion, and Carrington and Selwyn are by no means in complete agreement. Carrington with great restraint allows himself to speak only of an oral pattern within which he distinguishes three groups of ideas.[3] Selwyn goes much further and posits the existence of three distinct forms : an early baptismal form, more or less contemporary with the apostolic letter of Acts xv, and coloured by the same levitical associations; a later bap-

---

[1] I Thess. i. 3; v. 8; I Cor. xiii. 13; Gal. v. 5 f.; Rom. v. 1–5; Col. i. 4 f.; Eph. iv. 2–5; cf. Heb. vi. 10–12; x. 22–24; I Pet. i. 3–8, 21–22.

[2] Isa. lix. 17.

[3] The weakest point in Carrington's argument is his attempt to base a " Christian Holiness Code " on Leviticus. He treats the ritual ablution of Lev. xvii. 15 f. as though it were the prototype of Christian baptism. assumes that the use of the word " walk " for Christian behaviour is an echo of Lev. xviii. 4, though the word is exceedingly common in all parts of the O.T., and overlooks the fact that in the Epistles the commandment to love one's neighbour is derived from Jesus' summary of the Law and does not necessarily imply a direct reference to Leviticus. On the basis of this dubious parallelism he then goes on to speak of the church as a " neo-levitical community ".

tismal form more fully adapted to Gentile use;[1] and a persecution form.

However greatly opinions may vary concerning the rest of the material, in the case of Carrington's fourfold scheme we may be reasonably confident that we are dealing not merely with traditional ideas but with a fixed and accepted pattern. No other hypothesis will account half so well for the recurrent key words, the uniform order of the sections, and the many detailed resemblances between the epistles concerned; and it may be that this was the very pattern to which Paul alluded in writing to Rome. Moreover, Carrington is surely right in thinking that the pattern was introduced by some reference to baptism as a new birth or a new creation. This means that already at an early date the Hellenistic church had discovered a sound alternative to the legalism of the Judaists, and was regularly demanding from its converts a high ethical standard as the logical outcome of that inner change which they underwent at the time of their admission to the church.

In compiling this catechism the missionaries made use of all the suitable matter that lay ready to their hands. The code of subordination (*subiecti*) followed a plan already developed by Stoic teachers.[2] The participial imperative suggests that Rabbinic models also were copied. But whatever the sources employed, the final result was essentially Christian, inasmuch as every duty was to be undertaken " in the Lord ".

3

One of the most potent instruments of missionary education is the hymn, and there is evidence that in the Pauline churches not only the Psalter but hymns and spiritual songs of Christian composition were employed.[3] It is generally

---

[1] This chronological distinction is based on the Epistles of Paul, where the early form is represented by the Thessalonian correspondence, which stands apart from the rest of the Pauline corpus. But it seems to be a serious objection to Selwyn's analysis that in I Peter the two types of material are closely interwoven.

[2] Weidinger, *Die Haustafeln.*

[3] Col. iii. 16; Eph. v. 19; I Cor. xiv. 26.

H

agreed that the words " Awake, O sleeper, and rise from the dead, and Christ shall shine upon thee ", which are quoted in Ephesians as though they came from a familiar source, are a fragment of an early Christian hymn.[1] It is probable, too, that the credal passage in I Tim. iii. 16 is another example of early hymnody. Many attempts have been made to discover other passages of the same sort,[2] but few of the proposals have met with any general acceptance. In the Pauline Epistles the undertaking is exceedingly precarious in view of Paul's propensity to break forth into lyrical and rhythmical prose.

It has been argued, for example, that in Phil. ii. 6–11 Paul must have been quoting from a hymn, because neither the language nor the theology of the passage is quite in the Pauline vein.[3] Now it is true that the passage contains three *hapax legomena* and one word used in an unusual sense.[4] But one of the *hapax legomena* is a compound word of a kind that Paul delighted to create,[5] and several of the other words in the passage are typically Pauline. Moreover, Philippians has a higher proportion of *hapax legomena* than any other Pauline Epistle.[6] The linguistic evidence, therefore, is by no means incompatible with Pauline authorship. On the theological side, also, the case is very far from being clear cut. The passage is a detailed contrast between Christ and Adam to which the Pauline Epistles provide two excellent parallels.[7]

A much stronger case for the existence of an early hymn, quoted *in extenso* in I Pet. ii. 4–10 and more briefly in Rom. ix. 32 f., has been put forward by Selwyn in two closely reasoned notes.[8] His arguments may be summarized briefly as follows. Both epistles cite Isa. xxviii. 16 and Isa. viii. 14 in combination, but in I Peter the two texts are

[1] Eph. v. 14. [2] E.g. II Tim. ii. 11–13; Tit. iii. 4–7.
[3] See A. M. Hunter, op. cit., Ch. III.
[4] Μορφή, ἁρπαγμός, ὑπερυψόω; and κενόω.
[5] Paul uses in his Epistles no less than 20 compounds with ὑπερ.
[6] P. N. Harrison (op. cit., pp. 21, 23) gives the following figures for Philippians : words not found elsewhere in the N.T.—6·2 per page of Westcott and Hort's text; words not found elsewhere in the Pauline Epistles—12·7 per page.
[7] I Cor. xv. 20–23, 45–49; Rom. v. 12–21. [8] Op. cit., pp. 268–281.

held together by a third citation from Ps. cxviii. 22, so that the juxtaposition of the texts cannot be due to borrowing from Romans. Yet Romans and I Peter agree in certain minor deviations from the Septuagint text, which indicates that both were dependent on some source other than Scripture. Whatever the precise nature of this source, it must have consisted in a cento of Old Testament quotations or references. One possibility is that the source was a compilation of proof-texts of the kind envisaged by Rendel Harris in his Testimonies, but in view of Dodd's treatment of this subject, to which reference has been made in Chapter V, this is less probable than it once seemed to be. A much more likely theory, then, is that the Scriptural quotations had been woven together in a hymn. This was the method of composition employed for the canticles of the Lucan nativity story and for the hymns of the Revelation, and many a fine English hymn has been compiled on the same principle.

CHAPTER IX

PAUL

1

AMONG the characters of antiquity none, with the exception of Cicero, is so well known to us as Paul. His own letters and the diary of his companion Luke provide us with a fund of information which enables us to reconstruct much of the story of his missionary work. There remain, it is true, tantalizing gaps and unresolved controversies. Nevertheless, on this one brief period history has directed a spotlight which tends to throw into a deeper obscurity the period which preceded and that which followed. Histories of the apostolic age have accordingly tended to move lightly over the " hidden years " of the early church in order to concentrate on the better documented period. Even Johannes Weiss, who drew attention to the danger, produced a history dominated by the apostle to the Gentiles. That Paul was by far the greatest figure of his time need not be denied, but it does not increase his stature to represent him as a solitary giant, nor can we properly understand his unique contribution to Christian development unless we see him as the inheritor of a living, growing tradition, which he in turn stimulated to more vigorous and more splendid vitality.

In the foregoing chapters we have tried to delineate that tradition, and have found good reason to believe that Paul's thought and practice, as revealed in his Epistles, included much of the common thought and practice of the early church. The apostolic Gospel, in which Christ's death and Resurrection were interpreted as vicarious humiliation and triumph, and in which the church was presented as the new Israel, united by the closest of ties with her messianic head ; the two Gospel sacraments of baptism and the Lord's Supper ; the experience of the Spirit as the directing power within the church and the bond of the church's fellowship ;

the teaching of Jesus, containing both ethical instruction
and a key to the understanding of the Scriptures—all this
belonged to the primitive tradition. To this tradition the
Hellenistic church had added a new emphasis on the lordship of Christ over all hostile powers and a new form of
ethical instruction designed to meet the needs of Gentile
Christianity. This means that in none of the central
affirmations of the Christian message can Paul be regarded
as an innovator. It now remains for us to discover wherein
lay his original and distinctive contribution to the progress
of the early church.

Paul's contribution can be summed up in the words which
he himself used to describe the Christians of Macedonia :
he first gave himself to the Lord.[1] He had an intense and
passionate nature, which was always prompting him to
throw himself totally into every experience and to savour
it to the full. Whatever beliefs he held he pursued to their
logical conclusion. Whatever tasks he undertook he performed to the limit of his power. Whatever he met went
through the crucible of his experiencing soul. As a Jew he
never spared himself in his zealous pursuit of righteousness
under the Law. At his conversion he " underwent with
elemental vehemence the experience of Christ ".[2] In his
missionary work he asked only the chance to " spend and
be spent ".[3] His great secret with his fellow men was that
all there was of him went into his friendships. He held
Jewish and Gentile Christians together in one fellowship
because he refused even to consider the possibility that the
church could be divided. And he left an abiding monument
to his intellectual power and spiritual perception because it
was not in him to be content with present achievement or
present understanding. " I count myself not yet to have
apprehended . . . I press on toward the goal."[4] Nothing
less could satisfy him than to know the love of Christ that
passes knowledge and to plumb the unfathomable riches of
God.

[1] II Cor. viii. 5.   [2] A. Deissmann, *St. Paul*, p. 229.
[3] II Cor. xii. 15.   [4] Phil. iii. 13 f.

2

This trait of Paul's character led him early in life to join the Pharisees—the strictest sect of his religion. But even Pharisaic standards were not enough; he must advance beyond his contemporaries.[1] Jewish apologists have often taken Paul to task for misrepresenting the Judaism of the first century. Not all of their objections are well-founded, but it may be granted that Paul's experience of the Law was not typical, for the simple reason that he took both sin and righteousness more seriously than the majority of his compatriots. Like them he believed that God was merciful to the penitent sinner, but not even the divine mercy could detract from the ultimate demands of the divine righteousness.[2] The Law demanded perfect obedience, and by that norm he must be found blameless.[3] The Law set before him life and death, the blessing and the curse, and in no particular must he deviate from the path that led to life and blessing.[4] Above all the Law required that he should keep himself and the commonwealth of Israel free from the contamination of sinners, and it was this requirement that set him on his career as a persecutor. The ministry of Jesus had been a challenge to all that the Pharisee stood for. He had broken the Law, befriended notorious sinners, threatened the destruction of cherished institutions; and when he claimed divine authority for what he did and said, he had laid himself open to the charge of blasphemy on which he was condemned. The Cross was the proof that divine justice had been exacted and that the curse of God had rested on the breaker of the Law. When, therefore, the challenge to Judaism was renewed by Stephen's declaration that Christ was the end of both Law and temple, Paul believed that in persecuting the church he was doing the will of God.

[1] Gal. i. 14.
[2] "What Paul really does is to abstract the dominant principles of Judaism from their concrete setting and press them to their logical conclusion." W. Morgan, *The Religion and Theology of Paul*, p. 85.
[3] Phil. iii. 6 f.
[4] Deut. xxx. 19; Lev. xviii. 5; cf. Rom. x. 5; Gal. iii. 12.

But the zeal that made Paul a persecutor had another side to it. A man who took his religious responsibilities less seriously than Paul could never have become such a trenchant critic of the Law. Just because Paul had availed himself of all that the Law had to offer and was considered blameless by the standards of legal righteousness, he was in a position to know the limitations of legal religion. In Romans vii Paul has described the inner struggles of the man for whom the Law has provided a rule of life without providing the power to turn rule into reality. It is generally agreed that the chapter is in some sense autobiographical, though there is less agreement concerning the period of Paul's life to which the experience belongs. Some have wanted to place it before, some after, his conversion, and neither theory is without difficulty. If we regard the chapter as a description of Paul's feelings of frustration before his conversion, it is hard to see how a person so pathetically conscious of inner division could ever have become an ardent and wholehearted persecutor of the church. On the other hand it is quite out of keeping with all that Paul has to say elsewhere about the nature of the Christian life to consider that he is here describing a normal post-conversion experience. Denney is surely right in saying that Romans vii represents Paul's pre-conversion life " seen through regenerate eyes "; [1] though probably we should add, with Mitton, that Paul the Christian had enough acquaintance with the unregenerate life to remind him that left to himself, he was still a slave to the law of sin.[2] In the light of the power and peace which Christ had given him, Paul was able to review his past life and to see the impotence of the Law to which he had once devoted himself. Yet even though full disillusionment came only with conversion, the process must have begun at an earlier date with many a disappointment and misgiving. In the third Lucan account of Paul's conversion the voice from heaven says, " It hurts you to kick against the goads ".[3] Paul had felt

---

[1] James Denney, *Expositor's Greek Testament*. ii. p. 639.
[2] C. L. Mitton, " Romans vii. Reconsidered ", *Expository Times*. lxv, pp. 78–81, 99–103, 132–135.   [3] Acts xxvi. 14.

twinges of doubt which he had done his best to ignore, and his violent attempt to suppress the Christian critics of the Law was at the same time an attempt to suppress the critic of the Law in his own conscience.

3

Paul's conversion convinced him of three facts : that Christ was alive, that in some way the risen Christ was to be identified with the disciples whom Paul had persecuted, and that in this revelation of Christ God was commissioning him for a great new enterprise.   These facts changed completely his attitude to Christ, to Christians, and to himself, and with characteristic thoroughness he started to think through their implications and to reconstruct around them the edifice of his religious belief.   How long this reconstruction took we can only guess, because the evidence is all contained in epistles written from fifteen to thirty years later.   No doubt Paul continued to grow in spiritual wisdom throughout his lifetime, and we know that what he learnt from personal experience was later enriched by the traditions he received from the church.   But he emphatically asserts that his Gospel came to him by revelation and was in no way dependent on the Jerusalem apostles,[1] so that the period of readjustment was probably quite short and the main outline of his message must have been clearly formulated within the three years that elapsed before his first visit to Jerusalem.[2]

Paul had seen the risen Christ.   But if God had raised Christ from the dead, Paul could no longer hold that the Cross was the seal of God's disapproval on an ungodly life. God had vindicated the Crucified.   God's sovereign justice had in some way to be reconciled with the Crucifixion of the innocent.   Only one explanation was possible.   The innocent had died in the place of the guilty.[3]   He had so identified himself with sinful men, had so made himself responsible

---

[1] Gal. i. 11–17.
[2] Gal. i. 18.   C. H. Dodd thinks that Paul underwent a " second conversion " at Ephesus, but this affected his acceptance, not his understanding of the Gospel (*New Testament Studies*, pp. 67–82).   [3] Rom. v. 6.

for them, that he had taken to himself their sin with all its consequences.[1] It is a mark of Paul's quality of mind that this general truth came home to him as a personal conviction that Christ " loved me and gave himself for me ".[2] There could be but one response to that gift of love. If Christ had identified himself with Paul, Paul must respond by identifying himself with Christ; and since Christ was the Crucified One this meant entering into " the fellowship of his sufferings ".[3] " I have been crucified with Christ."[4] With sympathetic imagination Paul relived the experience of Christ with whom he now felt himself to be united. The utter devotion he had bestowed upon the Law was now redirected towards Christ, but with an added intensity of adoration and gratitude because his inner conflict had been first laid bare, then resolved by the all-controlling love of Christ, which so filled his heart that there was no room left for the wordly passions and motives against which he had striven in vain. Henceforward he was Christ's man with all his ransomed powers.

Once he had abandoned his worldly estimate of Christ, he could not again have a worldly estimate of any man.[5] In the church, which he had despised and persecuted for its repudiation of the standards of legal righteousness, he now came to see " brothers for whom Christ died ".[6] Christ had identified himself with them in their sinfulness in order that they might be identified with him in his righteousness. In all their persecutions he had been persecuted.[7] To be a member of the church was to be " in Christ ". Paul's use of this phrase has been much discussed, and no doubt many elements from his intellectual background combined to produce his full doctrine of Christ and the church. But the religious foundation of it all was laid when he first became aware that whatever he had done to the least of Christ's disciples he had been doing to Christ himself.

Paul's new attitude to himself had two aspects. In the first place, he experienced a great revulsion of feeling. His

[1] II Cor. v. 21; Gal. iii. 13.   [2] Gal. ii. 20.
[3] Phil. iii. 10.   [4] Gal. ii. 20; Rom. vi. 6.
[5] II Cor. v. 16.   [6] I Cor. viii. 11; Rom. xiv. 15.
[7] Acts ix. 4 f.; xxii. 7 f.; xxvi. 14 f.

whole life had been a battle against sin in the cause of righteousness, and now he found that what he had thought to be righteousness had betrayed him into persecuting God's Messiah. His fellow Jews were in no better case, for Christ had been condemned not by the irreligious or the immoral, but by conscientious men who believed that they were defending the honour of God's Law. It was Judaism at its best that had put Jesus on the Cross. But now the Resurrection had brought about a reversal of judgment. The old order which men had built around the Law, trying to establish a righteousness of their own, now stood condemned, nailed to the Cross of Christ. Not only had that order failed to bring men to God; it had hidden God from them, so that they had rejected him in the person of his Son; and in the Cross, in the very instrument of their rejection, God had provided a new way of putting men right with himself which rendered the old way out of date. Christ was " the end of the Law, that all who had faith may be justified ".[1] Whenever Paul mentions the Law, we can feel in the violence of his paradoxes the repercussions of the shock he felt when he first realized where the pursuit of legal righteousness had led him. The Law was holy and just and good; but to be under the Law was to be in the dominion of sin, to be ruled by principalities and powers, to be blinded by the god of this world.[2] The Law still retained its ancient glory, but before the radiance of Christ which had been revealed to Paul that glory had faded into insignificance as stars grow pale at the rising of the sun.[3] Beneath the piercing rays of that splendour Paul felt all his past attainments shrivel into worthlessness : all his gains he now counted as loss, and poured contempt on all his pride.[4]

But Paul did not believe that the work which God was accomplishing in him was a work of demolition only, nor did he ever regard his Christian life simply as the antithesis of the life he had lived under Judaism. The God whose glory he now saw revealed in the face of Jesus Christ was the

[1] Rom. x. 4.
[2] Rom. vii. 7–13; I Cor. xv. 56; Gal. iv. 9; II Cor. iv. 4.
[3] II Cor. iii. 10.   [4] Phil. iii. 7–9; Rom. iii. 27.

same God whom he had tried to serve with his unenlightened zeal. All through his life, unknown to him, God had been leading him to this hour. God had set him apart from before his birth, had called him by his grace, and finally had granted him this vision of Christ.[1] It is of the utmost significance that Paul became aware of his sin against Christ only in the moment of forgiveness. The fact of his sin was as nothing beside the fact that God had accepted him. He had fallen into the hands of the Living God, and the confidence that those hands were to be trusted came to him as a vast liberation. All that Paul ever wrote about freedom is a reflection of the freedom into which he entered at his conversion. He was free now to be what God had always meant him to be, what in his heart of hearts he had always wanted to be. The Creator who had said, " Let there be light ", had sent a flood of illumination into his heart, so that he could now see in Jesus Christ all that God had intended when he made man in his own image,[2] and he had a sense of being caught up into the eternal purposes of God.

Paul emphatically associates both his apostleship and his call to preach to the Gentiles with his conversion.[3] He was an apostle because the risen Christ had appeared to him and had sent him to preach the Gospel.[4] The question of his Gentile mission, however, is complicated by the inconsistencies of the three accounts of Paul's conversion in Acts. According to the first of these accounts the command to go to the Gentiles was given through Ananias, according to the second it came to Paul in a vision during his first visit to Jerusalem, and according to the third it was spoken by Jesus on the Damascus road.[5] The third account agrees more closely than the other two with Paul's own description, and it is best to follow this version and to assume that the Gentile mission was an integral part of Paul's original call to apostleship. For Paul's Gospel of the Cross was a universal Gospel. If the love of Christ could constrain the chief of sinners who had persecuted the church of God, there

[1] Gal. i. 15 f.   [2] II Cor. iv. 4–6.   [3] Ga 1, 16.l. i.
[4] I Cor. xv. 8; ix. 1; i. 17.   [5] Acts ix. 15; xxii. 21; xxvi. 17 f.

could be no limit to its saving power : Christ had died for all.[1] The intensely personal faith with which Paul emerged from his conversion pointed directly toward the vision of a world redeemed. The eclipse of the Law, too, meant the end of Jewish privilege. The barrier which had once stood between Jew and Gentile was a barrier no longer, and all alike must enter the presence of God through the door of faith.[2]

4

To the task of carrying the Gospel to the Gentiles Paul bent all his energies of body and spirit. His was " a life-work that as a mere physical performance challenges our admiration ".[3] The account of his journeys in Asia Minor, Macedonia, and Greece, which Luke has given us in Acts, makes a thrilling adventure, and when we turn to the Epistles we soon discover that Luke has not given us the whole story. There was a ten year period of missionary work in Syria and Cilicia before the " First Missionary Journey ".[4] There were repeated hardships to which Acts can furnish only a handful of parallels.[5] There were troubles in Ephesus at which Luke barely even hints.[6] At some point in his travels Paul visited Illyricum.[7] And all this was endured by a body weakened by chronic illness.[8] If Paul had accomplished nothing else, the expansion of Christianity throughout so large an area under the austere conditions of travel which prevailed in his day and in the face of unremitting opposition would have been a note-worthy achievement. But we cannot rightly appreciate even Paul's geographical contribution to the church of the apostolic age until we have learnt the secret that drove his battered body through long journeys and many afflictions.

Paul's movements were governed by many motives. His preaching in Galatia was the result of illness,[9] he was led to Macedonia by the guidance of the Spirit,[10] he would settle

---

[1] II Cor. v. 14 f.; Rom. xi. 32.
[2] Rom. iii. 30.
[3] A. Deissmann, op. cit., p. 65.
[4] Gal. i. 18–ii. 1.
[5] II Cor. xi. 23–27.
[6] I Cor. xv. 32; II Cor. i. 8.
[7] Rom. xv. 19.
[8] II Cor. xii. 7; Gal. iv. 13.
[9] Gal. iv. 13.
[10] Acts xvi. 6 f.

for a prolonged ministry wherever the door of opportunity opened to him,[1] he avoided going where Christ had been preached, lest he build on another man's foundations.[2] But all this concerns what we may call the tactics of missionary work, and behind the tactics it is possible to discern also a grand strategy.

Paul was a Roman citizen and proud of the imperial franchise which he had inherited from his father. Whenever he referred to districts he had visited, he always used the name of the Roman province rather than the local or ethnic names which Luke frequently employed. His missionary work was conducted almost entirely in the great cities of the Empire, and he seems to have had a preference for the centres of communication and of Roman government. In this connexion his unfulfilled intentions are particularly revealing. When he arrived with Barnabas and Mark at Perga, he had no intention of going up into the highlands of Galatia, nor would he have done so except for the sake of his health. His original purpose must have been either to take the overland route through Laodicea to Ephesus, or to work his way along the coast of Lycia, visiting the towns which were ports of call for Roman merchantmen. In either case his ultimate objective was the province of Asia with its many important cities. This purpose of entering Asia he resumed on his second journey, and when he was compelled by the Holy Spirit to abandon it for the second time, he set out in the direction of the cities of Nicaea and Nicomedia in the province of Bithynia. Finally, although there is no evidence that he actually succeeded in doing so, Paul informed the Roman Christians of his intention to visit Spain. Thus in three instances, quite apart from the actual course of his journeys, Paul seems to have been trying to follow a master plan. Sir William Ramsay has suggested that the master plan was nothing less than the conversion of the Roman Empire, that Paul had learnt to see the world through Roman eyes, that he had come to appreciate the Roman statesman's ideal of a unified world, and that he saw Christianity as the one bond which could give to the Empire

[1] 1 Cor. xvi. 9.   [2] Rom. xv. 20 f.

unity and cohesion.[1] It might be nearer to Paul's own way of thinking to say that he saw the Roman Empire as the divinely ordained means of providing the framework of law and order within which the Gospel could be freely preached to all the world.[2] But Ramsay is surely right in holding that Paul's missionary enterprise was coterminous with the Empire. The field was the world, and the world was Rome. In Romans ix–xi Paul has set forth his philosophy of history. There he declares that God's purpose is that " everyone who calls on the name of the Lord shall be saved ". To this end God has sent out preachers whose task it is to elicit saving faith from those who hear the Gospel. Of these preachers it may be said that " their voice has gone out to all the earth and their words to the end of the world ". This is a citation from Psalm xix, where the words refer to the praise of God by the heavenly bodies, and it can hardly be considered an obvious passage to quote in a description of the Christian mission. The idea of a world-wide mission came not from Scripture but from Paul's own conception of his apostolic calling.[3] The full number of the Gentiles must be brought in before God could complete his purposes by redeeming his rebellious people Israel.[4] God had been in Christ reconciling the world to himself, and it was Paul's vocation to see that the world heard the message of reconciliation.[5]

We may picture Paul, then, enduring the toils and hardships of his many journeys because a great necessity had been laid upon him.[6] He owed to Christ a debt of gratitude, and that debt must be paid in full, not directly to Christ himself but " to Greeks and barbarians, to the wise and to the foolish ".[7] He must be constantly breaking new

---

[1] *Pauline and Other Studies*, pp. 49–100. [2] Rom. xiii. 1–7.

[3] There are passages in the O.T. which envisage the coming of the Gentiles to Jerusalem to learn the ways of God (e.g. Isa. ii. 2–4; xlix. 6; Zech. viii. 23), but no O.T. writer seems to have thought that Israel should go out to bring in the Gentiles. [4] Rom. xi. 25 f.

[5] II Cor. v. 21; Col. i. 23. [6] I Cor. ix. 16; Col. i. 29.

[7] Rom. i. 14; this verse may be taken to mean that Paul regarded his preaching as repayment for the many benefits he had received from Graeco-Roman civilization, but in that case it is hard to see why he should have included the foolish among his benefactors. For this reason the interpretation adopted above is to be preferred.

ground, or he felt cramped and restricted.[1]   The love of God
which was moving in his heart was a love which embraced
all mankind, and all mankind must know of it.

5

Paul's impetuous nature and sterling honesty won for
him both enemies and friends.   He was not a man to whom
you could remain indifferent; you had either to love him
or to hate him.   He has often been described as a " man of
conflict," and it is only too easy to emphasize this aspect of
his character to the exclusion of the other.   For many of
Paul's greatest doctrinal statements were made in the heat
of controversy, and the student of theology tends to concentrate on the controversial chapters of the Epistles and to
pass rapidly over the greetings and personalia which show
us the other side of the picture.   Yet Paul's friendships
carry us nearer to an understanding of his lifework than
many of the severities with which he was accustomed to
silence opposition.

Whatever his detractors might say about his unpre-
possessing appearance,[2] Paul must have been a man of
remarkable charm.   There was that within him which cap-
tivated his fellow men at the first encounter and grappled
them to his soul.   He arrives in Galatia, weakened by a
bout of recurrent illness which had come upon him in the
enervating summer climate of Perga, and the Galatians
received the sick stranger as an angel of God.[3]   During his
brief stay in Philippi he made lifelong friends, to whom he
was later to write the most affectionate of all his letters,
when one of them, Epaphroditus, had risked his life in the
service of the apostle.[4]   Two of his closest friends, Priscilla
and Aquila, also risked their necks for his life.[5]   And the
long list of men and women who find mention in his correspondence is eloquent testimony to his winsome personality.

Men always love and admire those who bring out the best
in them, and this Paul did for all with whom he associated,

---

[1] Rom. xv. 23.   [2] II Cor. x. 10.
[3] Gal. iv. 13–15.   [4] Phil. ii. 20.   [5] Rom. xvi. 3.

because he always expected the best from them. He spared them as little as he spared himself, and they responded to his infectious enthusiasm. He was deeply grieved that Mark " had not gone with them to the work ",[1] and that Demas should feel the call of the world stronger than the call of Christ.[2] But such experiences were too rare to shake his confidence in his friends. He is confident that the Galatians will come round to his point of view.[3] Even when the situation at Corinth is at its blackest, he remains confident of ultimate reconciliation, and his confidence communicates itself to Titus.[4] He sends the runaway slave, Onesimus, his very heart, back to his master, confident that Philemon will do the right thing.[5] He trusts Timothy, Epaphras, Tychicus, Onesimus, and finds them worthy of his trust.[6]

Friendship implies mutual dependence, and Paul needed his friends. For all his independence, he did not thrive on solitude.[7] He was never afraid to rely on the good offices of his friends, and so he left behind him wherever he went a host of people endeared to him because they had been given a chance to be of service to him. There was the mother of Rufus, for example, who had become a mother to Paul also.[8] Paul had the happy gift of making people feel that they were as important to him as he was to them. Thus he writes to the Romans of his coming visit which is to be a mutual benefit, " that we may be mutually encouraged by each other's faith, both yours and mine . . . that by God's will I may come to you to our mutual refreshment ".[9] T. R. Glover has pointed out the significance of Paul's syn-compounds in this connexion. Fourteen fellow workers are mentioned by name in his letters, four fellow prisoners, two fellow soldiers, two fellow slaves, one yokefellow.[10]

---

[1] Acts xv. 38.   [2] II Tim. iv. 10.   [3] Gal. v. 10.
[4] II Cor. ii. 3; vii. 16; viii. 22.   [5] Phn. 21.
[6] II Cor. iv. 17; Col. i. 7; iv. 7, 9.
[7] I Thess. iii. 1.   [8] Rom. xvi. 13.   [9] Rom. i. 12; xv. 32.
[10] Fellow worker : Priscilla, Aquila, Urbanus, Timothy, Titus, Epaphroditus, Clement, Aristarchus, Mark, Jesus Justus, Philemon, Epaphras, Demas, and Luke; fellow prisoner : Andronicus, Junias, Aristarchus, Epaphras; fellow soldier : Epaphroditus, Archippus; fellow slave : Epaphras, Tychicus; and an anonymous yokefellow. Glover identified Epaphras with Epaphroditus and credits him with four syn-compounds.

The Philippians have shared in his work as partners, and are invited to share in his imitation of Christ; [1] and some women among them have shared his " athletic struggle ".[2] " The dearest of all ties for Paul is to find men sharing things with him. The work, the ' athletic life ', the yoke, the slavery, the imitation—these are all expressions of his relation with Jesus Christ, the very essence of life; how much more it is to him when he finds his friends standing with him in that great loyalty!" [3] And what must it have meant to his friends to share a prison cell with him, to fight the good fight of faith shoulder to shoulder with him, to bow the knee at his side as slaves of the one Lord ! One example of Paul's gracious treatment of others is to be found in the salutations of his Epistles, where he always places beside his own name that of any friend known to the church who happens to be with him at the time of writing. In all his vast labours Paul never had any assistants or underlings—only partners and colleagues.

But the strongest bond which united Paul to his friends was the sympathy which enabled him to put himself in their place and live through their experiences with them. This was a burden of care which he carried daily upon his heart. " Who is weak, and I am not weak ? Who is made to fall, and I am not indignant ? " [4] His converts are his children whom he had begotten in Christ through the Gospel,[5] and he feels a father's responsibility for their spiritual growth and well-being. If they go astray, he is in travail again until Christ be formed in them.[6] When he is separated from them, he longs for the intimacies of personal contact, in which so much may be conveyed by the changing tones of the voice.[7] If they suffer, he suffers with them : and twice we are allowed to see him in a ferment of unrest— once over the church in Thessalonica and once over the church in Corinth. At Thessalonica, encouraged by the warmth of his reception, he had shared his own self with his converts, and they had become very dear to him. But

---

[1] Phil. i. 7; iv. 14; iii. 17.   [2] Phil. iv. 3.
[3] T. R. Glover, *Paul of Tarsus*, p. 180.
[4] II Cor. xi. 29.   [5] I Cor. iv. 14f .; cf. Phn. 10.
[6] Gal. iv. 19.   [7] Gal. iv. 20.

I

he had been compelled to leave them to face unknown hazards with only a very inadequate preparation. At Athens he cannot get them out of his mind, and at the thought of what they may be undergoing he agonizes with them. Again and again he plans to visit them, but Satan prevents him, perhaps by an attack of the illness that he calls " Satan's messenger ". At length he can bear the suspense no longer, and sends his one companion, Timothy, to find out how they are faring. " I live if you stand fast in the Lord." [1] At Corinth the trouble came from within the church, but the effect on Paul was the same. After a " painful visit " which accomplished nothing, he wrote a letter " out of much affliction and anguish of heart and with many tears ". No sooner had Titus been despatched with the letter than Paul regretted writing it. Perhaps he had been too severe, perhaps he should have gone in person. In a frenzy of anxiety he went to Troas, hoping to meet the returning Titus. The door of opportunity opened wide to him there, but he was too restless to settle down to steady work. He moved on to Macedonia, and still Titus did not come with the news, and still Paul's restlessness persisted. Then at last Titus reported that all was well, and Paul wrote back to Corinth out of a full heart : " You are so much in my heart that I share with you in death and in life ". [2] In a quieter mood he showed his profound appreciation of other people's feelings by sending Epaphroditus home to Philippi. Epaphroditus had come to minister to Paul in prison, and Paul would dearly have loved to have his " fellow soldier " beside him for the ordeal which he expected shortly to face. But the Philippians were worried because they had heard that Epaphroditus was ill, and Epaphroditus was upset because he had heard that they were worried, and Paul shared in the anxiety of both. [3]

In all this Paul was making good his claim that " it is no longer I who live, but Christ who lives in me." [4] He saw his brethren with the eyes of the Master's love, and this more than anything else stamped his ministry with the seal

[1] I Thess. ii. 7–iii. 8.   [2] II Cor. ii. 1–4; vii. 2–9.
[3] Phil. ii. 25–30.   [4] Gal. ii. 20.

of Christ. In particular, his sufferings were transfigured by
the pastoral care which he lavished on his churches. It was
the lot of all Christians that they must suffer with Christ,
because the life which he communicated to his church was
his own life with all its superabundance of suffering.[1] But
Paul believed that his own sufferings had a peculiar significance. As a persecutor he had contributed to the
burden of suffering which the church had been called to bear
in the name of Christ, and as a Christian he believed that he
was given the opportunity of making amends by drawing off
upon himself some of the suffering which would otherwise
have fallen upon the churches under his care. "I rejoice
in my sufferings for your sake, and in my flesh I fill up for
my part that which is lacking of the afflictions of Christ on
behalf of his body, which is the church." [2] All that happened to him was on their account; and so it came about
that when others could see in him only a man crushed
beneath an insupportable load of affliction, Paul felt himself
to be labouring under an incomparable load of glory.[3]

6

Paul has sometimes been called the champion of Gentile
liberty; and although this is a true description, it is apt for
several reasons to be a most misleading one. Paul certainly
insisted that Gentile converts should not be made to accept
circumcision and with it the whole bondage of the Mosaic
Law. But there had been a Gentile mission at Antioch
before Paul, and no attempt had been made to force circumcision on the Gentiles. Barnabas, the official representative from Jerusalem, had given his approval to this
policy, and at no subsequent date did the Jerusalem
leaders ever go back on this decision. James and Peter were
in agreement with Paul that obedience to the Law was not
to be required as a condition of church membership. The
opposition to Paul came from unauthorized and unorganized
groups of Jewish Christians, and it is important to notice

[1] Rom. viii. 17; II Cor. i. 5–7.
[2] Col. i. 24.   [3] II Cor. iv. 7–18.

that, where such groups existed, theirs was not the only opposition that Paul had to face. From the Epistle to the Galatians, for example, it is clear that Paul was fighting a battle on two fronts : there were those who claimed that the full blessings of the Gospel were only for those who, by birth or adoption, were sons of Abraham, living by the Law which God had given to Abraham's seed; [1] but there were others who were only too ready to be emancipated from the Law, ritual and moral alike.[2] There was a double danger that, while the one side was demanding a narrow adherence to the Law, the other side would throw off its allegiance to the Old Testament altogether. It was Paul's great triumph that he dealt faithfully with both parties without siding with either, and without allowing either party to split the church.

In so far as Paul was the apostle of liberty, it was a liberty in which Jew and Gentile alike could share. Both had been baptized with the same Spirit, and " where the Spirit of the Lord is, there is liberty ".[3] Both had left behind the old life and had put on the new : " for neither is circumcision anything nor uncircumcision, but a new creation ".[4] It is more accurate, therefore, to describe Paul as the champion of church unity. He had had a vision of the one church, in which the Gentiles were fellow heirs with the Jews, inheriting with them the Old Testament promises, now fulfilled in Jesus Christ; and all his life he remained true to that vision. When his enthusiastic supporters claimed him as the leader of their party, he sent them a stern rebuke; and when he heard that others were proclaiming Christ in such a way as to cause him personal distress, he could rejoice that one way or another Christ was being proclaimed.[5]

For Paul there could be only one church because there was only one Christ. " For as many of you as were baptized into Christ have put on Christ. There is neither Jew nor Greek, there is neither slave nor free, there is neither male

[1] Gal. iii. 3, 7, 9, 14. [2] Gal. v. 13–21.
[3] II Cor. iii. 17. [4] Gal. vi. 15.
[5] I Cor. i. 12–17; Phil. i. 16–18.

nor female; for you are all one in Christ Jesus." [1] Within
this one church divisions were unthinkable—" Is Christ
divided ? " [2] The symbol of unity was the Lord's Supper :
" We who are many are one loaf, one body; for we all
partake of the one loaf ".[1] From this context Paul adopted
one of his favourite pictures of the church's unity : " As
the body is one . . . so also is Christ." [4] Those who
participated in the sacrament without regard for the one
fellowship which it both symbolized and sustained were
eating and drinking to their own condemnation, not discern-
ing the Lord's body.[5] A man might be severed from Christ
if he relied on his own obedience to the Law and not on
Christ's saving grace for his redemption.[6] A man might
be handed over to Satan if he persisted in a sin which un-
fitted him for the Kingdom of God.[7] But those who lived
by the Gospel belonged to an indissoluble fellowship.

There could be only one church because there was only
one Israel. The Jewish nation had forfeited this title,
which had now passed to Christ and through him to the
church.[8] All the promises of the Old Testament now
devolved upon those who were Abraham's sons, not by
physical descent but by sharing Abraham's faith.[9] This
concept of the church not only gave to the Gentiles equality
with the Jews in God's new people, but it made them heirs
to the Old Testament, interpreted not as a system of Law
but as the story of God's gracious dealing with the men to
whom in the fulness of time Christ was to come; and it thus
ensured that Gentile Christianity should be firmly rooted
in the soil of the Scriptures.

These two expositions of the church's unity are magnificently combined in Ephesians, which, if it is not by Paul,
is a masterly summary of Paul's theology by a disciple who
was capable of thinking Paul's thoughts after him. " You
were at that time far from Christ, alienated from the commonwealth of Israel and strangers to the covenants of

[1] Gal. iii. 27 f ; cf. Col. iii. 10 f.
[2] I Cor. i. 13.   [3] I Cor. x. 17.
[4] I Cor. xii. 12; cf. Rom. xii. 5; Col. i. 18; Eph. ii. 16; iv. 12–16.
[5] I Cor. xi. 29.   [6] Gal. v. 4.   [7] I Cor. v. 5.
[8] Gal. vi. 16.   [9] Gal. iii. 6–14; Rom. iv. 16.

promise, having no hope and without God in the world. But now in Christ Jesus you who were once far off have been brought near by the blood of Christ. For he is our peace, who has made us both one and has broken down the dividing wall of hatred. He has abolished in his flesh the Law with its rules and regulations, so that he might make peace by creating in himself one new man in place of the two, and might reconcile us both in one body to God through the Cross, having slain the hatred thereby. He came and preached peace to you who were far off and peace to those who were near; for through him we both have access in one Spirit to the Father. Now therefore you are no longer foreigners and strangers, but fellow citizens with the saints and members of the household of God . . . the Gentiles are fellow heirs, belonging to the same body and sharing the same promise in Christ Jesus through the Gospel. '' [1]

This doctrine of the church was implicit both in the traditions of the primitive church and in Paul's own conversion experience. But to Paul belongs the credit that he was the first to expound this unity openly, to think through the practical consequences of the church's nature, and to demand that nothing in the communal life of the church should be allowed to obscure the essential unity of all Christians in Christ. It was on this ground that he took his stand in the dispute at Antioch which he records in Galatians ii. 11 ff. The church there included both Jewish and Gentile Christians, and they had been accustomed to meet together for the common meal of which the Lord's Supper formed the climax. Barnabas and Peter saw nothing wrong in joining in this meal, until some men from James arrived, who pointed out that the Jewish Christians were breaking their national food laws by eating with the Gentiles. At their suggestion the Jewish Christians, Peter

---

[1] Eph. ii. 12–19; iii. 6. One of the differences supposed to exist between the Epistle and Colossians concerns the use of the word mystery—the eternal secret of God which is a secret no longer. But the difference is only a matter of emphasis. In Colossians God's secret purpose is said to be that the indwelling Christ should be, for Gentiles as well as Jews, the hope of glory. In Ephesians the secret is that in Christ the Gentiles are fellow heirs with the Jews. Both Epistles look beyond the human fellowship to the reconciliation of the heavenly powers.

and Barnabas among them, withdrew from the common act
of fellowship, presumably intending to hold a separate celebration of their own. At this point Paul appeared on the
scene, accusing Peter of compelling the Gentiles to adopt
Jewish customs. The form of Paul's attack is significant,
because it shows that he refused even to contemplate the
possibility that there should be two separate communions
within the one church. Those who belong to the one body
must be able to partake of the one loaf. Christ could not be
divided. If, then, the Jewish Christians felt bound by the
levitical food laws not to eat under conditions of ritual
impurity, that was tantamount to imposing their food laws
on their Gentile brethren. Paul's own solution was not that
the Gentiles should live like Jews, nor that the Jews should
live like Gentiles, but that both ways of life should be transcended in the greater unity of Christ.[1]

The same principle governed Paul's relations with the
church of Jerusalem. Although he asserted that his Gospel
and his apostolic authority had come to him independently
of the other apostles, it never occurred to him that either he
or his converts should live independently of those who were
in Christ before them. It would no doubt have been much
easier for him to forget about Jerusalem and to concentrate
on the building up of his own congregations. But interde-
pendence, not independence, was the keynote of life in the
church. "We who are many are one body in Christ and
individually members of one another." [2] The collection
for the needy Christians of Jerusalem which Paul organized
throughout the churches he had founded was undertaken
in the hope that it would make both givers and receivers
aware of their common membership in Christ. For the
Gentiles it was to be the acknowledgment of a debt of gratitude,[3] the acceptance of responsibility for the wider brotherhood to which they belonged, the realization of their equal
status in the commonwealth of Israel; to the Jerusalem
church it was to be a proof that the Pauline churches had
really been brought into subjection to the Gospel of Christ,[4]

---

[1] Gal. iii. 28; vi. 15. [2] Rom. xii. 5.
[3] Rom. xv. 27. [4] II Cor. ix. 13.

and for both it was to be a token of unity. How much store Paul set by this gesture we may judge from what he wrote on the eve of his departure from Corinth and from Luke's description of his journey to Jerusalem. He was apprehensive of danger from the Jews and of a cool reception from the Christians, but he set his face steadfastly to go to Jerusalem.[1] As his journey progressed he received repeated warnings that bonds and afflictions awaited him, but he was not deterred from his purpose.[2] His journey cost him his liberty, and ultimately his life. " It is no exaggeration to say that Paul died a martyr to the cause of Christian reunion." [3]

7

Paul was a great thinker, but he was not a systematic theologian, and his Epistles defy all who would make a system out of them. This is due in part to inconsistencies in his thinking, but partly also to the rugged vigour of his mind, and it is as well to be aware of his limitations so that we may the better appreciate his true greatness.

Many of Paul's ideas were hammered out in the heat of controversy, and it is useless to expect from the debater the consistency of the detached philosopher. Even parts of his fullest theological treatise, the Epistle to the Romans, are couched in the form of an argument with imaginary opponents. His letters are written to deal with specific situations, without any notion that generations yet unborn would weigh his every word, and it is hardly surprising if some of his arguments do not bear an academic scrutiny. He could press his points in a thoroughly one-sided manner, and twice at least he laid himself open to a misunderstanding which had to be corrected in a subsequent letter. It is possible, too, that some of his most characteristic terms— e.g. justification and *pleroma* [4]—were not of his own choosing, but were wrested by him from the vocabulary of his adversaries and turned to good account.

---

[1] Rom. xv. 31.   [2] Acts xx. 22 f.; xxi. 10 ff.
[3] J. A. Findlay, *The Acts of the Apostles*, p. 32.   [4] Col. i. 19; ii. 9.

We have already seen that Paul was never able to be thoroughly consistent in his attitude to the Torah. Nor did he ever reach a consistent belief about the future destiny either of the individual or of the world; or perhaps it would be more accurate to say that he started with the traditional belief and outgrew it. Like all other Christians of his day he expected an imminent return of the Lord, and thought of those who died in the interval as sleeping until the day arrived.[1] He still retained this belief when he wrote to the Philippians; yet his experience of communion with Christ and his confidence that his true life was hidden with Christ in God gave rise to a hope which could not be expressed in traditional terms, and in the same epistle he can speak of being ready " to depart and be with Christ ".[2]

In practical matters Paul could be just as inconsistent. In theory he was the great champion of equality between the sexes, since in Christ all disparity between Jew and Gentile, freeman and slave, man and woman, had been done away.[3] But in practice he required that women should wear on their heads a sign of their subjection and should keep silence in church.[4] If he had been content to put forward this teaching as a counsel of expediency, on the grounds that the Christian emancipation of women was liable to be misconstrued in pagan society and to bring the church into disrepute, he would not have contradicted his own principles; but in fact he could not forbear to back his injunctions with arguments designed to give them universal validity. Similarly, he could not bring himself to accept the logic of his own proof that Jew and Gentile meet in Christ on equal terms, and tried to find some way of retaining advantage for the Jew.[5]

Some of the difficulties of Paul's thought are paradoxes of the sort that delighted the Semitic mind. Like a true Hebrew Paul was never afraid to hold in tension two ideas which he made no attempt to reconcile. He could declare God's sovereign, unconditioned choice—" he has mercy on

[1] I Thess. iv. 15; I Cor. xv. 51.
[2] Phil. ii. 23; cf. iii. 20 f.; iv. 5.
[4] I Cor. xi. 2–16; xiv. 33–36.
[3] Gal. iii. 28; Col. iii. 11.
[5] Rom. iii. 1 ff.

whom he will, and whom he will he hardens "—and at the same time hold Israel responsible for her repudiation of God's word of grace.[1] He could think of history as the working out of God's unalterable purpose of love, and also as man's repeated frustration of that purpose through disobedience. He could proclaim the " larger hope ", that the fulness of the Gentiles and all Israel would be brought into the church, without sacrificing anything of the urgency which comes from believing that " the night is far spent, the day is at hand." [2]

Paul wrote in the language of religious experience, which avoids precise definition. It is notoriously difficult to distinguish in his theology the part played by the indwelling Christ from the part played by the Holy Spirit. In some passages Christ and the Spirit are clearly differentiated;[3] in others the distinction is almost obliterated : " You are not in the flesh, but in the Spirit, if the Spirit of God dwells in you. Anyone who does not have the Spirit of Christ does not belong to him. But if Christ is in you . . ." [4] The reason is that Paul had come to know Christ as a life-giving Spirit,[5] and he could never dissociate the experience of the Spirit from his experience of Christ. This is confusing for those who go to the New Testament to find the origins of a doctrine of the Trinity, yet it is here that we find one of the main sources of the influence that Paul's letters have always exercised over the lives of those who have read them. Paul constantly referred to the apostolic tradition as the standard by which his own experience must be tested, " lest by any chance I should be running or had run in vain ",[6] but he preached and wrote that which he knew. His readers have always found in his letters " some things hard to understand," [7] but they have also found something that spoke directly to their hearts and consciences.

One of Paul's greatest assets was his ability to rise from the particular to the general, to see the eternal principles involved in the various practical problems with which he

[1] Rom. ix. 18; x. 21. [2] Rom. xi. 25 f.; xiii. 12.
[3] I Cor. xii. 4–6; II Cor. xiii. 14.
[4] Rom. viii. 9 f.; cf. II Cor. iii. 17. [5] I Cor. xv. 45.
[6] Gal. ii. 2. [7] II Pet. iii. 16.

was constantly being confronted. At Thessalonica there was trouble over the Parousia, some Christians being worried about the fate of those who had died without seeing the great day, others giving way to a nervous excitement which made them neglect their daily duties. Paul dealt with these difficulties by providing an answer out of the traditional eschatology, but before the discussion is closed he has lifted his readers to a new plane by bidding them to see their whole life, here and hereafter, in the light of their fellowship with " our Lord Jesus Christ, who died for us so that whether we wake or sleep we might live with him ".[1] At Corinth the question was posed whether Christians ought to attend pagan banquets or eat meat which was offered for sale in the open market after being slaughtered at a pagan sacrifice. In his reply Paul went beyond the immediate subject under discussion to lay down a general rule for Christian conduct that the strong ought to help the weak and consider the effect which their behaviour was likely to have on the brother for whom Christ died. At Corinth, too, there were disorders in public worship, because some members had an exalted view of the importance of their own ability to speak with tongues. Again Paul has his practical instructions to give, but not before he has shown that ecstatic speech is only one of the minor gifts of the Spirit, who within the organic unity of the church provides not only for all the activities which build up the corporate life of the community, but also for those graces of character which give that life a permanent meaning.

This last passage exemplifies yet another quality of Paul's mind ; for in the course of his treatment of the Spirit-filled community he breaks out into his great hymn on love. Argument and disputation sink into nothingness as the theologian gives place to the poet. We can see the same thing happening repeatedly in other parts of Paul's correspondence. In I Corinthians xv the careful argument concerning the resurrection body works up to a song of triumph over vanquished sin and death. In Philippians an appeal for unity among church members leads on to a

---

[1] I Thess. v. 9 f.

hymn on the Incarnation.[1]   In Romans Paul expounds the nature of salvation as a past fact, a present experience, and a future hope; and then on the wings of faith he ascends to his majestic vision of a world delivered from the bondage of decay through the unconquerable might of the ever-present Lord.   Three chapters later, when he has wrestled with the problems of predestination and free-will, and won his way through to a confidence in universal salvation, his spirit soars for a second time : " O the depth of the riches both of the wisdom and of the knowledge of God ! how unsearchable are his judgments and his ways past finding out ! "[2]   For all his clarity of thought, Paul was content that knowledge should disappear into ultimate mystery before which he must bow in wonder, love, and praise.

It is tempting to leave Paul on the mountain-tops, but his own Epistles persistently bring us back to the plain. One of Paul's most remarkable gifts was his ability to return to earth from the heights without any sense of incongruity. " Thanks be to God who gives us the victory through our Lord Jesus Christ . . . Now concerning the collection . . ."[3] There spoke a man upon whom the light of the Gospel had so shone, that even mundane things had been touched for him with the glory of a new creation.

---

[1] Phil. ii. 5–11.   [2] Rom. xi. 33 ff.   [3] I Cor. xv. 57—xvi. 1.

CHAPTER X

THE PERIOD OF CONSOLIDATION

1

IN the sixties of the first century three events occurred
which were to change profoundly the character of the
apostolic church : the final break between Christianity
and Judaism, the beginning of persecution by Rome, and
the death of many of those who had been pillars of the early
church.

During the interregnum between the death of Festus and
the arrival of Albinus, James the Lord's brother was killed
in an outbreak of mob violence.[1] Soon afterwards the
Christian community of which James had been the leader
withdrew from Jerusalem across Jordan to the Gentile city
of Pella, and the last link between church and synagogue
was destroyed.[2] Throughout the Empire Jewish feeling
against the Christians was hardening into implacable
opposition, and the Pharisaic school which was established
at Jamnia after the fall of Jerusalem was strongly anti-
Christian. It was this school which was responsible for
adding the curse against apostates (*birkath hamminim*) to
the Eighteen Benedictions, and there is general agreement
that this " blessing " was directed mainly against the
Christians.[3] The Epistle of James is often cited as evidence
for the existence of at least one community where Christians
continued to attend the synagogue, in spite of harsh treatment from wealthy, unconverted Jews ; [4] but the date and
provenance of this epistle and the interpretation of the
passage in question are all open to dispute, and if there ever
was such a community after A.D. 70 it must have been quite
exceptional. On the Christian side feeling ran equally high,

---

[1] Jos., *Ant.* xx. 9. 1; Eus., *H.E.* ii. 23.
[2] Eus., *H.E.* iii. 5. It is commonly assumed that Judaistic Christianity
reappeared in the sects of the Ebionites, Nazarenes, and Elkesaites, but
this development belongs to the second century and lies outside our period.
[3] E. Schürer, op. cit. II. ii. pp. 85 ff.   [4] Jas. ii. 2.

as may be seen from the anti-Pharisaic tone of Matthew's Gospel, the frequent references to " the Jews " in the Fourth Gospel, and the attacks in Revelation on " those who say that they are Jews, and are not, but are a synagogue of Satan ".[1]

We shall see in the next chapter that the first official persecution of the Christians in A.D. 64 changed their legal status, so that from that time they were compelled to live in permanent insecurity, depending for their lives on the continuing good will of their pagan neighbours. After Nero's orgy of slaughter actual martyrdom was rare and was met with a steadfast courage.[2] But the precarious nature of the Christian calling was bound to have an unnerving effect on some of those who followed it. All the Synoptic Gospels contain warnings against treachery within the ranks of the church, and Tacitus' account of the Neronic persecution shows that these warnings were not out of place.[3] On those who remained faithful persecution had a more subtle effect. The Epistle to the Hebrews, whatever its date and destination may have been, illustrates the threat to the spiritual life of a church which could arise during a temporary relaxation of persecution. The letter was addressed to Christians who had previously been subjected to violence and legal action and had borne their hardships with fortitude. When the crisis passed, they had suffered a reaction, a slackening of the moral fibres, and were now exposed to the more insidious danger of drift.[4] A similar lowering of morale is described in three of John's letters to the seven churches of Asia : Ephesus had forsaken her first love, Sardis had the mere name of life, Laodicea was neither hot nor cold.[5]

The enmity of Jew and Roman, however, did not produce such far-reaching effects on early Christianity as did the disappearance of that generation which had seen and heard Jesus. The church to which the Epistle to the Hebrews was addressed had been evangelized by eye-witnesses of

---

[1] Rev. ii. 9; iii. 9.   [2] Rev. ii. 13.
[3] Mk. xiii. 12; Mt. x. 21; xxiv. 10; Lk. xxi. 16; for Tacitus see Appendix B.
[4] Heb. ii. 1.   [5] Rev. ii. 4; iii. 1, 15.

Jesus' ministry, but they had died, and with them the church had lost its direct link with the historic foundations of its faith.[1] There must have been many churches in this position during the later apostolic age. According to Clement of Alexandria the ministry of the apostles came to a close during the reign of Nero.[2] In particular we know of the deaths of James the Lord's brother in Jerusalem and of Peter and Paul in Rome. The Gospel and First Epistle of John claim to record the testimony of an original disciple who survived at Ephesus until the closing years of the first century,[3] but this is an exceptional case, and the author is deeply sensitive to the needs of second-generation Christianity.[4]

2

The most obvious result of these changes was the growth of heresy. As long as the church was led by men who had known Jesus, and had as its nucleus a substantial number of Jewish Christians, educated in the strongly ethical religion of the Old Testament, the apostolic tradition was relatively safe from distortion. But henceforward the church was to be a predominantly Gentile institution, and there was an increasing danger that the originally Semitic Gospel should be diluted by an admixture of ideas drawn from the syn-cretistic religions of the Graeco-Roman world. Pliny's letter to Trajan indicates that Gentile converts had been received into the church in very large numbers, and that many of them had too slight a grasp of their new faith to withstand the pressure of persecution.[5] From scattered references in Christian literature we can identify some of the pagan prejudices which kept these converts from a fuller appreciation of Christianity.

Among the Greeks ethics and religion had long been separated from one another, and the Hellenistic world knew little of the Jewish and Christian union between faith and conduct. To some of the converts the Gospel presented

---

[1] Heb. ii. 3; xiii. 7.   [2] Strom. vii. 17.
[3] Jn. xix. 35; xxi. 24; I Jn. i. 1.
[4] Jn. xvii. 20; xx. 29.   [5] See Appendix B.

itself as a new mystery religion which delivered them from
the demands of morality. This antinomianism is attacked
by Jude and by the author of II Peter, who makes it clear
that this heresy involved a misunderstanding of Paul's
teaching about the primacy of faith.[1] If the Epistle of
James belongs to the latter part of the first century, it too
must be taken as a protest against a corrupt Paulinism.[2]
But the Greek dichotomy between faith and morals affected
others besides the antinomians. The author of the Pastoral
Epistles, who wrote to provide an antidote to heresy, was
himself deeply influenced by the Greek point of view. To
him Christianity is " godliness "—a juxtaposition of sound
doctrine and sound morals; but his moralistic teaching is
in no way derived from his doctrine, and, though he is an
enthusiastic disciple of Paul, he shows no appreciation of
Paul's ethical principles that faith works itself out through
love and that the Christian virtues are the fruit of the Spirit.
But it may be that he owed his popularity and influence to
this very deficiency. For, being himself one of the epigoni,
he was able to appreciate and provide for the needs of his
day. As a transformer reduces electric current to a voltage
suitable for household use, so through this writer the power
of apostolic Christianity came to a later generation in a form
adapted to the household virtues which were most urgently
needed for the ongoing life of the church.

The Greek belief in the impassibility of God and the
corresponding depreciation of the world of matter led other
Christians to repudiate the Incarnation. Christ was divine :
but God could not really have been manifest in the flesh, nor
could he really have suffered on the Cross. Docetism of this
kind was rife in Asia Minor in the closing years of the first
century, for it is explicitly denounced in I John as " the
spirit of Antichrist ",[3] and the emphasis on " the flesh "
in the Fourth Gospel is probably due to the same cause.
Along with Docetism went Gnosticism, which had already
made a preliminary appearance in Paul's time at Colossae.
According to Polycarp, John once fled from the baths at

[1] II Pet. iii. 16.   [2] Jas. ii. 1–18; cf. Rev. ii. 14, 20.
[3] I Jn. ii. 18; iv. 1–3.

Ephesus when he saw the heretic Cerinthus there, for fear that the baths would fall to crush the enemy of truth.[1]

The widespread practice of magic also had its effect on Christianity, and particularly on the interpretation of the sacraments. Already Paul had had to warn the Corinthian church that they must not count on the efficacy of formula and ritual act, since sacraments without obedience had failed to save the Israelites in the wilderness.[2] But his protest was not enough to protect Christian sacramental teaching from further corruption. In the early second century we find Ignatius describing the Eucharist as " an antidote to death ".[3] Similar tendencies must have been well established at the end of the first century, and this supposition helps to explain the cautious treatment of the sacraments in the Fourth Gospel. Against the Docetists John asserts that flesh can be the vehicle of spirit, but against the magicians he declares that the flesh profits nothing, that it is the Spirit that gives life, and that the Spirit is not controlled by human word or act.[4]

Heretical teachings commonly derived their authority from prophetic inspiration, and in later New Testament writings we find frequent warnings against false prophecy. Matthew adapted for this purpose a Q saying about the tree and its fruit, which appears in Luke as a general test of Christian discipleship, and it is probable that his " wolves in sheep's clothing " were antinomians.[5] The woman Jezebel at Thyatira called herself a prophetess.[6] The Docetists of Asia Minor claimed inspiration, which John attributed to the spirit of Antichrist.[7] There had, of course, been false prophets in ancient Israel, but they derived much of their influence from the popular belief that ecstasy and trance were infallible signs of inspiration. It may be, therefore, that false prophecy in the Christian church owed something to the Hellenistic conception of inspiration as divine possession.

---

[1] Iren., *Adv. Haer.* III 3. 4.   [2] I Cor. x. 1–16.
[3] Eph. xx.   [4] Jn. iii. 3–8; vi. 51–63.
[5] Mt. vii. 15–20; Lk. vi. 43–45; Did. xi. 1 ff.
[6] Rev. ii. 20.   [7] I Jn. iv. 1–3.

K

3

Because of all these changes it was inevitable that the second generation of Christian history should be different from the first. The first generation had been a period of creative enthusiasm, when the tides of the spirit were running strongly and obstacles served only to promote the furtherance of the Gospel, an age of " power and the Holy Spirit and full conviction ".[1] The second generation, though not without its creative minds, was on the whole an age of stocktaking. The initial impulse of the Christian movement slackened, and the church, deprived of apostolic leadership and endangered by persecution without and heresy within, turned to the less romantic but necessary tasks of consolidating the gains of the past and adjusting to new conditions. The dominant note of the period is a concern for " the faith once for all delivered to the saints ",[2] a zealous guarding of " the noble heritage ".[3]

By far the most important manifestation of this concern was the writing of the Synoptic Gospels. Doubtless the three evangelists had other subsidiary motives, but Luke declares that he himself and other Gospel-makers before him were prompted by a desire to put on record what had been handed down to them by those " who from the beginning were eye-witnesses and ministers of the word ".[4] In Matthew's Gospel we can see the same motive controlling the life of a church. For it is generally agreed that Matthew is a revised edition of Mark, produced to meet the need for authoritative teaching, and this implies that the church for which it was written was determined to put itself under the authority of the apostolic witness.

This literary activity was, in fact, the church's response to the loss of the eye-witnesses. An eye-witness is clearly irreplaceable, and among the eye-witnesses there were some who had occupied positions in the life of the church to which no successors could be appointed. Jesus had chosen twelve men " that they might be with him, and that he might send them out to preach, and to have authority to heal sicknesses

<hr>

[1] I Thess. i. 5.   [2] Jud. 3.   [3] II Tim. i. 4 ; I Tim. vi. 20.   [4] Lk. i. 1–4.

and to cast out devils ".[1] These men had two distinct parts to play—as members of the college of Twelve and as apostles. As the Twelve they were the symbolic nucleus of the new Israel. Hort was undoubtedly right when he said of the Last Supper that " the Twelve sat that evening as representatives of the Ecclesia at large ",[2] but there is no reason why we should limit their representative character to that one occasion. Most of the sayings which Jesus spoke to them were addressed through them to the whole church. The apostasy of Judas caused a vacancy in the Twelve which was filled by the election of Matthias, but death caused no vacancy. There is not the slightest justification for the common assumption that the place of James the son of Zebedee was taken by James the Lord's brother. For the Twelve were destined to occupy their unique position not only in this world but in the world to come.[3]

The Twelve were also apostles, but this was a designation they shared with others, including Paul, Barnabas, James, Andronicus, and Junias.[4] The apostles were men directly commissioned by the risen Jesus to be witnesses to that which they had seen and heard, and especially to the Resurrection.[5] They carried a double authority—the natural authority of those who speak out of their own experience and the delegated authority of Christ. The New Testament, however, has very little to say about apostolic authority. Christ had warned his disciples against setting up distinctions of rank within the church, and had made it plain to the Twelve that he was bequeathing to them not rights and dignities but humility and service.[6] Paul, it is true, has frequently to defend his apostleship, and he does so with vigour, but only because he recognizes that the real object of attack is not himself but his Gospel. As an apostle it was his duty to call men to obey not himself but

---

[1] Mk. iii. 14 f. [2] *The Christian Ecclesia*, p. 30.
[3] Mt. xix. 28; Lk. xxii. 30; Rev. xxi. 14.
[4] Acts xiv. 14; Gal. i. 19; Rom. xvi. 7.
[5] Acts i. 8, 22; xxii. 15; xxvi. 16; I Cor. ix. 1; xv. 7 f.; see K. H. Rengstorf, *Apostleship* (tr. J. R. Coates), p. 43.
[6] Mt. xxiii. 8–12; Mk. x. 42–45; Lk. xxii. 26–27; cf. Rengstorf, op. cit. pp. 35 f.

his Gospel.[1] Wherever apostleship is mentioned in the New Testament the emphasis is never on the person or the office, but always on the task to be performed. Peter has an apostolic mission to the circumcision.[2] Paul has an apostolic mission " to bring about obedience of faith among the Gentiles ".[3] Nor was it considered fitting that the apostles should become involved in church administration to the neglect of their proper function, the ministry of the word.[4]

With the passing of the first generation the ministry of the word had to be handed on to others, but the apostolate, resting as it did on eye-witness and personal commission, was incommunicable.[5] The one thing that could and must be preserved was the apostolic testimony, and the Gospels are an abiding memorial to the zeal with which the church undertook this task.

Second only in importance to the Gospel tradition were the apostolic writings. E. J. Goodspeed has conjectured that by about A.D. 90 some member of the church of Colossae, perhaps Onesimus, prompted by the publication of the Acts of the Apostles, had collected the letters of Paul and published them with an introductory essay on Pauline theology, which is now known as the Epistle to the Ephesians.[6] Few scholars are prepared to accept the whole of Goodspeed's theory, though some such hypothesis is necessary if we reject the Pauline authorship of Ephesians.[7] But this much is beyond dispute, that the author of the Pastoral Epistles knew and imitated the genuine letters of Paul; and when II Peter was written (c. A.D. 120), there was in existence a corpus of Pauline Epistles which had by general consent been granted the status of Scripture.[8]

---

[1] Rom. vi. 17; x. 16; I Thess. i. 8; cf. Acts vi. 7.
[2] Gal. ii. 8.   [3] Rom. i. 5.   [4] Acts vi. 2–4.
[5] " The episcopate was formed not out of the apostolic order by localization but out of the presbyteral by elevation." J. B. Lightfoot, *Philippians*, p. 194; cf. F. J. A. Hort, op. cit. p. 35; K. H. Rengstorf, op. cit. p. 45. An attempt has been made in *The Apostolic Ministry* (ed. K. E. Kirk) to reopen the question of apostolic succession in the N.T., to which a complete answer has been provided by T. W. Manson in *The Church's Ministry*.
[6] *New Solutions to New Testament Problems*, pp. 1–20.
[7] See C. L. Mitton, *The Epistle to the Ephesians*.
[8] II Pet. iii. 16.

4

The death of the apostles and the prevalence of heresy and false prophecy meant that sooner or later the church would have to face the problem of church order, and in the later New Testament writings we find the first traces of an interest in this subject. Matthew has gathered together in a single paragraph a number of sayings which bear on the theme of discipline.[1] The sayings are included in one of his long collections of general Christian teaching, so he manifestly believed them to be addressed to the church as a whole. Disciplinary authority for dealing with breaches of the Christian fellowship resided in the church, and to the church Christ had entrusted the authority to bind and loose. These powers could be exercised by any local church, however small, because Christ had promised that wherever two or three were gathered in his name, he would be present with them to grant their requests and to ratify their decisions.

The author of the Pastoral Epistles is also concerned about church order, but from a different point of view. He is deeply anxious that men and women shall not be appointed to office in the church unless they have the necessary moral and spiritual qualifications. The epistles contain one reference to the practice of *dokimasia*—enquiry into a man's character and gifts before he is appointed to office.[2] Similarly Clement of Rome attributed to the apostles the rule that only proved men (δεδοκιμασμένοι) should be admitted to the presbyterate.[3]

In spite of the new difficulties and dangers, however, it was not until the beginning of the second century that any significant change took place in the organization of the church. At an early date the church in Jerusalem had taken over from the Jewish synagogues a form of church

[1] Mt. xviii. 15–20; the relation of Mt. xvi. 18–19 to this passage raises questions of notorious difficulty, but it is possible that the words spoken to Peter have nothing to do with church order, but concern his individual qualifications for the leading part which he was to play in the early church.
[2] I Tim. iii. 10.   [3] I Clem. xliv.

government by elders,[1] and the churches of the Gentile mission seem to have been equipped with a similar ministry.[2] The evidence of Acts on this second point has often been challenged on two grounds : firstly, that Paul never refers to the eldership in any of his Epistles, as he surely would have done if he had been in the habit of establishing the office in every church ; and secondly, that Paul had a conception of the church as an organism in which Christ through his Spirit was constantly directing every member into ministerial service. Now it is true that in the New Testament the ministry is always Christ's ministry, his work of redemption and revelation, which he seeks to continue through the church wherein he abides. He is *par excellence* apostle,[3] teacher,[4] pastor,[5] *episcopos*,[6] minister,[7] and all ministerial functions derive from his living presence in the church. But among the ministerial functions listed by Paul we find " government ",[8] and it is difficult to see how any Christian could have exercised a spiritual gift of this kind unless his gift had in some way been formally acknowledged by the church. In two other letters Paul refers to those who " bear rule ",[9] and he opens his letter to the Philippians with a greeting to the *episcopoi*. It has long been an accepted fact that in the New Testament *episcopos* is a synonym for elder. " The admissions of both mediaeval and modern writers of almost all schools of theological opinion have practically removed this from the list of disputed questions." [10] It seems, then, that the Pauline churches had men who performed the functions of eldership though they were called by other names. Luke was apparently familiar with this difference of terminology, for, although he himself writes of elders in Galatia and at Ephesus, he is careful to make Paul speak of them as *episcopoi*.[11] Yet another synonym is furnished by Hebrews, where there are three references to the " leaders " of the

---

[1] Acts xi. 30; xv. 2, 4, 6, 23; xxi. 18.   [2] Acts xvi. 4; xx. 17.
[3] Heb. iii. 1.   [4] Mk. iv. 38, etc.
[5] Jn. x. 11; Heb. xiii. 20; I Pet. ii. 25; v. 4.   [6] I Pet. ii. 25.
[7] Rom. xv. 8; cf. Mk. x. 45.   [8] I Cor. xii. 28.
[9] I Thess. v. 12; Rom. xii. 8.
[10] E. Hatch, *The Organization of the Early Christian Churches*, p. 39 n. Cf. J. B. Lightfoot, op. cit. pp. 93–97.   [11] Acts xx. 17. 28.

church, whose duties include the preaching of the word and the care of souls.[1]

The only other regular office in the church at this time was that of *diakonos*.[2] About the nature of this office little can be said, for *diakonia* is normally used in the New Testament in the general sense of ministry, and *diakonos* is frequently used in this wider sense also. There is, however, a consensus of opinion that the duties of the diaconate in the narrower sense were mainly charitable and financial.

The twofold ministry of elder and deacon continued unchanged throughout the first century. In I Peter the elders of Asia Minor are addressed by one who calls himself their fellow elder, and are bidden to shepherd the flock of God, exercising an episcopal care over them.[3] If Peter was the author of this exhortation, we may say that in his day there could have been no more exalted office in the church than the eldership in which he professed to participate; and if the Petrine authorship be rejected, then it is the more remarkable that a follower of Peter should consider " your fellow elder " to be a suitable designation for the apostle. Luke, as we have seen, used elder and *episcopos* interchangeably, and so did the author of the Pastoral Epistles [4] and Clement of Rome.

When we turn to the letters of Ignatius we find that by *c.* A.D. 115 a threefold ministry of bishop, presbyters, and deacons had been established at Antioch and in several churches in Asia; and in one place he actually says, " Without these there is not even the name of a church " [5]—" a typical extravagance which ", as G. Johnston has remarked, " would have unchurched most of Christendom if it had been taken seriously ".[6] This new polity was a congregational rather than a diocesan episcopacy, for the Ignatian bishop was the pastor in charge of a local church : " Where the bishop is, there let the congregation be ".[7] From the

---

[1] Heb. xiii. 7, 17, 24. [2] Phil. i. 1.
[3] I Pet. v. 1–2; some MSS. omit ἐπισκοποῦντες, but this does not make any serious difference to the sense, since earlier in the Epistle the titles " bishop and shepherd " are found in close association (ii. 25).
[4] Tit. i. 5–7. [5] *Trall.* iii.
[6] *The Doctrine of the Church in the New Testament*, p. 117.
[7] *Smyrn.* viii.

violence with which Ignatius states his case, it seems likely that this new development had been vigorously opposed.

Many theories have been put forward to explain the elevation of a single presbyter-bishop to a place of pre-eminence over his fellows, and it is necessary to consider them here, since some of them trace the beginnings of the change back into the apostolic period with which we are dealing. The theories fall into two classes. It may be held, on the one hand, that certain leaders of the church occupied during the apostolic age a position analogous to that of the second-century bishop, though without the name, and that second-century episcopacy was either instituted on their instructions or deliberately modelled on the precedent which they had provided. On the other hand, we may argue that episcopacy came into existence for reasons of expediency, and that the second-century churchmen subsequently defended the new regime by fathering it on the apostles, by confusing the second-century bishop with the presbyter-bishop of earlier times, and by generally reading back into the apostolic age the ecclesiastical conditions which obtained in their own day.

Among theories of the first type the least plausible is that which sees an incipient episcopacy in John of Patmos' letters to the churches of Asia; for John's authority is that of the prophet and owes nothing to formal appointment. Other scholars have found the precedent they were looking for in the Pastoral Epistles, where Timothy and Titus are instructed to act as the representatives of Paul in the appointment of a ministry for the churches. But these letters are certainly pseudonymous, and the names of Paul, Timothy, and Titus are only a part of the literary convention which the author has adopted; the fictitious Timothy and Titus are men with a roving commission, not resident ministers of a local church; and the title *episcopos* in these letters is still a synonym for presbyter. Lightfoot believed that the change was due to the influence of the apostle John at Ephesus, and declared that no other view could be entertained " without violence to historic testimony ".[1]

[1] Op. cit. p. 232.

More modern scholars are less disposed to believe in the prolonged residence of John the apostle in Asia.[1] Lightfoot's theory has also to reckon with the formidable silence of Ignatius, who musters every argument he can to the defence of episcopacy without so much as suggesting that it was of apostolic foundation. There are also the positive statements of later writers, cited by Lightfoot himself, to the effect that the supremacy of the bishop over the presbyters was " more owing to custom than to any actual ordinance of the Lord ".[2] The same difficulties attend the theory, recently revived by A. Ehrhardt, that episcopacy originated with James of Jerusalem.[3] Besides, Ignatius' own church of Antioch—one of the first churches to adopt episcopacy—was, on the evidence of Matthew's Gospel, more intimately associated with Peter than with James, and it has been plausibly suggested that the exaltation of Peter in this Gospel was an attempt to offset the reputation of James. Nor is it easy to see why, if James was the real founder of episcopacy, the first traces of it should appear more than fifty years after his death.

The second theory, that episcopacy arose spontaneously out of the pressure of pastoral necessity, has the combined support of Clement and Ignatius. For Clement tells us that the apostles appointed presbyter-bishops in every church and left instructions that the office should be perpetuated;[4] he knows nothing of the single bishop, and clearly regards the eldership as the universal apostolic ministry. Ignatius, who must have lived through the inauguration of episcopacy in his own church, sponsors it not on grounds of apostolic command or precedent, but simply because the bishop constitutes a necessary centre of unity for the church. "Time after time he insists, Obey the bishop, and presses it in every way he can. His urgency has not been exaggerated; and indeed it hardly can be exaggerated. So much the more significant is the absence of the one decisive argument which would have

---

[1] See R. H. Charles, *The Revelation of St. John* (ICC), pp. xlv. ff; and for the other side A. C. Headlam, *The Fourth Gospel as History*.

[2] Jerome on Tit. i. 5; cf. Aug., *Epist.* lxxxii. 33.

[3] *The Apostolic Succession.*   [4] I Clem. xliv.

made all the rest superfluous. With all his urgency, he never says, Obey the bishop as the Lord ordained, or as the apostles command. . . . The continued silence of so earnest an advocate as Ignatius is a plain confession that he knows of no such command : and the ignorance of one who must have known the truth of the matter would seem decisive that no such command was given. The theory of an apostolic command is needless as well as unhistorical." [1] What Gwatkin has said about an apostolic command applies with equal force to an apostolic precedent. The obvious inference from Ignatius' arguments is that episcopacy was first introduced for purely practical reasons as a safeguard against the danger of internal dissension or schism.

The records of the apostolic age are silent on three other points of church order also. There is no evidence from our period that the administration of the sacraments was the monopoly of any ministerial office, that ordination involved the laying on of apostolic hands, or that the ministry was ever regarded as a priesthood. Ignatius demands that only the bishop or his authorized representative shall preside at the Eucharist,[2] but this is a requirement which could hardly have been made before the emergence of episcopacy; and the Pastoral Epistles have nothing to tell us about the relation of the ministry to the sacraments. A man might be ordained by an apostle,[3] by a presbytery,[4] or " by other men of repute with the consent of the whole church ".[5] The church in the New Testament inherits from the old Israel the designation " royal priesthood ",[6] but no individual Christian is ever called a priest, and sacerdotal language is used only once to describe any distinctively ministerial function, when Paul in a violent metaphor claims to have been called to " a priestly administration of the Gospel of God, that the sacrificial offering of the Gentiles may be acceptable, sanctified in the Holy Spirit ".[7]

The picture which we have obtained of the ministry in the

---

[1] H. M. Gwatkin, *Early Church History*, p. 294.
[2] *Smyrn.*, viii. [3] II Tim. i. 6.
[4] I Tim. iv. 14. [5] I Clem. xliv.
[6] I Pet. ii. 9; Rev. i. 6. [7] Rom. xv. 16.

late apostolic age conforms with the general character of the period. The Christians of the second generation were concerned to preserve intact their inheritance from the apostles, and maintained unchanged till the end of the century that form of ministry which the apostles had instituted.

CHAPTER XI

CHRIST AND CAESAR

1

ACCORDING to Roman law religion was a department of state, so that political loyalty involved religious conformity.[1] In the imperial settlement of Augustus this principle was given a broad interpretation : the traditional worship of subject peoples was respected, and the control of religion was assigned to local government.[2] The Roman citizen must worship Roman gods, and the provincial must join in the established rites of his own municipality. Throughout the Empire there were organizations responsible for the maintenance of these civic ceremonies. In most places established religion entered deeply into the fabric of daily life. The trade guilds, for example, held feasts which were bound up with the local religion, so that the legal obligation of conformity was reinforced by social and economic pressure. But no roll was kept of attendance at public worship, and, if an Epicurean like Horace chose to stay out of public life and to be " a sparing and infrequent worshipper of the gods ",[3] nobody would be greatly concerned.

In every city there were large numbers of foreigners, who brought with them their own religions. These foreigners had no legal status, and their religions were in theory illegal. But cosmopolitanism was a fact which had to be accepted, and it had become a custom of Roman administration that foreign religions should be tolerated, provided that they did not interfere either with the celebration of official religion or with the maintenance of law and order. It was conclusively established by Mommsen that any

[1] *Ne quis privatim habesset deos.*
[2] The one exception was Druidism, which was put down with severity, because it was believed to involve human sacrifice, and because it was bound up with Celtic nationalism and was therefore a menace to imperial unity. See Pliny, *Hist. Nat.* xxx. 1, 13.   [3] *Odes* i. 34. 1.

action taken by Rome against foreign religions was in the nature of *coercitio*, i.e. police procedure, which operated independently of the criminal code and the regular law courts.[1] The enforcement of public order by *coercitio* lay within the *imperium* of emperor, governors, and magistrates, all of whom had considerable powers of discretion; and a new religion was likely to have a different reception in different parts of the Empire. New cults were constantly being ejected from Rome because of their disruptive influence on Roman society, whereas in the East a new religion would excite only a benevolent curiosity. The general tendency towards syncretism made it easy for new gods to be identified with old ones, just as the citizens of Lystra[2] tried to absorb the Gospel into the framework of established religion by identifying Paul with Hermes and Barnabas with Zeus. If a citizen of Rome or of a provincial city deserted his national religion to adopt a foreign one, he could be put on trial for atheism. But such trials were rare; there was no need for one religion to oust another, when one man could serve many masters.

Wherever the imperial cult was instituted, it came under the authority of the *concilium* or *koinon*, and carried the same degree of obligation as the local cult. For most subjects of the Empire the observance of the imperial cult was no more burdensome than it is for us to stand at the playing of the national anthem. They could make their act of grateful homage, and turn elsewhere for spiritual satisfaction.

The Jews throughout the Empire were exempt from all forms of state religion, but they were not exempt from the general obligation to keep the peace. On this score they were constantly in trouble not only in Palestine but elsewhere, including Rome. Tiberius, who attempted to rid Roman society of all foreign influences, was particularly hostile to the worship of Isis and to Judaism; and Claudius also expelled the Jews from Rome for repeated acts of sedition. As long as the distinction between the Jews and

---

[1] T. Mommsen, " Der Religionsfrevel nach römischen Recht," *Historische Zeitschrift*, lxiv. (1890), p. 398.
[2] Acts xiv. 12.

the Christians was not recognized by the Roman government, the Christians benefited from the legal protection of Judaism and suffered also from the prevalent anti-semitism.[1] If a Christian was brought before a Roman governor or provincial magistrate, it was on some charge that was not strictly religious. On the one occasion when the Jews accused Paul of practising an illicit religion, the proconsul Gallio ruled that no law had been broken, and that disputes on religious matters between Jews had no standing before a Roman seat of judgment.[2] But once the difference between Jew and Christian had been officially established, the Christians automatically lost their legal security.

The worst aspect of the Roman religious system was that it encouraged the informer, and most trials on religious charges were the result of delation.[3] Officials, who would not on their own initiative have taken any action against illegal religions, often felt themselves compelled to do so because of information received. The devotee of a foreign cult, therefore, enjoyed a religious freedom of which he might at any moment be deprived by a stricter application of the law, and in practice his fate depended in a large measure on the goodwill of his neighbours. If he happened to antagonize public opinion, his position became extremely precarious.[4]

2

In the early part of the apostolic age, then, there was no danger that Christianity would become a proscribed religion. But Christians were constantly exposed to other dangers which arose out of conflict with a hostile environment.

[1] Acts xvi. 20; xix. 34.   [2] Acts xviii. 12–17.

[3] There was, for example, the case of Pomponia Graecina, who was denounced as an adherent of a foreign religion; the court left the judgment of her case to her husband, who pronounced her innocent (Tac., *Ann.* xiii. 32).

[4] For a modern parallel we might cite the theft of the Stone of Scone from Westminster Abbey by a Scottish student. The British public was mildly amused and reluctantly admiring, and the government decided to take no action. But if any considerable section of the population had felt sufficiently outraged to work up a volume of public indignation, the offender could have been accused on a criminal charge and the jury would have had to find him guilty.

Jesus had taught his disciples to submit to constituted authority, to pay taxes to Caesar, to carry the baggage of the Roman army beyond the legally compulsory mile,[1] and he himself had scrupulously avoided anything that savoured of subversive activity. But he had founded a kingdom of his own, based on principles antithetic to those of worldly power, and had demanded that his disciples, faced with a clash of loyalties, should put first their allegiance to himself and the Gospel. These disciples had to live both in the world and in the Kingdom, and they had been warned that the world would hate and persecute them.

To the ordinary pagan the Christians seemed anti-social. For reasons unintelligible to the pagan mind they withdrew from the idolatry and immoralities of feasts and festivals in which they had formerly participated.[2] The Christians themselves could not help being aware of the strained relationship with their pagan neighbours, and at Corinth there were some members of the church who were seriously concerned about it. How far were they to carry their withdrawal from pagan society? Must they have nothing whatever to do with those who lived by lower standards of morality? Could a Christian man or woman continue to live with a non-Christian wife or husband? On what terms was it right for them to attend a pagan dinner-party? Must Christian women be governed by pagan conventions of respectability?[3]

The Christian leaders were also aware that they might appear to an outsider to be revolutionaries, bent on overturning the accepted order of society and in particular the institution of the family. There must have been many occasions when one member of a family was converted to Christianity, so that the Gospel brought not peace but division.[4] Moreover, the church was a fellowship of brotherly love, and in Christ Jesus there was neither slave nor free, neither male nor female. The oppressed classes, who found in the church dignity and freedom, could hardly

---

[1] Mk. xii. 17; Mt. v. 41.   [2] I Pet. iv. 4.
[3] I Cor. v. 9–10; vii. 12–16; viii. 1–xi. 16.
[4] Mt. x. 34–36; Lk. xii. 51–53; xxi. 16.

return unchanged to the daily life of a pagan household or neighbourhood, and there was a danger that they might be tempted to throw off the restraints of the pagan social order. Hence the ethical teaching of the Hellenistic mission included, as we have seen, a code of subordination in which Christian wives, children, and slaves were bidden to submit to the authority of the head of the household, whether he was a Christian or not. In particular, Christians had to avoid the charge of tampering with another man's slaves.[1] The vast numbers of slaves in the Empire were a constant source of anxiety to the Roman government, which would not countenance any weakening of the slave-owner's authority, except through the limitations laid down by law. This explains Paul's conscientious treatment of Onesimus. All personal considerations urged him to keep the runaway slave beside him as a friend to lighten the burden of his imprisonment. But he did not dare to lay himself or the church open to the accusation of harbouring a fugitive from justice.

In the story of Paul's missionary career we find two other threats to the security of the church. Wherever he went, Paul was received by Roman officials with polite and friendly interest, and he seems to have had the knack of making influential friends.[2] Opposition, when it arose, was due either to mercenary considerations or to Jewish jealousy.

At Philippi and again at Ephesus, Paul was attacked by men whose pockets had been affected by the coming of the Gospel,[3] and in both cities an attempt was made to arraign him on a political charge. At Philippi he was accused of anti-Roman activities, and at Ephesus of bringing the established religion into disrepute. In these two incidents we can see the shadow of coming events, for they show how easily public sentiment could be inflamed against the Christians and how difficult it could be for Christians to defend themselves against any accusation once public opinion had turned against them. There was, moreover, a

---

[1] This may be what is meant by the obscure word ἀλλοτριοεπίσκοπος in I Pet. iv. 15. Moffatt and Beare, however, prefer the rendering " revolutionary ".

[2] Acts xix. 21.   [3] Acts xvi. 19; xix. 25.

certain amount of justice in the second of these charges. The town clerk of Ephesus declared that Paul and his friends were not guilty of sacrilege, but a man who, on his own admission, went about the world calling on people to turn " from idols to serve a living and true God ",[1] cannot be wholly acquitted of contempt for the Ephesian Artemis.

In other places Paul became involved with the authorities because of Jewish hostility. In one city of Galatia after another it was the Jews who stirred up the Gentile population against the missionaries.[2] Indeed, the Jews of Antioch and Iconium actually pursued them to Lystra. Luke does not tell us by what arguments they carried their point, but presumably their methods were similar to those used at a later date in Thessalonica.[3] There the Jews first hired a gang of ruffians to stage a riot outside Jason's house, then laid a charge of treason against Paul and Silas. The two apostles made their escape from the city, but their converts were subjected to continued ill-treatment by the Jews, who also started a malicious whispering campaign against Paul, insinuating that he was a victim of hallucinations, that he was a moral pervert, that he was charlatan, that he preached only what people wanted to hear, that he had taken to preaching for what he could make out of it, that his one desire was to force himself into the public eye.[4]

What part the Jews had in the uproar at Ephesus is not clear. Luke tells us that at the height of the confusion in the theatre the Jews put forward Alexander as their spokesman, but he was shouted down by the mob.[5] If we could be sure that this man was Alexander the coppersmith, whom Paul regarded as a dangerous enemy,[6] his connexion with the metal-workers' guild would be established, and we should have reason for suspecting Jewish influence behind the original riot; but the name Alexander was a common one, and the identification must be dubious. It has been suggested that the charge of temple-robbing (ἱεροσυλία) [7]

---

[1] I Thess. i. 9. [2] Acts xiii. 50; xiv. 2, 19.
[3] Acts xvii. 5–7. [4] I Thess. ii. 3–6.
[5] Acts xix. 33. [6] II Tim. iv. 14 f.
[7] Acts xix. 37; see G. S. Duncan, *Paul's Ephesian Ministry*, pp. 34–45, 202.

L

was brought by the Jews, who found that Christian Jews were diverting into church funds money which they had formerly contributed as temple tax for the upkeep of the Jerusalem temple; but ἱεροσυλία was also used in a wider sense which covered any offence against established religion.

It is clear, however, that the Jews of Asia were no better disposed towards Paul than those of Galatia, Macedonia, or Achaea, for some Asiatic Jews were responsible for his final imprisonment.[1] Whether they had followed Paul to Jerusalem in order to cause trouble for him or had come up as pilgrims for the feast of Pentecost, we are not told. But they saw Paul in the city accompanied by Trophimus, whom they recognized as a Gentile from Ephesus, and jumped to the conclusion that Paul had taken his Gentile friend into the temple. This was an offence for which Roman law allowed the Jewish authorities to carry out the death penalty even on Roman citizens. Less than ten years before the outbreak of the Jewish war tempers were running high in Jerusalem, and the Jews were in no mood for dispassionate inquiry. Paul was fortunate, then, to be taken into protective custody by Roman soldiers. For his two years' imprisonment at Caesarea there was no legal justification : the charge against him could not be proved, the key witnesses were never produced, and he would have been acquitted, had not Felix been afraid that the Jews would then make his own position untenable. Paul's two years of house-imprisonment in Rome, however, were quite legal. He had appealed to Caesar, and Roman law provided that in appeal cases, where the prosecution and witnesses had to come from remote parts of the Empire, two years' grace should be allowed after which the case would go by default.[2] Luke's abrupt ending of Acts seems to imply that Paul's accusers failed to appear within the legal limit, and that Paul was accordingly released from his imprisonment. On the other hand, there can be little doubt that Paul met his death, sooner or later, as a martyr in Rome.[3]

---

[1] Acts xix. 9; xxi. 27; xxiv. 18.
[2] See H. J. Cadbury, *The Beginnings of Christianity*, V, pp. 297–338.
[3] I Clem. v.

Paul was by no means the only victim of Jewish anti-
pathy. Suetonius tells us that Claudius expelled the Jews
from Rome because they were repeatedly rioting at the
instigation of one Chrestus.[1] In this garbled account
Chrestus is certainly an error for Christus. The riots may
have been outbreaks of Jewish nationalism, provoked by
messianic expectations. But it is far more likely that they
were anti-Christian riots, and that in Rome as in other
places the unpopularity of the Christians was in no small
measure due to Jewish enmity.

Thus for one reason or another Christians of the first
generation incurred the mounting antagonism of their
neighbours. Once they had fallen under suspicion, ignorance and imagination combined to produce in the public
mind a horrifying picture of their enormities, and it was this
popular animosity which brought down upon them the
scourge of persecution.[2]

3

In A.D. 64 a fire broke out in Rome which raged for nearly
a week and destroyed a large part of the city. A rumour
sprang up that Nero had ordered the fire because the ugliness
of the city revolted his aesthetic sensibilities. Nero decided
to shift the blame on to the Christians, and so began the
first persecution of the church by Rome.

From Tacitus' description [3] it is evident that the persecution passed through three stages. The first arrests were
made solely because Nero needed to divert suspicion from
himself, and had learnt—perhaps from his wife, Poppaea
Sabina, who is known to have had Jewish sympathies—that
the Christians were popularly believed to be capable of any
atrocity. From the examination of this first group, probably under torture, information was obtained which led to

---

[1] Claud. xxv.
[2] The punishments inflicted by Nero were those meted out to magicians
(see W. M. Ramsay, *The Church in the Roman Empire*, p. 236 n.). In the
second century Christians were believed to be guilty of cannibalism and
incest (Iren. fr. xiii; Tert. *Apol.* vii., Orig. *Cels.* vi. 27), and this is presumably the type of atrocity covered by the less precise term flagitia used by
both Tacitus and Pliny.   [3] See Appendix B.

further arrests and also to a change in procedure. The charge of arson was dropped and a charge of hatred of the human race was substituted. The natural interpretation of Tacitus' extremely laconic diction is that at the first trials the Roman authorities inquired into the nature of the Christian religion, came to the conclusion that it was a public menace, and decided to treat its adherents as outlaws. We are left to conjecture what there was about the Christians that created this fatal impression. The change of policy must have been based on real evidence, however much this evidence may have been coloured by public suspicion and hysteria. Some indications of the nature of the evidence may be obtained from Tactitus' description of the Jews, as a nation which " had an implacable hatred against all others ".[1] This description is so closely parallel to the charge brought against the Christians that we may safely assume that in Roman eyes the two groups were guilty of the same offences—but with this difference, that Jewish intransigeance was protected by a law of long standing. The supposed enmity of the Christians against society, then, must have consisted in their obstinate refusal to show loyalty to Rome by worshipping Roman gods, their unconditional allegiance to another power than Rome, their open contempt for many time-honoured customs of Roman life, their prayers for the downfall of the present world order, including the Roman Empire. The final stage of the persecution came about when the Roman mob felt its appetite for horrors to be satiated, and experienced a revulsion of feeling in favour of the Christians; nobody believed them to be innocent, but it had become obvious that Nero's actions were prompted by other motives than concern for the public interest.

Thus in two ways the Neronic persecution determined the course of future relations between church and state. A Roman court of inquiry had ruled that Christianity was tantamount to an attack on the Roman way of life, and thenceforward Christians could at any time be brought to trial on a capital charge. But whether in fact any action

[1] *Hist.* v. 5.

was taken against them depended on the condition of public opinion and on the personal feelings of the officials concerned.

The interpretation we have given to Tacitus' account of the persecution is borne out by the evidence of Suetonius, who mentions the proceedings against the Christians not in connexion with the fire but in a chapter devoted to Nero's administrative policy.[1] " Every other regulation which is mentioned in the list is the permanent institution of a custom, or the lasting suppression of an abuse. It would be quite inconsistent with the others to introduce in the midst of them a statement which meant only that a number of Christians were executed on the charge of causing a fire. The fair and natural interpretation of Suetonius' words is, that he considered Nero to have maintained a steady prosecution of a mischievous class of persons, in virtue of his duty to maintain peace and order in the city, and to have intended that this prosecution should be permanent." We shall find further confirmation of this view in Pliny's correspondence with Trajan.

4

According to Tertullian,[3] Vespasian was not to be counted among the persecutors of the church. Ramsay has contested this assertion on the basis of a passage in Sulpicius Severus, which describes a council of war held by Titus after the fall of Jerusalem : " Others, including Titus himself, expressed the opinion that the temple especially must be destroyed, in order that the religion of the Jews and Christians might be the more completely eradicated. . . . Christianity had been derived from Judaism, and once the root was removed the stock would perish forthwith." [4] It is probable that Sulpicius was following the lost *Histories* of Tacitus, and that Tacitus was accurately representing the sentiments of the Flavian emperors concerning Judaism and Christianity. But there is no evidence that these sentiments led to actual persecution. The opinions ascribed to Titus suggest rather that no further persecution was

[1] *Nero* xvi.   [2] W. M. Ramsay, op cit. pp. 230 f.
[3] *Apol.* v; cf. Melito in Eus., *H.E.* iv. 26.   [4] ii. 30.

necessary after the destruction of the temple, since both religions could be expected to die without additional assistance from Rome. We shall see later that there may have been sporadic prosecutions of Christians in accordance with the precedent established under Nero, but we cannot ascribe either to Vespasian or to Titus personally an actively anti-Christian policy.

A strong Christian tradition grew up during the second century that Domitian was the second great persecutor of the church, " a replica of Nero's cruelty ".[1] But it is extremely difficult to discover any positive evidence to account for this belief. Domitian, as we have seen in an earlier chapter, was acutely sensitive to any opposition, and struck out savagely against those who appeared to be questioning his authority. He attacked the Stoics because their belief that succession to the principate should be by election rather than by dynastic inheritance seemed to be a direct criticism of his own position and his own practice of nepotism. The same sense of insecurity led him to demand the title *dominus et deus*, and to prosecute any prominent citizens who withheld their worship. Less than a year before his assassination he brought such a charge against the consul T. Flavius Clemens and his wife Domitilla, his own cousin and niece, whose eldest son had been unmistakably designated heir to the principate. According to Suetonius, Clemens, " a man of the most despicable sloth ", was executed " on very slender suspicion ". Domitilla was banished. According to Dio Cassius, the charge against both was " atheism ", and other distinguished Roman citizens, including a former consul, M'. Acilius Glabrio, were executed on the same charge.[2] There can be little doubt that Clemens and his wife were Christians,[3] but it is clear, too, that their high rank contributed to their downfall, which need not have been part of any general persecution.

The Revelation belongs to this critical period at the end of Domitian's reign, but its evidence must be used only with

[1] Tert., *Apol.* v ; for other passages see Lightfoot, *Clement* i. p. 104.
[2] Suet., *Dom.* xv ; Dio Cass. lxvii. 14 ; Eus., *H.E.* iii. 18. 5.
[3] Lightfoot, op. cit. i. pp. 29 ff.

the greatest caution. At the time of writing John knew of one Christian who had suffered martyrdom for his faith at Pergamum, though this event had apparently taken place some years earlier and was not directly connected with the present crisis; [1] he had himself spent a period of imprisonment in the penal settlement of Patmos; [2] and he was able to commend the patient endurance which his fellow Christians had shown in times of testing. [3] But the greater part of his work is concerned with a more severe trial which lay still in the future. [4] In his prophetic vision he had been allowed to see accomplished on the heavenly plane, i.e. in the predestining counsels of God, events which, he believed, would shortly be worked out on the stage of history. He saw these events as the fulfilment of the prophecy of Daniel, and supposed his vision to mark the beginning of Daniel's three and a half year period of final distress. We are justified, therefore, in looking for historical events only in those parts of John's vision which antedate the three and a half years. Thus the attack of the dragon upon the woman clothed with the sun covers the incarnate life of Christ; the war in heaven, whereby the accuser is cast out, corresponds to the atoning death of Christ; the rise of the beast from the sea indicates the emergence of Rome as a totalitarian power in Domitian's demand for worship; and the second beast represents the imperial priesthood of Asia, which had obviously gone to great lengths to secure compliance with the emperor's demand. [5] But the Great Tribulation had not yet begun, and John appears to imply that it could not begin until the three and a half years had run their course, since during that period the church was to rest secure under the special protection of God. [6] We may safely say, then, that all the conditions had been

[1] Rev. ii. 13; there may have been others, but John would hardly have singled out one man for special mention if the numbers had been large.
[2] Rev. i. 9; cf. Pliny, *Hist. Nat.* iv. 12. 23.
[3] Rev. ii. 2, 9, 19; iii. 10.
[4] Rev. i. 1, 3; iv. 1; xxii. 6, 10.
[5] Rev. xii–xiii.
[6] Rev. vii. 3; xi. 3–7; xii. 6. To these may be added xvii. 10 f., which suggests that John expected the return of the Neronic persecution not in the present reign but in the next reign but one. But it would be hazardous to rest any weight on a passage of such doubtful interpretation.

established for mortal combat between church and state, between the Lamb and the Beast, that John with prophetic insight discerned the eternal principles underlying the struggle, and that in vision he saw the battle fought to a finish—destruction for Rome and victory for Christ. But the Revelation provides no more solid evidence for a widespread persecution of the church at the end of the first century than it does for the fall of Rome and the inauguration of the Millenium. It is probable that Domitian's death postponed the clash of empires, and that his bad reputation among Christians of a later age was due more to his intentions as a persecutor than to any considerable accomplishment.[1]

5

The reign of Trajan falls outside the limits of our period, but the correspondence between Pliny and Trajan concerning the Christians contains evidence relating to the first century as well as to the second.[2] Pliny had been sent out by Trajan as a special administrator to restore order to the combined provinces of Bithynia and Pontus, which had been scandalously mismanaged by senatorial governors. He was a lawyer and a financial expert with no previous experience of provincial government, and was accustomed to write to the emperor for instructions whenever he was in doubt about even the smallest detail of his work.

Pliny found that official religion in Bithynia-Pontus was being seriously neglected, because no steps had been taken to check the rapid growth of Christianity. He himself was forced to take action by a series of informers. He knew that in other parts of the Empire Christians had been prosecuted, but he had never attended their trials and was ignorant of the correct procedure. His ignorance must

[1] It is significant that the three other writings which belong to this period give no indication of any persecution. I Clement (A.D. 96 or 97) refers only to the Neronic persecution. The Fourth Gospel speaks of the hostility of "the world" toward the church, but the world which hated Jesus can hardly be identified with the Roman Empire (xv. 18 f.). In I John "the whole world lies in the Evil One", but the Antichrist shows himself in heresies which undermine the church's life from within and not in political action which threatens it from without (iv. 3; v. 19).

[2] For the text of these letters see Appendix B.

not, however, be exaggerated. He was obviously familiar
with the general principles of imperial policy, and found
himself at a loss only when he had to deal with the com-
plexities which arose in the later stages of the case. He was
quite sure that confessing Christians were guilty of a capital
offence, and without hesitation pronounced the death sentence on them. His first doubts arose when he was confronted with a large group of prisoners who admitted that
they had been Christians, but claimed that they had abandoned their former faith. Their treatment must depend
on a more precise legal definition of their offence. If
Christians were condemned simply for the name (i.e. for
being Christians), then their case must be dealt with under
the governor's power of *coercitio*, and this meant that those
who had ceased to be Christians might be acquitted.[1] But
if Christians were condemned in respect of crimes inseparable from the practice of their religion, crimes punishable
under the regular criminal code, then they could still be
put on trial for those crimes even after they had renounced
their Christian profession, and a penitent Christian could
no more be pardoned than a penitent thief or a penitent
murderer. Pliny had been unable to discover evidence of
any such crimes, and accordingly referred the case to the
emperor for an authoritative ruling. His own view was
that the penitent should be pardoned, and he firmly believed that, if such a policy were to be publicly proclaimed,
a general recantation would follow.

Trajan's answer is simple and brief: Pliny's general
procedure has been correct, he should not be bound by any
one rule, he may pardon the penitent, he must act on information received (anonymous letters excepted), but need
not act on his own initiative.

From this correspondence it is apparent that Trajan was
not formulating a new anti-Christian policy of his own.[2]

[1] According to Minucius Felix (Octav. 28), renunciation of the name in his
day purged the Christian of all guilt.
[2] " This rescript does not initiate procedure against the Christians. It
is absurd to suppose that Trajan for the first time laid down the principle,
'The Christians are criminals deserving death; but you may shut your
eyes to them until an accuser insists on your opening them'." (W. M.
Ramsay, op. cit. p. 212.)

Like Pliny, he felt himself bound by a long-established precedent with which he had little sympathy, but intended that the law should be administered as leniently as possible. Unfortunately Trajan did not give a direct answer to Pliny's question concerning the nature of the charge against the Christians, but we can arrive at an answer by a process of elimination :

(*a*) The charge had nothing to do with the law against *collegia*. On taking up office Pliny had issued an edict against the holding of club meetings, and the Christians had immediately complied with his order by discontinuing their fellowship meal.

(*b*) The charge had nothing to do with emperor-worship. It is true that Pliny brought the emperor's image into court along with the images of the gods in order to give the accused persons an opportunity of proving their loyalty ; but he did not charge them with *maiestas*, nor would Trajan have countenanced such a charge. In an earlier rescript Trajan had written to Pliny : " You knew very well that it was not my policy to win respect for my name by intimidation or by prosecutions for *maiestas* ".[1] This means that the legal precedent on which Trajan's ruling was based was older than Domitian's self-deification.

(*c*) Christians were not to be condemned for " the crimes that attach to the name ", since in that case the penitent could not have been pardoned.

(*d*) It follows, therefore, that Christians under Trajan were prosecuted " for the name ", and had long been liable to such prosecution.

(*e*) If we ask what there was about the Christians that laid them open to a capital charge, we have to rely on Pliny's remark, of which Trajan seems to approve, that they were guilty of obstinacy, i.e. defiance of Roman *imperium*.[2]

[1] Pliny, *Ep.* x. 82.
[2] John Knox in a recent article (" Pliny and I Peter ", *Journal of Biblical Literature*, LXXII (1953), pp. 187–189) has suggested that *obstinatio* describes not a persistent confession of faith but a truculent refusal to answer questions. He thinks that I Peter was written at this time to encourage the Christians to co-operate with the government by giving a rational defence of their faith, which could make clear that they were not criminals and that the only count against them was their religion. Pliny,

However gently and sympathetically Rome might rule her subject peoples, the structure of Roman government depended in the last analysis on *imperium*, the absolute right of the state to command obedience; and it was precisely this that Christians were unable to admit.

The evidence of Pliny confirms the deductions we have already made from Tacitus' story of the Neronic persecution. The police regulations instituted by Nero continued in force throughout the Flavian period, and resulted in sporadic prosecutions. Domitian's claim to the worship of his subjects temporarily accentuated the danger in which all Christians lived, but after his death Rome reverted to what had become her normal policy; and this policy found concise expression in Trajan's rescript.

6

The attitude of the church towards Rome during the first century oscillated between two points of view, both of them inherited from the Jews, who had always had two streams of thought with regard to the Gentile world—one particularist and one universalist. At the outset of her history Israel had been designated " a kingdom of priests and a holy nation "; [1] that is to say, she was to be the means of mediating God's sovereignty to the world, and to that end she must maintain her religious identity, since only a people with a unique religion has any right to embark upon

---

it seems, would have been totally disarmed by such frankness, since he had " grave scruples about putting persons to death for the mere profession of an apparently innocuous religion "; the contemptuous attitude of certain Christians to his investigations had led him " to suspect the truth of the charges of other more serious crimes "; so he had put them to death " not for confessing themselves Christians . . . but for the manner in which they did so ". This theory, however, suffers shipwreck on four distinct counts. (1) Pliny expressly says that he had found no evidence of other crimes. (2) Pliny is a lawyer who claims to be giving Trajan a detailed account of the legal procedure he has employed, but he does not mention any question which the Christians refused to answer; on the contrary, he says he put only one question, to which they thrice gave an affirmative reply. (3) Trajan clearly understands Pliny to mean that he has condemned the Christians on the ground of their faith, and he approves this procedure. (4) The use of I Peter to throw light on Pliny's letter begs the question of the Epistle's date.

[1] Exod. xix. 6.

a world mission. From her calling it was possible for her to fall away in two directions : towards religious nationalism, which was a denial of her mission, or towards syncretism, which was a denial of her unique religion.

The force of circumstances had compelled Israel to concentrate on the second of these dangers. The prophets, from Elijah to Ezekiel, Nehemiah and Ezra, the Maccabees, and the Pharisees were all prompted by the one continuing necessity of resisting the encroachments of foreign religion. This atmosphere of unremitting struggle encouraged the survival and growth of the primitive belief that the enemies of Israel were also the enemies of God. When Antiochus Epiphanes made his ill-conceived attempt to spread a uniform Greek culture throughout his domain, this Jewish belief hardened into the apocalyptic dogma that the pagan world would shortly be hurled to irretrievable disaster under the accumulated weight of its own corruption. But throughout this whole period there had been a parallel development of a more optimistic and generous feeling towards the Gentiles. The prophets had taught that Yahweh controlled the destinies of other nations besides Israel, and had even suggested that he could use pagans in the working out of his sovereign purpose.[1] They had looked forward to the day when the nations should recognize the sovereignty of Yahweh, and in that knowledge find their salvation;[2] and this hope had found a place in Israel's worship.[3] Along with this hope came a dawning appreciation of the noble elements in pagan culture and religion.[4] By the beginning of the Christian era the Rabbis had developed a theory that in making his covenant with Noah God had revealed to all nations certain basic moral obligations, so that pagan ethics and government could be deemed to rest ultimately on the secure foundation of natural law.[5] This side of Jewish thought had been strongly emphasized

---

[1] Amos ix. 7; Isa. x. 5; xlv. 1.
[2] Isa. ii. 2–4 (Mic. iv. 1–4); Isa. xlv. 22–23; xlix. 6; xix. 23–25; xxv. 6–8.
[3] Ps. xxii. 27–28; xlvi. 10; xlvii. 8; lxvii. 1–2; lxxxix. 9; xcvi. 7; xvii. 6.
[4] Amos i. 11.   [5] See G. F. Moore, *Judaism*, I 274 f., 462.

by Jesus, who had attempted to summon Israel back from nationalism to her universal mission,[1] and had been at all times ready to show his approval of Gentile response to God.[2] But Jesus had also used apocalytic imagery, and the book of Daniel in particular, to interpret his own mission.

Both Jews and Christians received a forceful reminder of the apocalyptist's predictions when Caligula decreed that his statue was to be set up in the Jerusalem temple. Here surely was the " Desecrating Horror " of Daniel's prophecy,[3] and the judgment of this world's empire could not be far distant. This event still found an echo ten years later in the mind of Paul when he wrote his Second Epistle to the Thessalonians. He believed that " the mystery of lawlessness ", which had manifested itself in Caligula, was being kept in check by a " restraining power," but would shortly break out in open revolt against God, when " the man of lawlessness " would " take his seat in the temple of God, making himself out to be God ", thus achieving what Caligula had only attempted.[4] This " rebellion " would be followed by the return of Christ to " destroy with the brightness of his coming " the enemies of God. But if Paul the apocalyptist was alive to the demonic quality in Roman imperial power, Paul the Roman citizen could recognize that this was not the whole truth about the Empire. The " restraining power " of which Paul speaks in this passage was Rome in her nobler aspect—the guardian of justice and of world peace. Not long after he wrote this Epistle Paul experienced at the hands of Gallio the benefit of Roman impartiality, and in the years that followed he became more deeply appreciative of Roman rule. When he wrote his Epistle to the Romans he was ready to assert that the state had been instituted by God for the restraint and punishment of wrongdoers and that the magistrate was a man " ordained to a sacred ministry ".[5] He would

---

[1] Lk. xiii. 28 (Mt. viii. 11); Mk. xi. 17.
[2] Lk. iv. 24–27; vii. 9; x. 33; xi. 31–32; xvii. 18.
[3] Dan. xi. 31; xii. 11; cf. Mk. xiii. 14.   [4] II Thess. ii. 1–12.
[5] Rom. xiii. 1–7; the word λειτουργός is used later in the same Epistle to describe Paul's own ministerial calling.

presumably have said that the Christian's duty to obey the state existed only so long as the state continued to fulfil its God-given function. But in the tranquil *quinquennium Neronis*, when there was no immediate reason to fear any change in Roman policy, it must have seemed unnecessary to mention such a condition. Paul had now moved on from his earlier vision of world judgment to a new vision of world salvation,[1] and had come to hope that even the principalities and powers, the demonic agencies behind the pagan world order, would in the end be reconciled to God.[2]

7

Apart from the Epistles of Paul there are only two New Testament writings, Hebrews and I Peter, which can with any degree of likelihood be assigned to the period prior to the outbreak of persecution, and in each case many scholars have preferred a later date. The only possibility of dating either book lies in identifying from somewhat slender internal evidence the crisis for which it was written.

The people to whom Hebrews was addressed had at some time in the past been the victims of abuse, mob violence, imprisonment, and looting, but there had not so far been any case of martyrdom among them.[3] The disciples of Jesus from whom the community had first received the Gospel were now dead, but there is no suggestion that they died an unnatural death.[4] Nor is there any immediate prospect of persecution. Those who come out to Christ from the camp of this world's society must be ready to bear abuse on his account, just as Moses preferred abuse borne for the sake of Christ to all the treasures of Egypt; but that is all.[5] Now it is probable that the Epistle was addressed to Rome, either to the church as a whole or to a Jewish Christian group within the church. The salutation, " Those who are of Italy greet you ",[6] comes more naturally from a man writing to Rome from a city outside Italy where

---

[1] Rom. xi. 25–32. [2] Phil. ii. 10; Col. i. 20; Eph. iii. 10.
[3] Heb. x. 32–34; xii. 4. [4] Heb. ii. 3; xiii. 7.
[5] Heb. xiii. 13; cf. xi. 26. [6] Heb. xiii. 24.

there is a small company of Italian Christians, than from a
man in Rome writing to a church in one of the provinces;
and the external evidence agrees best with this hypothesis.
But it is difficult to see how the author could have written
to any group of Christians in Rome, referring as he does to
their past tribulations and to their former leaders without
mention of the Neronic persecution, unless he wrote before
that persecution took place. On the other hand, we have
reason to believe that the Jews in Rome had organized anti-
Christian riots in A.D. 49, and that in the years immediately
preceding the fire of Rome the Roman mob had learnt to
distinguish the Christians from the Jews and had begun to
regard the Christians with suspicion and hatred. In these
circumstances the Jewish Christians might have been
tempted to avoid needless unpleasantness by an observance
of the Torah which would keep them formally within the
boundaries of Judaism.[1]

I Peter i. 1–iv. 11 shows the same confidence in Roman
justice that we have seen in Paul's Epistle to the Romans.
Christians may have to suffer from the ignorance of fools,
but they have nothing to fear from the emperor or his
representatives.[2] They are liable to undergo " various
trials ", including the malicious attentions of scandal-
mongers, but a clear conscience and a ready answer will
provide them with an adequate defence.[3] The reason for
their unpopularity is that they refuse to join in pagan
profligacy.[4] But their tribulations have also a positive
value as a test of their faith and as a participation in the
redemptive suffering of Christ.[5] In the final section of the
Epistle the situation seems to have deteriorated. The
expectation of suffering is no longer qualified by such phrases
as " if necessary " or " if that should be God's will ".[6] The
testing of faith in the furnace of affliction has ceased to be a
remote contingency and is becoming a present experience.
All through the world the devil—the slanderer—is at work,
and the calumnies which are directed at the church are now

---

[1] See also W. Manson, *The Epistle to the Hebrews.*
[2] I Pet. ii. 13–17.   [3] I Pet. i. 6; iii. 13–17.   [4] I Pet. iv. 4.
[5] I Pet. i. 7; ii. 21–25; iv. 1; cf. iv. 13.   [6] I Pet. i. 6; iii. 17.

likely to lead to more serious consequences than before
Christians are in danger of being prosecuted on charges of
murder, theft, magic,[1] or tampering with another man's
household. It is their duty, therefore, to make it plain to
the authorities that these charges have no foundation, so
that, if they suffer any legal penalty, it shall be solely on
the ground that they are Christians. It is no longer to be
expected that a candid defence will secure an acquittal :
for this crisis is the Crisis, the Last Judgment, which is
about to begin at the household of God ; and the judgment
of the church by persecution will be followed rapidly by the
judgment of unbelievers.[2]

A few scholars have argued that this Epistle must have
been written in the reign of Trajan, because Pliny's letter
provides the first datable reference to the persecution of
Christians " for the name ". It should be noticed, however,
that in I Peter iv. 14 ff. this phrase has no legal significance :
Christians may be abused for the name of Christ, and this
abuse may lead to subsequent legal action in which they
will suffer " as Christians ". Now we have the evidence of
Luke and Mark that from the earliest times Christians had
been accustomed " to suffer dishonour for the name ",
and that Jesus had predicted that this would happen.[3] It
has sometimes been held that the two evangelists were
reading back into the Gospel record the terminology of their
own day. But in that case their phraseology becomes all
the more significant, and we have two weighty pieces of
evidence, one from the reign of Nero and the other from the
reign of Domitian, that Christians in those days regularly
spoke of their tribulations as suffering endured for the name.
Again, Luke and Tacitus agree that from Antioch and
Caesarea to Rome the followers of Jesus were popularly
known as Christians, and it was under that name that they
incurred, before the fire of Rome, the contempt and hatred
of the Roman mob. The conduct advocated in I Peter iv.
15 for Christians in court is that regularly attributed by
Luke to Paul : " I have lived before God in all good con-

---

[1] This is Tertullian's interpretation of κακοποιός (*Scorp.* xii).
[2] I Pet. iv. 12-19; v. 8-10.   [3] Acts v. 41; Mk. xiii. 13.

science up to this day "; " neither can they prove to you the charges they now bring against me. But this I admit to you, that according to the Way, which they call a sect, I worship the God of our fathers." [1]

The second part of the Epistle, then, could have been written at almost any time in early Christian history, but the same cannot be said of the first part. Only a writer totally out of touch with the local situation could have told Christians living in Bithynia-Pontus during Pliny's term of office that they had nothing to fear from the government, provided that their consciences were clear; and the same argument applies with only slightly less cogency to any province at any time from A.D. 64 onwards. The same attitude to the state is recommended in I Peter and in Romans, though in terms so different as to preclude dependence; and the natural assumption is that the two documents belong to roughly the same historical setting. We can account adequately for all the facts on the hypothesis that I Peter i. 1–iv. 11 was written in the early sixties, and that the postscript was added later when for some reason public feeling against the Christians had reached that pitch of frenzy which is presupposed by Tacitus in his story of the fire. This theory has the additional merit that it leaves us free to accept the Epistle for what it purports to be—a letter written by Silvanus on the instructions of Peter.

8

Not long after the outbreak of persecution in A.D. 64 Mark wrote his Gospel at Rome. His purpose was to provide a permanent record of the Jewish Christian Gospel of the apostles for a predominantly Gentile church, bereft now of apostolic guidance, but his book owes many of its secondary characteristics to the fact that it was addressed to a martyr church. To those who lived under the constant threat of suffering Mark declared that Jesus had been the Messiah, the Son of God, precisely because he had suffered,[2] and that he had called his disciples to carry the same cross, to drink

---

[1] Acts xxiii. 1; xxiv. 13–14.   [2] Mk. viii. 31; ix. 32; x. 33 f.

M

the same cup, to share the same baptism.[1] The Cross had won from the Gentile centurion the admission, " This man was truly son of God " ; [2] and the disciples could look forward to a like success as the result of their own suffering. The seed of the Gospel would bear abundant fruit in spite of all hindrance,[3] the light of the Gospel would not be hidden,[4] the trial of Christians before governors and kings was but an opportunity to testify to their faith, that the Gospel might be preached to all the world.[5] Behind the sombre realism of Mark's story there is a confidence in the ultimate triumph of the Christian cause which Nero's ferocities had not been able to subdue.

Only once is there any suggestion of recrimination against Rome. " When you see the Desecrating Horror standing where it ought not (let him who reads understand) then let them that are in Judaea flee to the mountains." [6] This saying has some literary connexion with Luke xxi. 20 : " When you see Jerusalem surrounded by armies, then know that her desolation has drawn near". There are two possible ways of explaining the relationship. If Luke was using Mark at this point, then he has recast the apocalyptic language of Jesus in order to show that the prophecy had been fulfilled in the destruction of Jerusalem.[7] But if Luke's eschatological passage was drawn from his independent source L, then Mark has wrapped up in apocalyptic imagery an explicit prophecy of the fall of Jerusalem.[8] Into this controversy we need not enter here, for in either case it is clear from Mark's parenthesis that he understood the prophecy to refer to events of his own day, of which it was dangerous to speak more openly; and those events included war in Judaea. This being so, we must suppose that Mark in some way identified the Horror of Daniel's prophecy with Rome.

Whoever Theophilus may have been, Luke's two books were manifestly written to commend the Gospel to the

---

[1] Mk. viii. 34; x. 38.   [2] Mk. xv. 39.   [3] Mk. iv. 1–20.
[4] Mk. iv. 21–22.   [5] Mk. xiii. 9–10.   [6] Mk. xiii. 14.
[7] See J. M. Creed, *The Gospel according to St. Luke*, ad loc.
[8] See V. Taylor, *Behind the Third Gospel*, pp. 109 ff. ; *The Gospel according to St. Mark*, pp. 511 f.

Roman reader, and his apologetic purpose reveals itself in two ways. Firstly, he shows that no Roman official had ever been able to find any fault with the Christian religion : Pilate had thrice pronounced Jesus innocent, Sergius Paulus had been attracted to Christianity, Gallio had dismissed the criminal charge which the Jews had brought against Paul, Claudius Lysias had reported to Felix in a similar vein, and Agrippa had declared to Festus that Paul could have been set at liberty if he had not appealed to Caesar.[1] Secondly, Luke is at some pains to show that Christianity is the true successor to Judaism, and ought therefore to receive from Rome the same toleration which Rome had always shown to the Jews. The tenor of Luke's writings fits exactly with the view we have put forward of the relations between church and state during the Flavian period : Christianity was a proscribed religion which needed defence, but the proscription was not so rigorously enforced as to make defence irrelevant.

9

The apocalyptic conception of the pagan world order, to which both Paul and Mark had made passing allusions, found its full expression in the vision of John of Patmos. Here Rome is represented by three successive symbols. First there is the city of this world—Vanity Fair—whose name is " Sodom and Egypt, where also our Lord was crucified ".[2] Sodom, whose name was the byword for unutterable vice ; Egypt, the first persecutor of the people of God ; Jerusalem, too blind to recognize her God when he came to her in the person of his Son ; all these have contributed to the character of the Great City, which will make holiday over the deaths of the saints. A more elaborate picture of Rome is given under the second symbol of the beast.[3] The beast rises from the sea, that epitome of all

---

[1] Lk. xxiii. 4, 14, 22; Acts xiii. 7 ff.; xviii. 12 ff.; xxiii. 26 ff.; xxvi. 32.
[2] Rev. xi. 8.
[3] Rev. xiii; it may be that the beast is the Antichrist, but the seven heads which are seven kings prove that John conceived the Antichrist to have historical embodiment in the Roman Empire.

that is hostile to the purposes of God : the chaotic deep
which God had cleft asunder by his creative word, the Red
Sea which God had cleft asunder to provide a passage for
his ransomed people, the sea of glass which stood in heaven
to bar man's access to the throne until a new Exodus should
call forth from the martyrs the song of Moses and the Lamb.[1]
The beast is a synthesis of all four beasts of Daniel's vision,
the final and total manifestation of pagan empire.[2] The
authority of the beast is derived from the dragon, " that
old serpent, called the Devil, and Satan ", and its title—
" who was and is not and is to come "—is a parody of the
title of God, whose worship the beast attempts to usurp.[3]
Finally, Rome is the great harlot, the city of vice and op-
pression, whose essential character is revealed as sheer
materialism, battening on the luxury trade of the whole
mercantile world.[4] The fall of Rome comes about by the
self-destructive power of evil, for the beast turns to rend the
harlot, who had been enthroned upon his back.[5]

Rome did not fall as quickly as John expected. Like a
true prophet he had seen the eternal principles governing
the contest between good and evil, which was being fought
out on the plane of history. Like a true prophet he had
seen the issues so clearly defined in black and white and the
final triumph of Christ so vividly assured, that the sands of
time seemed to be running out before his eyes. But Rome
was not yet ready to die of her own depravity.

---

[1] Rev. xiii. 1 ; cf. Gen. i. 2 ; Isa. li. 9 f. ; xxvii. 1 ; Rev. iv. 6 ; xv. 2 f. ;
xxi. 1.
[2] Rev. xiii. 1–2 ; cf. Dan. vii. 3–8.
[3] Rev. xvii. 8 ; cf. i. 4, 8 ; iv. 8 ; xi. 17.
[4] Rev. xvii–xviii.   [5] Rev. xvii. 16–18.

CHAPTER XII

THE COMING OF THE LORD

1

" I AM the Lord your God who brought you out of the land of Egypt, out of the house of bondage." This first sentence of the Decalogue expresses succinctly the two cardinal tenets of Old Testament faith. In the Exodus Yahweh had revealed himself as the Living God who acts in history, and he had chosen Israel to be his people, bound to him by a covenant of grace. Out of this experience was born the conviction that the future history of Israel would follow the pattern laid down by the creative act of God which had brought the nation into existence. The Exodus was a source of perpetual amazement not only to those who participated in it but to their descendants also; their God was the " great God of wonders ".[1]   He had made his ways known to Moses, and could therefore be relied on to perform acts of vindication and justice for all that were oppressed.[2]   He was " God their Saviour, who had done great things in Egypt, wondrous works in the land of Ham, terrible things by the Red Sea "; and he would continue to " command salvation for Jacob ".[3]

Every new act of God in history gave to the prophets the opportunity of deepening the twofold faith which had come down to them from the past, so that by the time of the Exile there had developed a mature belief that God was the Lord of all history, whose ways were mercy and truth, that he was working out a purpose which had man as its centre, and that the agent of that purpose was Israel. Almost every theological concept in the Old Testament in some way throws light on this central affirmation. God's word, for example, is both deed and speech, an outgoing activity which produces results in nature and history and a revelation of

[1] The word *niphlaoth* is used some forty times in the O.T. to describe the acts of God in creation and history.
[2] Ps. ciii. 6 f.   [3] Ps. cvi. 21–22; xliv. 4.

what those results are to be; "surely the Lord God will do
nothing, but he reveals his secret to his servants the
prophets".[1] The righteousness of God is no abstract
quality but an active power which achieves the chastisement
of the wicked and the redemption of the down-trodden.
Holiness and glory are more than eternal attributes of
deity; they are modes of divine revelation in the events of
time.[2] The convenant is the proclamation of God's gracious intentions towards Israel, and his covenant-love (*ḥesedh*)
is the loyalty with which he abides by his declared purpose.

Israel's faith arose out of history, and she looked to
history to justify it. But there were two ways in which
history regularly contradicted that faith. The pagan
nations did not recognize the sovereignty of Yahweh, but
oppressed Israel his servant; and Israel herself failed to be
a holy people, dedicated to the ways of God. Isaiah might
argue that Assyria was a rod in the hand of God for the
punishment of wayward Israel, and that the experience of
sin and judgment served to reveal a new aspect of God's
character. But this did not remove the whole contradiction : Israel failed to respond to discipline, and Assyria
was not content to have her imperial designs limited by the
educational purposes of God.[3] It was out of this conflict
between faith and fact that eschatology arose. For eschatology is the assertion that God's character cannot
change, and that his purpose cannot be frustrated inde-
finitely by creatures of flesh. "All flesh is grass, and all
its constancy is like the flower of the field . . . the grass
withers, the flower fades; but the word of our God shall
stand for ever."[4] God is the everlasting God, and he
will outlast all that resists his will. The day must come,

---

[1] Amos iii. 7.

[2] See especially the use of the niphals *niqdash* and *nikhbadh*, which should
be rendered as true reflexives: "he displays his holiness" or "he shows
himself holy"; "he displays his glory" (Lev. x. 3; Num. xx. 13; Isa.
v. 16; Ezek. xx. 41; xxviii. 22, 25; xxxvi. 23; xxxviii. 16; xxxix. 27;
and Exod. xiv. 4, 17, 18; Ezek. xxviii. 22; xxxix. 13).

[3] Isa. x. 5 ff.

[4] Isa. xl. 6–8; cf. Ps. ciii. 14–17. One symbol of this contrast is the
earthquake, which plays a prominent part in all eschatological writings and
represents "the removal of what is shakable . . . in order that what
cannot be shaken may remain" (Heb. xii. 27).

therefore, when the character of God will be fully revealed and his purpose fully realized.

Israel's belief in the Day of the Lord was thus an emphatic asseveration of her faith in God in the face of facts which cried out against her creed. It came into being not in the academic calm of theological discussion, but in a nation's wrestling with the mystery of iniquity. It is not surprising therefore that Israel never attained, nor sought to attain, consistency in her picture of the End. The character of the Day varied as one prophet after another tried to bring home to Israel different aspects of the divine nature and purpose. To a nation blinded by its own godlessness Amos declares that the Day of the Lord is darkness and not light.[1] But to the same nation broken by the suffering of the Exile the Day becomes a day of deliverance : " It is the day of the Lord's retribution, the year of recompenses for the controversy of Zion." [2] When Israel is in danger of losing in syncretism her distinctive revelation of God, the Day is represented as God's judgment on the idolatries and immoralities of paganism.[3] But when Israel turns in upon herself in nationalistic self-sufficiency, she must be reminded that God's salvation is to reach to the ends of the earth.[4] In each case the picture is different, not because the prophets were indulging in speculation about an unverifiable future, but because they were applying their knowledge of God to the pastoral necessities of the present.

In this respect apocalyptic eschatology was not fundamentally different from prophetic, in spite of an apparent increase in speculative thought. The apocalyptist faced a problem of evil which had grown beyond the limits of Israel's national scene to cosmic dimensions, and his solution had to be on a similar scale. Accordingly the Day of the Lord is represented as the climax of world history and is described in mythological terms.[5] But the purpose of apocalyptic writing was not philosophic but pastoral. The book of Daniel was written to provide spiritual strength for the

---

[1] Amos v. 18. [2] Isa. xxxiv. 8.
[3] Isa. xiii. 6–19. [4] Isa. xix. 23; xxvii. 13.
[5] " It was this fusion of myth and eschatology which produced what we call apocalyptic. In fact we may define apocalytic as the mythologizing of eschatology." S. B. Frost, *Old Testament Apocalyptic*, p. 33.

Jewish people during the persecutions of Antiochus Epiphanes, and the author of IV Ezra was agonizing over the spiritual problems created by the fall of Jerusalem. In each case the writer was concerned less with the future than with a present in which faith was beset by many a doubt.

The End is called by many names in the Old Testament. Sometimes it is " the Day of Yahweh ". Isaiah, Zechariah, and others refer to it as " the Day ". Jeremiah prefers the expression " days are coming ". In Lamentations and Ezekiel the phrase is sometimes " the Day ". Elsewhere it is " the issue of the days ". But all these are descriptions of the same divine event, which is conceived as being both final and imminent,[1] and it is of vital importance for our understanding of New Testament eschatology that we should do full justice both to the finality and to the imminence.[2]

2

The key to the understanding of this aspect of eschatology is to be found in a characteristic mode of Hebrew thought which may best be described as the telescoping of time. Three good illustrations may be drawn from the ceremonies of Israelite worship. In Deuteronomy xxvi. 1–11 a liturgy

---

[1] E.g. Isa. xiii. 6; lx. 22; Joel i. 15; ii. 1; Obad. 15; Zeph. i. 14; Dan. xii. 11. " The issue of the days " is a partial exception; it is sometimes used in a more limited sense " denoting the final period of the future so far as it falls within the range of the speaker's perspective ". S. R. Driver on Deut. iv. 30. For the finality of the Day of Yahweh see A. B. Davidson in H.D.B. I. p. 736.

[2] We must beware at this point of reading back into the O.T. distinctions which Hebrew writers had neither the linguistic nor the philosophic equipment to make. The distinction between *kairos* (time considered in relation to actions and purposes) and *chronos* (chronological or clock time) is valuable for the modern philosopher (see John Marsh, *The Fulness of Time*, pp. 19 ff. and J. A. T. Robinson, *In the End God . . .* pp. 44 ff.) but misleading for the biblical exegete. Marsh recognizes that Hebrew has no word for *chronos*, but thinks that the N.T. writers observed the distinction between the two terms—a thesis which is hard to defend in face of a comparison between Acts iii. 19 and 21; Mk. i. 15 and Gal. iv. 4; I Pet. i. 5, 20 and Jud. 18. Marsh's translation of Acts i. 7 (p. 119)—" it is not for you to know the epochs of history [*kairoi*] nor yet how long they will last [*chronoi*] " involves an inversion of the Greek and overlooks the source of the phrase in Dan. ii. 21 and iv. 34, where no such interpretation is possible. In the LXX the distinction between *kairos* and *chronos* is purely temporal and non-theological : *kairos* means a point of time at which something happens, *chronos* (which is rare) means a period of time; but even this distinction is not always maintained.

is provided for the offering of the firstfruits, in which the worshipper says : " A wandering Aramaean was my father, and he went down into Egypt and sojourned there, few in number; and there he became a nation, great, mighty, and populous : and the Egyptians ill-treated us, and afflicted us, and laid on us hard bondage; and we cried to the Lord . . . and the Lord brought us forth out of Egypt." There is more involved in this passage than the concept of corporate personality, whereby the Israelite of later times could be deemed to have taken part in the Exodus because " he was still in the loins of his ancestor ".[1] In the act of worship the Israelite was to make a positive identification of himself with the Exodus generation, so that God's past salvation should become to him a present reality. Similarly in the liturgy provided for the Passover the head of the household was to say : " It is because of that which the Lord did for me when I came forth out of Egypt ".[2] In the annual celebration of the Passover the Exodus became not merely a vivid memory from the distant past but a perpetually contemporary event. But if the past could be brought thus into the present, so could the future. In Psalms xciii, xcv-xcix it is generally agreed that we have part of a liturgy for a coronation feast of Yahweh. For our present purpose it matters little whether the festival was the New Year [3] or the Sabbath.[4] The psalm cycle moves from a declaration of God's mighty acts in creation and redemption to the future coming of the Lord as Saviour and Judge. Past and future meet at the point which is called Today,[5] and the festival thus becomes a present assertion of the ultimate sovereignty of God—" Say among the nations, The Lord reigns." [6] The enthronement of God at the

---

[1] Heb. vii. 10.

[2] Exod. xiii. 8. For later Jewish developments of this theme see W. D. Davies, *St. Paul and Rabbinic Judaism*, pp. 102 ff.

[3] S. Mowinckel, *Psalmenstudien* II.

[4] N. H. Snaith, *The Jewish New Year Festival*, pp. 195 ff.   [5] Ps. xcv. 7.

[6] Ps. xcvi. 10. This telescoping of time is facilitated by the structure of the Hebrew verb, which has no past, present, and future tenses. The Hebrew perfect can express a completed action in past, present, or future, and the time has to be determined from the context. There is no means of telling whether the sentence *malakh Yahweh* (the Lord reigns), taken by itself, refers to past, present, or future, and in the context of the coronation psalms it certainly refers to all three.

creation, his proclamation as King at Sinai, and the future coming of his eschatological kingdom are all gathered into one in a single ceremonial act.

This interpenetration of past, present, and future is the Old Testament's way of describing the relationship between time and eternity. The eternal God is not the changeless reality of the Greek philosophers, of which the temporal world is but a moving shadow. He is the First and the Last, who makes himself known in the events of time. His former acts do not belong to a lost past nor his last acts to an inscrutable future; for by remembrance men may inhabit God's past, and by faith they may lay hold on God's future.

S. B. Frost has reminded us that the prophets expected their prophecies to be fulfilled in two different ways.[1] They predicted the coming of historic events which would happen as part of a chain of cause and effect, and they also looked forward to an eschatological event which would impinge upon history from without. But the historic fulfilment was always seen in relation to the eschatological fulfilment, and in the prophet's vision the one tended to merge into the other. Thus Jeremiah's prediction of the Scythian invasion merges into a vision of the return of chaos,[2] and Joel's prophecy of a locust invasion fades into a description of the Last Judgment. Any crisis in which God confronted man with an urgent decision was liable to present itself as the Crisis. This did not mean that the temporal succession of events could be disregarded. God's purpose must move towards an End; but the End was repeatedly at hand, because the End was God.[3]

The prophet was peculiarly well qualified by his prophetic vision to appreciate this telescoping of time. To him God was more vividly real than all the obstacles that man could put in the way of God's purpose. " The Lord of hosts has sworn, Surely as I have planned, so shall it come to pass; and as I have purposed, so shall it stand . . . For the Lord

---

[1] Op. cit. pp. 46–56.　　　　[2] Jer. iv. 23–26.

[3] " To view the world *sub specie aeternitatis* is to view it *sub specie finis* . . . to see in history the hand of the eternal is to see in history the mark of the *eschaton*." J. A. T. Robinson, op. cit., p. 36.

of hosts has purposed, and who shall annul it? His hand is stretched out, and who shall turn it back?"[1] The prophet was aware, too, that God was demanding from man an immediate response to his word. "Seek the Lord . . . it may be that you will be hidden in the day of the Lord's anger."[2] Thus a prediction of an imminent Day of the Lord, however literally the prophet may have intended it, was a means of expressing utter confidence in the triumph of God's cause and the urgency of the present moment in which man must face the ultimate issues of life.

Round the expectation of the Day of the Lord there gathered a cluster of associated ideas. It was the day when God the King would assert his sovereignty over all the earth. Because he was "a just God and a Saviour", his reign would mean both judgment and salvation. He who had overwhelmed Egypt with plagues to bring about the release of his captive people would send his judgments into all the earth, that out of this final cataclysm there might emerge a redeemed and purified Israel. With this new Israel the God of Sinai would make a new convenant; and into the covenant people would come not only the righteous living but also the righteous dead, restored to life by a resurrection. Because God had promised to David, his anointed, that there should not fail a prince to sit upon his throne, he would raise up an anointed Son of David to rule over the age to come. And because he was the giver of life, the new age would see the outpouring of his spirit upon all flesh.

3

Any study of Jesus' teaching about the future must begin with what C. H. Dodd has called "realized eschatology". Dodd has pointed out that Jesus began his ministry with a proclamation that God's sovereign rule had arrived.[3] The decisive act of God foretold by all the prophets had now been

---

[1] Isa. xiv. 24–27; cf. Isa. xliii. 13; xlvi. 11–13; lv. 10–12; lx. 12.
[2] Zeph. ii. 3; cf. Joel ii. 11–12.
[3] Mk. i. 15; Mt. x. 7; xii. 28; Lk. x. 9; xi. 20. On the Aramaic background of these sayings see the note by M. Black in the *Expository Times*, lxiii (1952), pp. 289–290.

initiated, and had brought with it both salvation and judgment. In some sense the *eschaton* had entered into present
experience. Up to this point the argument is unassailable.
But Dodd goes on to claim that in the mind of Jesus this
entry of the *eschaton* into history was such as to preclude
any final denouement of history. " Jesus declares that this
ultimate, the Kingdom of God, has come into history, and
He takes upon Himself the ' eschatological ' role of ' Son
of Man '. The absolute, the ' wholly other ', has entered
into time and space. . . . The historical order however
cannot contain the whole meaning of the absolute. The
imagery [sc. of eschatology] therefore retains its significance
as symbolizing the eternal realities, which though they
enter into history are never exhausted in it. The Son of
Man has come, but also He will come; the sin of man is
judged, but also it will be judged. But these future tenses
are only an accommodation of language. There is no
coming of the Son of Man ' after ' His coming in Galilee
and Jerusalem, whether soon or late, for there is no before
and after in the eternal order." [1] In support of his thesis
Dodd then tries to show that all the parables of Jesus, and
particularly the parables of crisis, were originally intended
to apply to the historic crisis of the ministry, but that they
were recast so as to have a reference to a second coming of
Christ, because the early Christians misunderstood the
" realized eschatology " of Jesus and, finding that world
history continued after Pentecost, reconstructed a " futurist
eschatology " out of Jewish tradition.

This second part of Dodd's argument has evoked much
criticism. The phrase " realized eschatology " has been
attacked as a contradiction in terms. It has been said
with some justice that, although the disciples of Jesus
certainly misunderstood some of the things he said, any
theory which presupposes a wholesale misunderstanding
must be regarded with suspicion. The majority of the
New Testament writers show a firm grasp of the " realized
eschatology " of Jesus, but still look forward to a Parousia.
Mark and Luke were certainly aware that the parables of

[1] *The Parables of the Kingdom*, pp. 107 ff.

Jesus applied in the first instance to the historical situation in which they were uttered, but they took them to have a general application as well.[1] But underlying these comments there is the more serious question whether we ought to attribute to Jesus a conception of eternity which is unbiblical. "The absolute" and "the timeless" are categories of thought foreign to the Hebraic mind, and therefore foreign to eschatology which is the creation of the Hebraic mind. If we are to speak of eschatology at all in connexion with the ministry of Jesus, we must say that the coming of the Kingdom in his ministry was not the irruption into time of that which is timeless but the entry into the present of that which in its essence is future and final. The Kingdom had come, yet the disciples must pray for its coming. The prophecies of Israel's humiliation and glory were fulfilled in the vicarious suffering and triumph of Jesus, the Son of Man, but this representative fulfilment was meaningless without the further promise of a real ingathering of the people of God.[2]

In spite of the great emphasis on fulfilment, then, we cannot banish the element of futurity from the eschatology of Jesus. Like the prophets before him Jesus expected two types of event. He looked forward to an historic crisis which would mean for himself suffering and subsequent vindication, for his disciples persecution, for Jerusalem disaster. But his view of the historic future merged into a vision of the absolute future, and he regarded these historic events as eschatological events in so far as they were embodiments or expressions of the final Crisis. In this proleptic sense the Day of the Son of Man was always at hand and the disciples must always be on the watch for it.[3] But Jesus clearly indicated that in its final manifestation the Day was known only to God, not because God had fixed a date which he guarded as a close secret, but because the coming of the Day was contingent upon the full realization of the purposes of God.[4]

[1] Mk. xiii. 37; Lk. xii. 41.
[2] Mt. viii. 11; Lk. xiii. 29.
[3] Mk. xiii. 33–37.
[4] Mk. xiii. 22; cf. Acts i. 7.

4

We have already seen in a previous chapter that the early Christians believed themselves to be living in the age of fulfilment. Jesus had proclaimed the arrival of God's sovereign rule. He had mediated to men God's salvation. He had chosen twelve disciples to be the nucleus of the new Israel, they had confessed him Messiah, and with them he had entered into a new covenant. They had been eye-witnesses of his Resurrection, and upon them he had poured out the gift of his Spirit. All this could mean only one thing—that the last days had set in.[1]

It is probable that from the first the Christians expected the last days to be of short duration, but this does not necessarily mean that the future hope occupied the forefront of their minds. E. F. Scott has spoken of " that early period when the Christian mind was wholly possessed with forebodings of the end ".[2] T. W. Manson says that " the Early Church was certainly obsessed by the idea of the imminent return of the Lord ".[3] This is surely to go some-what beyond the evidence. In the primitive preaching, as it is represented in the speeches of Acts, this item of the creed is mentioned only twice, and in neither case is there any word of the shortness of the time.[4] As in the Old Testament, so also in the New, the surest guide to the under-standing of eschatology is to be found in worship, and in the Lord's Supper we have an excellent example of the tele-scoping of time, whereby past and future become contem-porary in the present rite, which is both a memorial of the death of Christ and an anticipation of the messianic banquet. Week by week the prayer *Maranatha* (Our Lord, come) was answered in the eucharistic presence of him who had come in the guise of a servant and would come again in the glory

---

[1] Acts ii. 17; I Cor. x. 11; Heb. i. 2; I Pet. i. 20; cf. I Cor. vii. 26, where the correct translation is " in view of the present distress ", i.e. the eschatological woes which have already begun (see E. De W. Burton, *The Epistle to the Galatians*, pp. 432 f.).
[2] *Varieties of New Testament Religion*, p. 165.
[3] *The Teaching of Jesus*, p. 260.
[4] Acts iii. 20 f.; x. 42.

of his Father.[1]   Thus the centre of interest in these early days was fellowship with the risen and regnant Christ.

This threefold character of the Christian religion as it appears in the Lord's Supper may be regarded as the permanent framework of New Testament thought.   Salvation is always a past fact,[2] a present experience,[3] and a future hope.[4]   This pattern is particularly evident in the Epistle to the Hebrews, where we are told repeatedly that the redeeming work of Christ has been acccomplished "once for all "; [5] but the word of the Gospel becomes operative only when it is "mixed with faith in those who hear it ", and faith is defined as "the present possession of the things we hope for ", a tasting of "the powers of the age to come ".[6] "Christ was once offered to bear the sins of many, and he will appear a second time, not to deal with sin, but to save those who are eagerly expecting him."   But the past and future comings meet in the moment of grace and opportunity which is called Today.[7]   For "Jesus Christ is the same yesterday, today, and for ever ".[8]

As time went on, however, this primitive eschatology with its centre in the present was modified by a number of conflicting influences.   The Gospel was carried to the Gentiles who tended to take literally the eschatological language in which it was expressed.   A series of events occurred which directed attention to the final crisis of history.   And all the while the new Christian faith was producing an eschatology of its own, in which the revelation that had come in Christ was profoundly altering the traditional hope of the Jews.

---

[1] "Past, present and future are indissolubly united in the sacrament. It may be regarded as a dramatization of the advent of the Lord, which is at once His remembered coming in humiliation and His desired coming in glory, both realized in His true presence in the sacrament."   C. H. Dodd, *The Apostolic Preaching*, p. 234; cf. *The Parables of the Kingdom*, pp. 203 f.; and "The Sacrament of the Lord's Supper in the New Testament " (in *Christian Worship*, ed. N. Micklem), pp. 68 ff.

[2] I Cor. vi. 20;   vii. 23;   I Pet. i. 18;   Rev. v. 9;   xii. 10.

[3] I Cor. i. 18;   II Cor. ii. 15;   vi. 2;   Phil. ii. 12;   I Pet. i. 9.

[4] Rom. v. 9;   viii. 23;   xiii. 11;   I Cor. v. 5;   I Pet. i. 5.

[5] Heb. vii. 27;   ix. 12;   x. 10.

[6] Heb. iv. 2;   xi. 1;   vi. 5.

[7] Heb. ix. 28;   iii. 13;   cf. II Cor. vi. 2.

[8] Heb. xiii. 8.

5

We have already seen that the Greek mind found great difficulty in apprehending the biblical doctrine of history and in particular the biblical eschatology. To the predominantly Gentile church of Thessalonica the proximity of the Parousia constituted a problem so great that Paul had to write twice in quick succession to deal with it. In his first letter Paul declared that the Day of the Lord would come without warning and might come at any moment; in his second letter he warned his readers not to get excited, because the Day would not come immediately. "The Day of the Lord will come as a thief in the night . . . that Day will not come unless the rebellion comes first." [1] Some modern scholars have been so perturbed by this apparent contradiction that they have denied the authenticity of II Thessalonians, and no doubt the Gentiles of Thessalonica were equally perturbed. But we find precisely the same juxtaposition of ideas in Mark xiii, and Mark was seemingly untroubled by any sense of incongruity. We must therefore reckon with the possibility that the Jew was able to take in his stride paradoxes which have perplexed Gentiles ancient and modern. Where we should make a guarded statement, the Semitic mind prefers to throw together two extreme statements and allow the one to qualify the other. The prophets repeatedly declare God's irrevocable judgment on human sin, and almost in the same breath call on men to repent before it is too late.[2] Jesus tells his disciples that they must love their neighbours but hate their father and mother. Paul can say that salvation "is not of man's willing or running but of God's mercy", and in the following chapter lay the blame for the rejection of the Jews at their own door because "they have not all obeyed the Gospel".[3] Doubtless all these pairs of statements can be reconciled by those who are interested in precise logic, but the point is

---

[1] I Thess. v. 2; II Thess. ii. 3.
[2] "Many things were foretold precisely that they might not come to pass." J. Paterson, *The Goodly Fellowship of the Prophets*, p. 6.
[3] Rom. ix. 16; x. 16.

that the Hebrew mind never felt the necessity of reconciling them.[1] Thus Paul and Mark (and perhaps we should add, Jesus himself) were content to say : " The End is at hand ; the End will not come until God is ready for it," and to leave it at that.

Throughout the apostolic age events were continually happening which, either in the traditional thought of Judaism or in the teaching of Jesus, had been given eschatological significance, and these events inevitably heightened the general feeling of expectancy. Caligula's threat to set up his statue in the temple at Jerusalem suggested that Daniel's prophecy of a " Desecrating Horror " was in process of fulfilment.[2] Wars and rumours of wars in Palestine made it seem to Paul as if the wrath of God was at last descending on the children of disobedience.[3] The outbreak of persecution was taken to be the first stage of the Judgment, beginning " at the household of God ".[4] The fall of Jerusalem was the signal that the great marriage feast of Christ was about to begin.[5] Domitian's demand for worship was the rise of Antichrist against the Kingdom of God.[6]

Most of the passages in the New Testament which speak of an imminent Parousia are bound up with one or other of these crises. Yet even so, these events had only a limited influence on Christian thinking. The further Caligula slips into the background of his thought, the less Paul has to say about the proximity of the End. The fall of Jerusalem impressed Matthew as one of the signs of the Lord's coming, but it had exactly the opposite effect on Luke, who records two warnings against those who suppose that the Kingdom is about to appear,[7] and interposes between the fall of

---

[1] On this cast of thought in the modern Arab see T. E. Lawrence, *Seven Pillars of Wisdom*, Ch. III : " This people was black and white, not only in vision, but by inmost furnishing : black and white not merely in clarity, but in apposition. Their thoughts were at ease only in extremes. They inhabited superlatives by choice. Sometimes inconsistents seemed to possess them at once in joint sway ; but they never compromised : they pursued the logic of several incompatible opinions to absurd ends, without perceiving the incongruity. With cool head and tranquil judgment, imperturbably unconscious of the flight, they oscillated from asymptote to asymptote."

[2] II Thess. ii. 1–12.   [3] I Thess. i. 16.   [4] I Pet. iv. 17.
[5] Mt. xxii. 7.   [6] Rev. xiii   [7] Lk. xix. 11 ; xxi. 8.

N

Jerusalem and the Day of the Son of Man an indeterminate period called " the seasons of the Gentiles ".[1]

The influence of these eschatological events on the Christian conception of the future was largely offset by the progress of the Gentile mission, which committed the church to an evangelistic task of unforeseeable dimensions. According to the most probable interpretation of I Peter i. 10–12, Christian prophets were concentrating their energies on ascertaining the date and circumstances of the Parousia, when a revelation came to them that the Gospel of salvation must first be preached to the Gentiles. In the Epistle to the Ephesians the same divine purpose is expounded to such effect that the Parousia drops out of sight altogether. And in Mark's Gospel a catalogue of eschatological events, leading up to the coming of the Son of Man, is interrupted by the warning : " The Gospel must first be preached to all nations ".[2]

6

It has sometimes been suggested that the Christians of the apostolic age turned their minds from the present experience of salvation to a future hope because they saw that not all the Old Testament prophecies had been fulfilled. No doubt there is an element of truth in this. But the Advent hope is never merely a repository for unfulfilled prophecies. It is rather, in the words of W. Manson, " the reassertion in Christianity of the eschatological impulse, the same impulse which in the older days raised men's eyes from sin to grace but now operates in Christianity to raise men's eyes from grace to glory ".[3] As the Exodus faith, confronted by the facts of pagan hostility and Israel's disobedience, gave rise to Old Testament eschatology, so the Resurrection faith, confronted by the facts of Christian imperfection and an unbelieving world, generated its own distinctively Christian eschatology. Because God had been at work in the events of the Gospel story, the Day of

[1] Lk. xxi. 24.   [2] Mk. xiii. 10.
[3] " Eschatology in the New Testament ", *Scottish Journal of Theology*, Occasional Papers No. 2, p. 6.

the Lord could now be redefined as the coming, the appearing, or the manifestation of Jesus, when all that had been apprehended by faith would be revealed to open sight. Because Jesus had been exalted to the right hand of God, it could now be affirmed that he must reign until he had put all his enemies under his feet.[1] Because he had died and risen as the inclusive representative of the new Israel, in whom the whole people of God had passed from death to life, his final triumph would be the signal for all the sons of God to appear with him in glory.[2]

Like the eschatology of the prophets, the eschatology of the apostles was primarily pastoral in its intention, and varied with the circumstances that called it forth. Thus Paul found himself called upon to minister to a Greek world which shrank in horror from the all-pervading decay of the natural order. His own experience of bodily weakness had engendered in him an intense sympathy with this Greek obsession, and so enabled him to meet the needs of his converts by erecting on the Resurrection faith an eschatology of bodily redemption which included all Nature in its scope.[3] The Revelation, for all its mystifying symbolism, is essentially a work of pastoral eschatology, written to assure Christians under an immediate threat of persecution that redemptive love is on the throne of the universe and that the scroll of the world's destiny is in the hands of Christ. There are times when John's apocalyptic imagery seems to escape the control of his central vision of Christ as the Lion of the tribe of Judah who is also the sacrificial Lamb, and we are compelled to wonder whether the power which vanquishes Satan is really the power of the Cross. But the dominant impression of the book is that the Christian can face the End with perfect confidence because the End is Christ.

The extent to which the historic revelation dominated the Christian view of the future is clearly to be seen in the Epistle to the Hebrews. The author writes under a sense

[1] I Cor. xv. 25; Heb. x. 37.
[2] Rom. vi. 5; viii. 17–19; Col. iii. 4; II Tim. iv. 8; I Pet. v. 4; I Jn. iii. 2.
[3] Rom. viii. 18–23

of overwhelming urgency, yet he derives this urgency not from his belief in the nearness of the Parousia but from the finality of the word which God has spoken in Jesus Christ. For those who disobeyed God's Law there remained a promise of future salvation, but for those who neglect God's salvation there remains only the certainty of judgment.[1] Christ will appear again, but only to consummate his work of redemption " for those who are eagerly expecting him ".[2] For those who commit apostacy the Epistle holds out no hope of a second repentance.[3]

> What more can he say than to you he hath said,
> You who unto Jesus for refuge have fled ?

In the Fourth Gospel the End is so wholly identified with Christ that eschatology is transposed into Christology. The evangelist takes one by one the terms which were traditionally associated with the Last Day, and shows how they have found their complete embodiment in the incarnate life of Christ. He is the Light of the world, in whose presence all men stand already before the judgment seat of God.[4] He is the Life, and to believe in him is to pass from death to life eternal.[5] He is the Resurrection, through whom death loses all its power.[6] He is the incarnate Word : in him the eternal purpose of God is both revealed and achieved. The Word goes forth from God and does not return to him void : " I have accomplished the work which thou gavest me to do." [7]

This is the logical conclusion of the process which began when Jesus said : " The time is fulfilled ". God alone is the First and the Last, and to say that the ministry of Jesus was an eschatological event is to say that God was in Christ. But John is not simply making exalted claims on Christ's behalf ; he is allowing the revelation of God in Jesus Christ to remint the currency of Christian speech, and nowhere is this more evident than in his use of the word glory. Since the time of Ezekiel glory had been a popular eschatological term to denote the radiant splendour of the divine presence,

---

[1] Heb. ii. 1.　　　　[2] Heb. ix. 28.　　　[3]Heb. vi. 3–6; xii. 17.
[4] Jn. viii. 12; iii. 19; xii. 31.
[5] Jn. xi. 25; xiv. 6; v. 24.　　[6] Jn. xi. 25.　　[7] Jn. xvii. 4.

which would be revealed on the Day of the Lord, and then imparted to God's people. It had become part of the primitive Christian tradition that the Jesus who had been known to men in his humiliation had now entered his divine glory, and would come again in the glory of the Father. It was necessary that he should first suffer and so enter his glory; and those who shared his suffering would also share his glory.[1] But for John the humiliation of Jesus is his glory, and his glorification is the Cross.[2] For over against the spurious glories on which the world sets its heart John sees the one true glory, which is the Father's redemptive love. This glory Jesus manifests in his life and supremely in his death, for throughout his ministry he loved his own and on the Cross he loved them to the end.[3] The only glory which Jesus ever sought for himself or offered to his disciples was to be caught up into God's redemptive purpose. John still looked forward to the Last Day, believed it to be near, and knew not what it would bring.[4] But it could bring with it nothing that had not been revealed when Jesus proclaimed that redemptive love had attained its end. "It is accomplished."[5] That for John was the kingdom, the power, and the glory for ever and ever.

[1] Lk. xxiv. 26; Rom. viii. 17.
[2] Jn. vii. 39; xi. 4; xii. 16; 23; xiii. 31 f.; xvii. 1, 5; cf. iii. 14; viii. 28; xii 32.
[3] Jn. iii. 16; xiii. 1.
[4] Jn. vi. 39 f., 44, 54; xii, 48; I Jn. ii. 18; iii. 2.
[5] Jn. xix. 30.

APPENDIX A

THE CHRONOLOGY OF THE APOSTOLIC AGE

1

THROUGHOUT the foregoing chapters every problem of chronology has been consistently and deliberately evaded, not because dates are unimportant, but because in the present state of New Testament studies the evidence is so equivocal and the assured results so meagre, that it is better for the student of the period to be acquainted with the difficulties than to be provided with a ready-made solution in which all awkward facts are conveniently ignored.

The standard work on this subject in English is still C. H. Turner's article in Hasting's *Dictionary of the Bible*, written over fifty years ago, but since he wrote there have been three developments which have rendered almost all of his conclusions invalid. The discovery of the Gallio inscription at Delphi has provided a fixed date in Paul's career; P. N. Harrison's work on the Pastoral Epistles has proved that the theory of a second imprisonment of Paul in Rome is without foundation; and Lightfoot's identification of the conferences of Galatians ii. 1–10 and Acts xv, which Turner accepted without question, has come under attack from many sides. By these changes the older systems of chronology have been demolished, and unfortunately we are not yet in a position to put in their place a new system which could command anything like universal assent.

The few events in the New Testament which are dated at all are dated relatively to other events. To reach an absolute system of chronology we have to start with those events to which a fixed date can be assigned from Roman or Jewish sources. With the exception of the Crucifixion, which occurred in either A.D. 29 or 30, not a single event mentioned in the Epistles can be dated in this way. Of the events described in Acts only five can be dated, and some uncertainty attaches to two of the dates.

The death of Herod Agrippa (Acts xii. 23): A.D. 44

The famine in the reign of Claudius (Acts xi. 28): A.D. 46

The edict of Claudius against the Jews (Acts xviii. 2): A.D. 49 or 50.[1]

The arrival of Gallio in Corinth (Acts xviii. 12): A.D. 51.[2]

The arrival of Festus in Caesarea (Acts xxiv. 27): A.D. 59.[3]

2

The task of filling in this framework from Acts and the Pauline Epistles is beset with frustrations. The first half of Acts contains few chronological data, and it is difficult to know how the events there recorded are to be distributed throughout the initial twenty years of the church's history.[4] In the second half of Acts there are many notes of time, but, while some of them are precise, others are tantalizingly vague. Thus we are told that Paul had been eighteen months in Corinth when he was brought before Gallio, and that afterwards he remained " yet a good while ".[5] Moreover, a comparison with the Epistles shows that Luke's account of Paul's missionary work has some serious gaps in it. At what point in Luke's narrative, for example, are we to place Paul's preaching in Illyricum ?[6]

Some of the gaps in Luke's information can be supplied

[1] This date is given by Orosius (vii. 6. 15), who cites Josephus as his authority, though no mention appears in the known works of Josephus. Dio Cassius (lx. 6. 6) seems to place the edict in A.D. 41.

[2] See A. Deissmann, *St. Paul*, pp. 235–260. The year 52 is a possible but improbable alternative.

[3] See W. M. Ramsay, *Pauline and Other Studies*, pp. 349–360. Ramsay's arguments are persuasive, but it is possible that Festus' arrival should be placed a year earlier. A later date is extremely improbable, for Festus died during the year A.D. 60–61.

[4] Luke must, however, be acquitted of the charge of having confused the order of events. The grounds for this charge are that Luke records the famine of 46 in the chapter before he records the death of Herod in 44. What Luke in fact does is to record Agabus' prophecy of the famine, and to remark in passing that, when the prophecy came true in the reign of Claudius (is it implied that the prophecy was given in an earlier reign ?), the church of Antioch was ready to act for the prompt relief of the Jerusalem church. Luke was well aware that the visit of Paul and Barnabas to Jerusalem took place after the death of Herod, and he records their return in due order (xii. 25). It would seem, therefore, that the endless conjectural rearrangements of Luke's material, based on the assumption that he was a careless and uncritical editor, are without justification.

[5] Acts xviii. 11, 18.   [6] Rom. xv. 19.

from the Epistles, but not all of Paul's statements can be taken at their face value. We cannot, for instance, assume that Paul actually left Ephesus at the feast of Pentecost which followed immediately on the writing of I Corinthians. He expressed his intention of doing so,[1] but immediately afterwards there occurred a series of events which compelled him to revise his plans. He had to make a flying visit to Corinth,[2] which was followed by the writing of another letter.[3] Then came a mysterious trouble, during the course of which Paul despaired of life.[4] As a result of all this he was accused of fickleness for not abiding by his original intentions.[5] What seemed to be a helpful piece of evidence thus turns out to be of little value.

3

The arrival of Gallio in Corinth provides us with a fixed point from which to reckon both backwards and forwards. But as soon as we begin to work backwards, we are confronted with the apparently insoluble problem of Paul's visits to Jerusalem. The evidence is contained in Galatians i–ii and Acts; each source presents several serious exegetical difficulties, and a third set of difficulties arises when we attempt to put the two accounts together.

In Galatians Paul describes one visit to Jerusalem three years after his conversion, when he met Peter and James, and another after fourteen years, when he went up with Barnabas and Titus and had a discussion with James, Peter, and John concerning the admission of the Gentiles to the church. This was followed by another meeting with Peter at Antioch, when there was an altercation about table fellowship between Jewish and Gentile Christians. But did the second visit take place fourteen years after Paul's conversion or fourteen years after his first visit? On that occasion was Titus actually circumcised or not?[6] At

---

[1] I Cor. xvi. 8.   [2] II Cor. xiii. 1.   [3] II Cor. ii. 4; vii. 8.
[4] II Cor. i. 8.   [5] II Cor. i. 17.
[6] "Who can doubt that it was the knife which really did circumcise Titus that has cut the syntax of Gal. ii. 3–5 to pieces?" F. C. Burkitt, *Christian Beginnings*, p. 118. But questions of this sort are not settled by an epigram.

what point in the series of events are we to place the Galatian mission ? And at what point in Paul's career was the Epistle written ?

Acts mentions five occasions when Paul visited Jerusalem, and the description of the third visit on the occasion of the apostolic conference is full of difficulties. First there is a textual problem. The conference decided to send a letter to the Gentile Christians asking them to refrain from certain practices,[1] but the list of practices is given differently in three different manuscript traditions : (a) the Alexandrian text has " from pollutions of idols and from fornication and from what is strangled and from blood "; (b) the Western text omits " and from what is strangled " and (in some forms) adds a negative version of the golden rule, thus making the whole requirement moral rather than ritual; (c) P[45] (Chester Beatty) omits " and from fornication ", thus making the requirement purely ceremonial. The majority of modern scholars prefer either the first or the third of these readings,[2] and are at once confronted with a further problem. Acts xv begins with a demand, made by some converted Pharisees, that circumcision be made a condition of church membership; but the chapter ends with a letter which has to do with table fellowship between Jewish and Gentile Christians. Did a single conference begin with the one theme and end with the other, or were there really two conferences ? If so, was Paul present at both ? For at a later date James informs Paul of the contents of the apostolic letter as though the decision had been taken in Paul's absence.[3] We are told that Paul delivered the decree to the Galatian churches, yet the decree itself was addressed only to the churches of Antioch, Syria, and Cilicia.[4]

The ambiguities and inconsistencies of Galatians and Acts make it a formidable task to correlate the evidence of the two books. To simplify the problem as far as

---

[1] Acts xv. 20, 29; cf. xxi. 25.
[2] For a detailed discussion see C. S. C. Williams, *Alterations to the Text of the Synoptic Gospels and Acts*, pp. 72–75.
[3] Acts xxi. 25.
[4] Acts xv. 23; xvi. 4.

possible let us label Paul's recorded visits to Jerusalem as follows :

A 1　Acts ix. 26–30.	G 1　Gal. i. 18–24.
A 2　Acts xi. 30 & xii. 25.	G 2　Gal. ii. 1–10.
A 3　Acts xv. 1–30.	
A 4　Acts xviii. 22.	
A 5　Acts xxi. 17 ff.	

G 1 may with reasonable confidence be identified with A 1. But with which visit in Acts are we to identify G 2 ? Answers to this question fall into five main types.

I. G 2 = A 3.

In support of this theory Lightfoot [1] argued that the geography of the two visits is the same—Antioch and Jerusalem ; that the persons are the same—Paul and Barnabas, attended by Titus, or, as Luke has it, " certain other Gentiles ", and on the other side James and Peter ; the subject of the dispute is the same—the circumcision of the Gentile Christians ; and the result is the same—the exemption of the Gentiles from the Law. According to Lightfoot, Paul in Galatians does not mention A 2 because he was concerned to enumerate only his contacts with the apostles, and on that occasion all the apostles were absent from Jerusalem, so that the embassy from Antioch was received only by " the elders ". The apostolic decree was not mentioned by Paul because it was intended only as a temporary expedient for the churches already in existence.

At almost every point this argument is open to question. The explanation of Paul's silence about his second visit to Jerusalem is thin ; where so much was at stake it would have cost him nothing to explain that this visit gave him no opportunity to meet the apostles, if this had indeed been the case.　The persons involved in the two conferences were

---

[1] *The Epistle to the Galatians*, pp. 123–128. Lightfoot's treatment of the problem was complicated by his adherence to the " North Galatian " theory, which has now been generally abandoned. But his arguments are largely independent of this complication.

not the same : Acts describes a public meeting of the whole Jerusalem church, but Paul asserts that he insisted on keeping the discussion private. The subject under discussion was not the same : the conference of G 2 concerned the admission of Gentiles to the church, but the pastoral letter of A 3 lays down the terms of table fellowship between Jewish and Gentile Christians. The result was not the same : Paul declares that no obligation was laid upon the Gentile mission except that they remember the poor, but in Acts the Gentile Christians are asked to observe certain ceremonial regulations. There is also the evidence of Galatians ii. 11 ff. : the controversy at Antioch over table fellowship must have happened after G 2, but it is scarcely credible that it should have happened after A 3. For in that case, within a year of the agreement at Jerusalem James must have gone back on the decision of the conference and persuaded both Peter and Barnabas to do the same.

In view of all these discrepancies we cannot identify the two conferences without seriously impugning the accuracy of either Paul or Luke; and since Paul is writing within a few years of the event and vouches for his version with an oath, it follows that Luke's narrative must be regarded as almost total fiction. This first theory, therefore, turns out to be a most desperate device.

II. G 2 = A 2 = A 3.

This theory [1] is based on the assumption that Luke drew his material from various sources. From his Antioch source he learnt that Paul visited Jerusalem with the famine fund; from his Jerusalem source he learnt that Paul was in Jerusalem for the apostolic conference; and he failed to realize that these were two accounts of the same visit. We thus eliminate one of the objections to Lightfoot's theory— Paul's silence in Galatians about A 2. But all the other objections remain unaltered, with a further charge of inaccuracy to be laid to Luke's account.

[1] See A. D. Nock, *St. Paul*; C. H. Dodd in *Helps to the Study of the Bible*, pp. 195–197.

III. G 2 = A 2.

This theory had a powerful advocate in Ramsay, and has proved highly popular among English scholars, though it has received little attention in Europe and America. It has one great advantage, that it provides an intelligible sequence of events. Paul and Barnabas are commissioned by the church of Antioch to carry the famine relief fund to Jerusalem, and take the opportunity to consult the Jerusalem apostles about a projected mission to the Gentiles. Full agreement is reached concerning the admission of Gentiles to church membership. Not long afterwards Paul and Barnabas are sent out on their first missionary journey. Either before or after this journey there occurred at Antioch a dispute over table fellowship between Jewish and Gentile Christians, precipitated by a message from James (Gal. ii. 11 ff.). The problem raised by this incident was finally settled at the Jerusalem conference (A 3).

It has been objected that Paul's claim that he went up to Jerusalem because of a revelation is incompatible with Luke's statement that he was sent up to carry the famine fund. But if we allow any weight to this criticism, it must weigh equally strongly against the identification of G 2 with A 3, since Luke says in Acts xv. 2 that Paul and Barnabas were sent to Jerusalem for the conference as delegates of the church of Antioch.

A much more serious difficulty is raised by Paul's dates in Galatians i. 18 and ii. 1. Paul arrived in Corinth about eighteen months before Gallio, i.e. early in 50. The apostolic conference must have been held in the spring of 49, and if we allow adequate time for the first missionary journey the famine visit (= G 2) cannot have been later than the autumn of 46. If Paul's first visit to Jerusalem happened fourteen years earlier, it can be placed in the spring of 33. Then his conversion, three years before, cannot have occurred later than the autumn of 31. This leaves an interval of one and a half, or at the most two and a half, years between the Crucifixion of Jesus and the conversion of Paul—not an impossibly brief period, but much briefer than we should otherwise have supposed. Ramsay avoided this difficulty by the hypothesis that Paul's dates were both reckoned from his conversion in 33, i.e. his first visit occurred three years after his conversion—in 36, and his second visit fourteen years after his conversion—in 46. But this is not the natural interpretation of Paul's words.

One further problem remains. Why did Paul, in writing to the Galatians, omit to mention the Jerusalem conference in his list of contacts with the apostles? The answer given by most English supporters of the theory (though not by Ramsay) is that Paul did not mention the conference because it had not yet taken place at the time of writing, that the Epistle was written in 48 or 49 between the first missionary journey and the conference, and that it is thus the earliest of Paul's Epistles. This early dating of Galatians, more than anything else, has brought into disrepute the theory to which it is attached. For whatever we may think of Lightfoot's own theory, which we have discussed above, there is no gainsaying the cogency of Lightfoot's argument that in language, in style, in subject matter, and in general tone Galatians forms the natural transitional link between II Corinthians and Romans.[1] Only as a last resort should we adopt any theory which requires us to remove Galatians from its natural place in the sequence of Paul's Epistles.

But the theory that $G\,2 = A\,2$ does not stand or fall with the early date of Galatians, for there is an alternative answer to our question. It is possible that Paul did not mention the apostolic conference in writing to the Galatians because it did not affect his argument. His apostolic authority had been challenged, and it was his intention to prove his independence of the Jerusalem apostles by demonstrating that he had had no opportunity to derive from them the Gospel message which he had preached in Galatia.[2] To this end he describes in some detail all contacts he had had

---

[1] Op. cit. pp. 42–50; cf. C. H. Buck, Jr., "The Date of Galatians", *Journal of Biblical Literature*, lxx (1951), pp. 113–122.

[2] The aorist participle in i. 11 shows that Paul was referring to a specific occasion in the past, viz. his first preaching in Galatia.

with the other apostles *prior to the Galatian mission*.[1] There
was no need to include the apostolic conference, since even
his worst enemy could hardly claim that this was the
occasion when he had received from others the Gospel which
he had preached in Galatia two years before the conference
met.

IV. G 2 = A 3a.

Johannes Weiss [2] began his treatment of this subject with
an analysis of Acts xv, and came to the conclusion that
Luke had confused two conferences—one which dealt with
the demand of certain Pharisaic Christians that circumcision should be made a condition of church membership
(vv. 1–4, 12), and one which dealt with the terms of table
fellowship between Jewish and Gentile Christians (vv. 5–11,
13–33). The first of these conferences was to be identified
with G 2, and took place between the first and second missionary journeys. It was followed by the dispute at
Antioch, which resulted in a permanent breach between
Paul on the one hand and Barnabas and Peter on the
other. On the evidence of Acts xxi. 25, where James
informs Paul, as though for the first time, of the contents
of the apostolic decree, Weiss asserted that Paul was not
present at the second conference. Since Silas had a hand
in the drawing up of the decree, this conference must have
happened after he had parted from Paul at the end of the
second missionary journey.

This theory explains Paul's silence about the apostolic
decree in Galatians and I Corinthians, but it fails to explain
his silence in Galatians about A 2. It repudiates Luke's
explicit and repeated statements that Paul and Barnabas
were present at the apostolic conference, and does so on the
evidence of a single verse, Acts xxi. 25, which does not
necessarily mean that Paul was ignorant of the provisions

[1] On this reading of the Epistle the dispute of Gal. ii. 11 ff. must have
occurred before the first missionary journey, otherwise there would have
been no point in mentioning it.
[2] *The History of Primitive Christianity*, pp. 259–276. A modification of
this theory has been put forward by J. R. Porter in the *Journal of Theological Studies*, xlvii (1946), pp. 169 ff.

of the decree; it may be interpreted as a gentle reminder
that James had made a concession in favour of the Gentile
Christians and had every right to expect Paul to make a
concession in return. The analysis of Acts xv, too, is
speculative. Nobody who has any experience of church
conferences will doubt that the apostolic conference could
have been diverted from its proper agenda by converted
Pharisees, who wanted to reopen a matter already settled
at a previous meeting. And the idea that there was a
permanent breach between Paul and the other apostles has
little to commend it.

V. G 2 = A 4.

The most drastic solution has been put forward by John
Knox.[1] He begins by discarding Luke's chronology as
totally unreliable, though he believes that Luke was using
material of high historical value. In the place of this
abandoned framework he tries to construct a new one from
hints thrown out in the Epistles of Paul. He finds the key
in Galatians ii. 10—the request made by the Jerusalem
apostles that Paul should remember the poor. Paul's
response to this request was the collection mentioned in I
Corinthians xvi. 1–4, II Corinthians viii–ix, and Romans
xv. 25–32. G 2 must therefore have occurred shortly
before the writing of these letters, and must be identified
with A 4. A 2 and A 3 can be dismissed as unhistorical.
Paul's career ran roughly as follows : the three years after
his conversion were spent in Damascus and Arabia (Gal. i.
15–17) ; then, after a brief visit to Jerusalem, he departed
to Syria and Cilicia (Gal. i. 18–21) ; the next eleven years
(Gal. ii. 1, using the inclusive reckoning) were spent in Asia
Minor and Greece in company with Barnabas; then
followed the second visit to Jerusalem (G 2 = A 4),
further missionary work in Galatia, Asia, Macedonia, and

[1] *Some Chapters in the Life of St. Paul.* Cf. D. W. Riddle, *Paul, Man of
Conflict*; P. S. Minear, " The Jerusalem Fund and Pauline Christianity ",
Anglican Theological Review, xxv (1943), pp. 389–396; C. H. Buck, Jr.,
" The Collection for the Saints ", *Harvard Theological Review*, xliii (1950),
1–29.

Achaea, and the final visit to Jerusalem. All this is based entirely on the evidence of the Epistles, but into this framework may be fitted select items from Acts, whereby the whole system may be anchored to an absolute date. The edict of Claudius is placed on the evidence of Suetonius and Dio Cassius in 41, which gives a date for Paul's first arrival in Corinth. The coming of Gallio cannot be moved so far back, and so this incident is assigned to Paul's last visit to Corinth. The final date is provided by Eusebius, who puts the replacement of Felix by Festus in the second year of Nero—55.

It need hardly be said that this theory avoids all the difficulties involved in the attempt to harmonize Acts with Galatians. It has also the additional advantage of filling with strenuous activity the " hidden years " of Paul's life between his first and second visits to Jerusalem. But it raises at least as many problems as it solves. Barnabas was with Paul when he went up to Jerusalem for his second visit (G 2), and on the slender evidence of I Corinthians ix. 6, and in face of the silence of the Thessalonian Epistles and the denial of Acts, Knox has to assume that Barnabas accompanied Paul to Greece. On the other hand he can give no explanation for the presence of Silas-Silvanus in Greece, vouched for by Acts and the Thessalonian Epistles. The dispute of Galatians ii. 11 ff. must be placed after G 2, but the clause " when Cephas came to Antioch " implies that at the time Paul was using Antioch as headquarters, and not merely paying a passing visit between two prolonged periods of residence in Greece and Asia. The behaviour of Barnabas on that occasion is extremely hard to understand if he had spent the previous eleven years in partnership with Paul and had shared in founding the predominantly Gentile churches of Philippi, Thessalonica, and Corinth. The selection and rearrangement of the evidence from Acts is arbitrary, and there seems to be no justification for the basic assumption that Paul's letters can be made to yield a complete outline of their author's career.

These five theories naturally produce different chronological results, which may be tabulated as follows (the figures given by Lightfoot and other early writers are revised in the light of the Gallio inscription) :

	I	II	III	IV	V
Conversion of Paul .	33	33	31 or 33	33	34 or 37
First visit to Jerusalem .	36	36	33 or 36	36	37 or 40
Famine visit . . .	46	—	46	46	—
First missionary journey .	47–8	47–8	47–8	47–8	37 or 40–51
Apostolic conference .	49	49	49	49	51
Paul's arrival in Corinth .	50	50	50	50	—

4

Gallio arrived in Corinth in the summer of 51, and soon after this Paul was brought before him on a charge of practising an illicit religion. Then, we are told, Paul " stayed a good while longer " [1] before leaving to pay a rapid visit to Jerusalem on his way to Antioch. " A good while " may mean a few weeks or a few months, so that this visit to Jerusalem occurred either in autumn 51 or in spring 52. It was followed by " some time " spent at Antioch and a tour of the Galatian region and Phrygia, ending at Ephesus.[2] Tentatively, then, let us place Paul's arrival at Ephesus in autumn 52. At Ephesus Paul spent three months plus two years plus a while and then set out for Corinth via Macedonia.[3] According to I Corinthians xvi. 8 Paul intended to leave Ephesus at Pentecost, and this must have been Pentecost 55. We know from the Epistles that his plans were upset at this point by a number of events which have left no mark on the story of Acts, including a visit to Corinth, the sending of Titus to Corinth with a letter, and the affliction which made Paul despair of life; and we have no means of estimating what length of time these events occupied. After leaving Ephesus Paul waited for a time at Troas in hopes of meeting Titus on his way back from Corinth, and then went on to Macedonia where Titus met him.[4] About the next six months we know nothing except that they must have been spent in Macedonia (and

---

[1] Acts xviii. 18.
[2] Acts xviii. 23; xix. 1.
[3] Acts xix. 8, 10, 22.
[4] II Cor. ii. 12 f.; vii. 6.

dare we say Illyricum ?)[1] In the following year (56) Paul spent three months in Corinth, celebrated the Passover at Philippi, and hurried on to Jerusalem to be there in time for Pentecost.[2] There he was arrested and kept in prison at Caesarea for two years, until Felix was replaced by Festus.[3] This brings us to the summer of 58 and to our first snag. For the most probable date for the arrival of Festus is 59. It cannot be said that this date is beyond all possible doubt, but we must face the possibility that our neat chronological scheme is too neat, and that we have somehow compressed eight years' activity into seven. It is barely possible that Gallio's term of office began in 52 instead of 51, and this would advance all our dates by one year. But if we disregard this remote possibility, the extra year must be inserted between Paul's departure from Jerusalem (A 4) and his arrival in Ephesus. For we can hardly find room for it between his departure from Ephesus and his final visit to Corinth : as it is, he seems to have spent at least six months on the way, and he was too deeply concerned about his collection for the Jerusalem church to spend a whole year more. For this period, then, we arrive at two alternative systems of dating, and our choice between them depends on the date we assign to Festus' arrival at Caesarea.

Paul leaves Corinth	Autumn 51 or spring 52
Paul arrives in Ephesus	Autumn 52 or 53
Paul leaves Ephesus	Summer 55 or 56
Paul arrives at Corinth	End of 55 or 56
Paul at Philippi	Passover 56 or 57
Paul arrives at Jerusalem	Pentecost 56 or 57
Paul appeals to Caesar	Summer 58 or 59
Paul arrives at Rome	Spring 59 or 60
Imprisonment in Rome	59–61 or 60–62

At this point we lose sight of Paul, and at the same time exhaust the chronological data of the New Testament.

[1] Acts xx. 2; Rom. xv. 19.   [2] Acts xx. 3, 6, 16.   [3] Acts xxiv, 27.

CHRONOLOGICAL TABLE

DATE	EMPERORS	PROCURATORS OF JUDAEA	EVENTS IN JEWISH OR CHRISTIAN HISTORY
37 B.C.		Herod the Great (king)	
31 B.C.	Augustus		
4 B.C.		Archelaus (tetrarch)	Antipas tetrarch of Galilee and Peraea. Philip tetrarch of Ituraea and Trachonitis.
6 A.D.		Coponius	Revolt of Judas of Gamala.
?		Marcus Ambivius	
?		Annius Rufus	
14	Tiberius	Valerius Gratus	
26		Pontius Pilate	
29 or 30			The Crucifixion.
36		Marcellus	
37	Caligula	Marullus	Herod Agrippa succeeds Philip.
39			Herod Agrippa succeeds Antipas.
40			Caligula orders his statue to be placed in the Jerusalem temple.
41	Claudius	Herod Agrippa (king)	Death of James, son of Zebedee.
44			Death of Herod. Revolt of Theudas.
45		Cuspius Fadus	
46		Tiberius Alexander	Famine.
48		Ventidius Cumanus	
49			Apostolic conference.
51–52			Gallio proconsul of Achaea.
52		Felix	
54	Nero		
59 ?		Porcius Festus	
61 ?		Albinus	Death of James, the Lord's brother.
64		Gessius Florus	The fire of Rome.
66			The Jewish revolt.
69	Galba		
	Otho		
	Vitellius		
	Vespasian		
70			The destruction of Jerusalem.
79	Titus		
81	Domitian		
96	Nerva		
98	Trajan		

APPENDIX B

I. Tacitus, *Annals* xv. 44.

" So in order to suppress the rumour Nero made into scape-goats and subjected to exquisite punishments persons detested for their outrageous practices and known to the populace as Christians. Christus, from whom the name took its origin, was executed in the reign of Tiberius by the procurator Pontius Pilate. Checked for a time, the pernicious super-stition broke out afresh, not only in Judaea, where the trouble started, but even in the City, where all that is vile and shameful flows in from every quarter and is welcomed with enthusiasm. Those therefore who openly admitted to being Christians [1] were first arrested, and on their information a large crowd was con-victed, not so much on the charge of arson as for hatred of the human race. Their execution was made an occasion for cruel mockery : some were sent to their death covered with the skins of wild beasts for dogs to tear, some fastened to crosses, some set up to be burned as torches and to serve, when daylight failed, for nocturnal illumination. Nero had opened his gardens for this entertainment, and provided a display of horse-racing, mixing with the crowd in the garb of a charioteer or driving his own chariot. And so it happened that, although the victims were guilty and deserving of extreme penalties, a feeling of compassion arose ; for it seemed as if they were being exterminated not for the public welfare but to gratify one man's brutality."

II. Pliny's Letter to Trajan (*Ep.* x. 96)

" It is my habit to refer to you, my Lord, all matters about which I am in doubt. For who can better direct my hesitation or instruct my ignorance ? I have never been present at investigations concerning Christians, and so I do not know the nature and limits of the customary procedure with regard to their punishment or prosecution. I have had no little hesita-tion over the following questions. Is any allowance to be made

---

[1] This must be the meaning of the phrase *qui fatebantur*. Some scholars have taken the phrase to mean " who confessed to the crime ". But Tacitus clearly did not believe that the Christians were guilty of arson, and, although under torture they might have confessed to a crime of which they were innocent, they would hardly have done so before they were arrested. But the imperfect *fatebantur* surely describes the class of person first arrested, not an action subsequent to their arrest. It has been argued that *confiteor* and *profiteor* were used to denote profession of faith, but not *fateor*; but it is one of the tricks of Tacitus' style to use a simple verb where other writers use a compound one.

for age, or are children, in spite of their tender years, to be treated exactly like adults ? Are penitents to be pardoned, or if a man has once been a Christian is it of no advantage to him that he has now recanted ? Is it the name itself that is punishable, if unaccompanied by crimes, or the crimes that attach to the name ? In the meanwhile, in dealing with those who have been denounced to me as Christians, I have adopted this method. I have asked them whether they were Christians. If they pleaded guilty, I have put the same question a second and a third time with threats of punishment ; and if they remained obdurate, I have ordered their execution. For I was never in any doubt that, whatever the precise nature of their confession, their insubordination and unyielding obstinacy deserved punishment. Others, who shared in the same sort of madness, I have remanded to be sent to the City for trial, because they were Roman citizens. In the course of these proceedings, as usually happens, the prosecution was extended to include several different types. There came into my hands an anonymous document containing the names of many persons. Some of them denied that they were or ever had been Christians ; at my dictation they repeated an invocation to the gods ; they offered prayer with incense and wine before your statue, which I had ordered to be brought into court, along with the images of the gods, for this very purpose ; and, above all, they cursed Christ. Since it is said that no true Christian can be forced to perform any of these actions, I decided that those persons should be acquitted. Others who were named in the information said that they were Christians and then immediately denied it : they had been formerly, but had recanted three years ago or more, some as much as twenty years before. All these, too, worshipped your statue and the images of the gods and cursed Christ. But they declared that the sum total of their offence or error was this : they had been accustomed to meet before dawn on a fixed day, to sing hymns antiphonally to Christ as to a god, and to bind themselves by an oath not for any criminal purpose but in a covenant not to commit theft, robbery, or adultery, not to break faith, nor to deny a deposit when called upon to restore it. When these rites were completed, it had been their habit to depart and to reassemble for food—a corporate meal and quite innocent. This second practice they had abandoned since my edict, by which in accordance with your instructions I forbade club-meetings. In view of this declaration I considered it the more necessary to make a further attempt to discover the truth by torture from two slavewomen, who were called deaconesses. I could discover nothing more than superstition, shameless and unrestrained. For this reason I have postponed judgment and have taken the precaution of consulting you. For the case seemed to me worthy of consultation, especially considering the numbers of those who are exposed to danger. This contagious superstition has spread not only through the cities but through the villages and rural areas as well, but I think it can now be checked and corrected. At least there is general agreement that temples, once almost deserted, are beginning to be frequented, that solemn rites long discontinued are being restored, and that there is a sale for the fodder which is given to sacrificial animals, for which it was formerly extremely unusual to find a buyer. From this you may easily estimate what a multitude of people can be reformed if opportunity be granted for repentance.''

III. Trajan's Rescript (*Ep.* x. 97)

" You have followed the right course, my dear Secundus, in dealing with the cases of those who were denounced to you as Christians. For it is not possible to lay down for all cases anything that resembles a fixed rule. They need not be hunted down. If they are denounced and found guilty, they must be punished, but with this proviso, that anyone who denies he is a Christian and proves his denial by the required action, that is by offering prayer to our gods, even if he were suspect in the past, shall receive pardon for his penitence. Anonymous documents that come into your hands should have no standing in any prosecution. It is a thoroughly bad practice and not in keeping with our era.''

BIBLIOGRAPHY

GENERAL

Bartlet, J. V.   *The Apostolic Age*, 1900.
Burkitt, F. C.   *Christian Beginnings*, 1924.
Lake, K. & Cadbury, H. J.   *The Beginnings of Christianity*, Vol. V, 1933.
Lietzmann, H.   *The Beginnings of the Christian Church*, tr. B. L. Woolf, 1937.
Rawlinson, A. E. J.   *The New Testament Doctrine of the Christ*, 1926.
Scott, E. F.   *The Beginnings of the Church*, 1914.
Wand, J. W. C.   *First Century Christianity*, 1937.
Weiss, J.   *The History of Primitive Christianity*, tr. F. C. Grant & others, 1937.

CHAPTER I

Angus, S.   *The Religious Quests of the Graeco-Roman World*, 1929.
Bevan, E. R.   *Stoics and Sceptics*, 1913.
Dill, S.   *Roman Society from Nero to Marcus Aurelius*, 1920.
Glover, T. R.   *The Conflict of Religions in the Early Roman Empire*, 1909.
Halliday, W. R.   *The Pagan Background of Early Christianity*, 1925.
Nock, A. D.   *Conversion*, 1933.
Tarn, W. W.   *Hellenistic Civilization*, 1927.
Wendland, P.   *Die hellenistisch-römische Kultur*, 1912.

CHAPTER II

Bevan, E. R.   *Jerusalem under the High Priests*, 1904.
Bousset, W.   *Die Religion des Judentums in neutestamentlichen Zeitalter*, 3rd ed. revised and edited by H. Gressmann, 1926.
Charles, R. H.   *The Apocrypha and Pseudepigrapha of the Old Testament*, 1913.
Danby, H.   *The Mishnah*, 1933.
Guignebert, C.   *The Jewish World in the Time of Jesus*, 1939.
Herford, R. T.   *Judaism in the New Testament Period*, 1928.
Juster, J.   *Les Juifs dans l'Empire Romain*, 1914.
Moore, G. F.   *Judaism in the First Centuries of the Christian Era*, 1927.
Schürer, E.   *A History of the Jewish People in the Time of Jesus Christ*, 1886–90.
Snaith, N. H.   *The Jews from Cyrus to Herod*, 1949.

CHAPTER III

Cullmann, O. *Baptism in the New Testament*, tr. J. K. S. Reid, 1950.

Dibelius, M. *From Tradition to Gospel*, tr. B. L. Woolf, 1934.

Dodd, C. H. *The Apostolic Preaching and its Developments*, 1936; *History and the Gospel*, 1938; *According to the Scriptures*, 1952.

Easton, B. S. *Christ in the Gospels*, 1930.

Flemington, F. W. *The New Testament Doctrine of Baptism*, 1948.

Gavin, F. *The Jewish Antecedents of the Christian Sacraments*, 1928.

Higgins, A. J. B. *The Lord's Supper in the New Testament*, 1952.

Hopwood, P. G. S. *The Religious Experience of the Primitive Church*, 1936.

Lietzmann, H. *Messe und Herrenmahl*, 1926.

Manson, T. W. *The Teaching of Jesus*, 1931.

Taylor, V. *The Formation of the Gospel Tradition*, 1933.

CHAPTER IV

Carrington, P. *The Primitive Christian Catechism*, 1940.

Cullmann, O. *The Earliest Christian Confessions*, tr. J. K. S. Reid, 1949.

Dix, G. *Jew and Greek*, 1953.

Harnack, A. *The Mission and Expansion of Christianity*, tr. J. Moffatt, 1908.

Hort, F. J. A. *Judaistic Christianity*, 1904.

Hunter, A. M. *Paul and His Predecessors*, 1942.

Knox, W. L. *St. Paul and the Church of Jerusalem*, 1925; *St. Paul and the Church of the Gentiles*, 1939; *Some Hellenistic Elements in Primitive Christianity*, 1944.

Latourette, K. S. *The History of the Expansion of Christianity*, Vol. I, 1937.

Selwyn, E. G. *The First Epistle of St. Peter*, 1946.

CHAPTER V

Davies, W. D. *St. Paul and Rabbinic Judaism*, 1948.

Deissmann, A. *St. Paul*, 1912.

Dodd, C. H. *The Meaning of Paul for Today*, 1920.

Glover, T. R. *Paul of Tarsus*, 1925.

Nock, A. D. *St. Paul*, 1938.

Ramsay, W. M. *St. Paul the Traveller*, 1895.

Schweitzer, A. *Paul and his Interpreters*, 1912.

Scott, C. A. A. *Christianity according to St. Paul*, 1927.

Stewart, J. S. *A Man in Christ*, 1935.

CHAPTER VI

Dahl, N. S. *Das Volk Gottes*, 1941.
Ehrhardt, A. *The Apostolic Succession*, 1953.
Harrison, P. N. *The Problem of the Pastoral Epistles*, 1921.
Hort, F. J. A. *The Christian Ecclesia*, 1897.
Johnston, G. *The Doctrine of the Church in the New Testament*, 1943.
Lightfoot, J. B. " The Christian Ministry " (Dissertation in *The Epistle to the Philippians*, pp. 181–269), 1883.
Manson, T. W. *The Church's Ministry*, 1948.
Rengstorf, K. H. *Apostleship*, tr. J. R. Coates from Kittel's *Theologisches Wörterbuch zum Neuen Testament*, 1952.
Streeter, B. H. *The Primitive Church*, 1929.

CHAPTER VII

Cadoux, C. J. *The Early Church and the World*, 1925.
Hardy, E. G. *Christianity and the Roman Government*, 1925.
Momigliano, A. *Cambridge Ancient History*, Vol. X, pp. 724 ff. 887 ff.
Ramsay, W. M. *The Church in the Roman Empire*, 1893.
Workman, H. B. *Persecution in the Early Church*, 1906.

CHAPTER VIII

Cullmann, O. *Christ and Time*, tr. F. V. Filson, 1951.
Dodd, C. H. *The Parables of the Kingdom*, 1935.
Frost, S. B. *Old Testament Apocalyptic*, 1952.
Manson, W. " Eschatology in the New Testament ", *Scottish Journal of Theology*, Occasional Papers No. 2, 1953.
Marsh, J. *The Fulness of Time*, 1953.
Mowinckel, S. *Psalmenstudien*, II, 1922.
Robinson, J. A. T. *In the End God. . .* , 1953.
Rowley, H. H. *The Relevance of Apocalyptic*, 1944.

INDEX OF AUTHORS

INDEX OF SUBJECTS

220